MW00414318

# The Practical Book of Bicycling

## New, Revised Edition

by Frances Call
with Merle E. Dowd

E. P. Dutton | New York

To
The Cyclemates

For information contact: Elsevier-Dutton Publishing Co., Inc.,
2 Park Avenue, New York N.Y. 10016

ISBN: 0-525-93203-8
Library of Congress Catalog Card Number: 81-67095

Published simultaneously in Canada by Clarke, Irwin & Company
Limited, Toronto and Vancouver.

10 9 8 7 6 5 4 3 2 1

# Contents

# Introduction

The
Bicycling
Schoolteacher
from Mercer Island

Each summer for more than a decade fifteen or sixteen junior high school boys and girls took a long-distance tour on their bicycles. These groups were called the Cyclemates, and they were organized and led by one of their teachers, Frances Call. Every one of those kids cycled the whole distance. On four of the trips they spanned the continent from their homes near Seattle—3,500 miles to New York City, 3,600 to Washington, D.C., 4,500 to Halifax, Nova Scotia, and 4,000 miles to Williamsburg, Virginia. Fran Call believes those 165 kids learned more about themselves biking around the country than they would from any similar number of hours in school.

What kind of a woman is Fran Call? She is quiet and would just as soon nobody make a fuss about her unique concept for throwing kids into a wide new world of experiences. But, she has a way of tossing out challenges that almost defy you not to accept them.

Cyclemates I began almost innocently. Fran was looking for some way to get her group of junior high students involved in an adventure that would "help them to gain an understanding of themselves and other people; teach them self-reliance and discipline; encourage them to learn how to save and spend money effectively; and acquaint them with this beautiful land." A monumental objective, you might say.

There were other reasons for the trips. "We wanted to show people," Fran says, "that all the bad news about kids their age doesn't represent the full or true story. We read about drug use, school dropouts, rebelling against authority, and other faults of this generation. Most kids just do not fall into those categories. Instead of sitting back and criticizing the few bad apples that appear to make news, let's demonstrate positive leadership and encourage constructive behavior."

At 40 Fran Call is slender and lithe, blonde, and with a lively smile that breaks out often. She plans ahead like a systems analyst and leaves little to chance. As for bicycling, she practices what she preaches. During the past decade she has bicycled at least 40,000 miles —on the Cyclemates' trips, training and conditioning for months before each trip, and weekend bike-tripping, rain or shine, somewhere around Puget Sound—usually with a bunch of young cyclists in tow. A trip around Lake Washington, sixty-six miles, can be an enjoyable Sunday afternoon jaunt. One training assignment she likes is to challenge the gang to ride ten round trips nonstop up and down Gallagher Hill on Mercer Island. Gallagher Hill is about half a mile long and most cars have to shift into second going up.

Fran was born in Washington, D.C., the daughter of an Army colonel, now retired. After earning a Master's Degree in educational psychology in 1962 from Seattle University she began teaching in the Seattle area. In 1968 she joined the faculty at North Mercer Junior High where she teaches history, English, and a special physical education class called Outdoor Fitness. It emphasizes cycling, running, hiking, and camping. Approximately 50 students fill the class every year, eager to accept the challenges found in the out-of-doors.

One question is often asked of Fran—"Why don't other teachers do things like bicycling all over the countryside?"

Fran figures that few others can follow her lead for several reasons. "First, I'm single. I can afford to take the time throughout the year and during the summer to work with those kids who respond to leadership. Second, I'm physically fit enough to keep up with them. I do my part. Other teachers serve in different ways.

"I never tell the kids that anything is going to be easy. I let them know how really hard it is pedaling uphill in the broiling sun or with rain pelting you in the face. Or, how hard each crank revolution can become at the end of a long day without a home-cooked meal, a soft bed, or a hot shower to look forward to. There's little satisfaction in completing a task or meeting a challenge if they think it's easy before they start. The important thing the kids learn is to cope with discomfort and adversity."

Fran tells parents and associates: "You might as well expect and demand a lot of kids these days because they're quite capable of meeting almost any challenge—if they feel it's worthy of the effort."

While the Cyclemates are Fran Call's own unique way for helping kids grow and mature, her program is solidly based on sound psychological grounds. She borrows heavily and often from behavior modification techniques. She encourages the students to "start small—but start. Get high on trying! Then build on success. Learn basic skills, learn them one at a time, and don't be afraid of making a mistake!"

"Preparation and anticipation build confidence," Fran likes to repeat. "Learning to be self-sufficient rather than depending on others really amounts to accepting a responsibility to others. When a kid takes care of himself and learns to be self-sufficient, he becomes responsible to others. Carelessness amounts to selfishness—and shows a lack of concern for others."

Fran accepted the challenge of writing this book because she recognized that it provided a rare opportunity for personal growth and for influencing others. She wants teachers and kids to know and understand and to love bicycling as she does. The book is a "practical" book because it reflects her own down-to-earth philosophy.

If there's one message in these pages, it's the challenge to the reader —to learn about bicycling, to enjoy touring, and to sense the feeling of accomplishment that follows setting a goal and achieving it. Even if a first goal may be to ride around the block without falling off, try it. Then, go on to longer tours and more demanding rides. Soon bicycling will become as natural as walking. At that point you can enjoy bicycling as much as Fran Call.

MERLE E. DOWD

# Part 1

## The
## How
## and Why
## of Bicycling

# 1.
# Bicycling for Everyone

Ecology — noise — energy crisis — physical fitness — cost of living — fun! All good reasons for enjoying the old-time new-time pleasures of bicycling.

Ecology buffs have adopted the bicycle as one sure way to reduce the pollution spewed into the air by the millions of automobiles crowding downtown areas. Their thesis—get rid of air pollution by getting rid of the automobile.

University students depend on their bicycles for economical transportation. In Davis, California, a large sign advises motorists entering the outskirts that many bicycles operate in the city. At latest count, there were over 28,000 being used by a population of only 37,000; the rate of bicycle ownership is probably one of the highest in the nation.

The Davis campus of the University of California accounts for many of the bicycles, but not all. A recent traffic count during the summer, when few university students were in town, noted that 40 percent of all traffic was by bicycle. During the rush hour on a downtown street, 90 percent of all the riders are adults.

Davis was one of the early leaders in proposing and building separate facilities for bicycles. The city began building a bicycle path network unique in the United States—but not for long. Now, with the specific approval of the Department of Housing and Urban Development, new housing tracts in many cities are required to set aside space for bicycle lanes separated from automobile traffic.

Bicycles in Davis are not merely owned, stored, or used for recreational purposes; they constitute an important part of that city's transportation system. Many business leaders in the community strongly support expansion of facilities for bicycles. The use of bicycles means no parking meters and tolerable rush-hour traffic; it has helped preserve the central city core as a viable shopping district by eliminating parking as a serious obstacle to downtown shopping. California climate accounts for part of this popularity but not all. Around rainy Seattle, I see more and more students, adult commuters, and shopping housewives taking to their bicycles for a variety of reasons.

All around the country governments are recognizing the potential of the bicycle as an alternative mode of urban transportation. City, state, and federal agencies have conducted development studies in the areas of safety, bike path and lane facilities, and bicycle security.

Money to build separate facilities for cyclists is always a problem. So I was heartened when Oregon became the first state to tap gasoline tax revenues for building bicycle paths. Oregon statutes require that not less than one percent of state gasoline taxes be spent for planning and construction of bikeways. In Oregon the standard bike path is 8 feet wide and constructed of 2 inches of asphalt over 4 inches of rock base. Highway engineers estimate it costs almost two million dollars per mile for a four-lane rural expressway, but only $75,000 per mile for a bikeway.

Shortly after the Oregon law was passed Washington State legislated ½ of one percent of highway funds for bikeways. Other states across the country were quick to follow this lead, and the Federal Department of Transportation supports bikeways by sharing at least half of the costs with the states on suitable projects.

Regular bicycling as an exercise helps youngsters and adults alike to feel better, head off cardiovascular disease, live with greater vitality, and control weight—all detailed in Chapter Seven. Dr. Stanley Stamm, head of the Cardiopulmonary Center at the Children's Orthopedic Hospital in Seattle, Washington, bicycles to and from work every day, rain or shine. He reports, "Since I ride the bike to work, we got rid of our second car."

Commuters from outlying suburbs need not be deterred by distances. Some cyclists ride from one to 10 miles from their home to a train station for the long ride into town. The Chicago & North Western Railroad offers Chicago commuters bike parking facilities at thirty-five suburban stations. C&NW commuters may also store bicycles over-night in the downtown station, and bicycle from the station to work after taking the train into town. Washington, D.C.'s Union Station provides similar facilities. When a Washington bike commuter arrives at his office or plant, there's no problem about parking; he racks his bicycle near the doorway to his office. In downtown areas, major buildings now provide bicycle parking space on sidewalks outside entries or on lower levels. An executive order passed down during the Carter Administration requires that adequate parking be provided when any new Federal building is built, or when any of the 450,000 existing Federal buildings are renovated. Finding parking in non-government buildings continues to be a problem, but many cities would much rather tackle the bike storage problem than try to find space for commuters' automobiles.

One physician I know now makes his rounds via bicycle to save time. Commuters and shoppers save not only time but money too. As the cost of living rises inexorably, families are examining their discretionary expenses—transportation, for one—with a sharp eye. They are asking, as Dr. Stamm did, "Is the second car really necessary?" Transportation may be necessary, but more and more families are considering whether that extra $1,500 to $3,000 a year they spend for a second car wouldn't be spent better on medical bills, college expenses, travel, a bigger house, a boat, or invested for higher retirement income. Few equipment purchases depreciate as fast as a car; during the first two years, a new car loses half of its original value in the marketplace. If the car is a gas-guzzler, it depreciates even faster. Operating costs averaged 23 to 25 cents per mile for a standard size car as of the beginning of 1981, according to the Department of Transportation. That figure almost tripled in ten years, and with oil prices rising steadily, it may go even higher.

As an exercise in family economics, one of my classes compared the cost of bicycle and automobile commuting. We considered a case where the commuter drove regularly five miles one-way to work. Minimum costs would average $2.30 a day or $575 for the year—just for commuting. A bicycle, on the other hand, could be expected to last five years and cost $50 per year. Even with $25 added for parts and maintenance, annual commuting costs would total only $75—for a saving of $500. We also considered time. At an average speed of

15 mph, the trip would take about twenty minutes by bicycle. Driving, allowing for time to fight traffic, parking in a far-off lot, and walking to the door, might save five minutes. A loaded example? Perhaps, but the point is clear—bicycling affords a viable alternative to buying a second car used mainly for commuting.

Weather seldom stops the confirmed bicycle commuter. But now the PPC (People-Powered Car) has been invented. At least one model offers complete protection from the weather, can be pedaled in one of five gears at speeds up to 15 mph, and includes space for a youngster or two big bags of groceries. And you pedal it yourself —no gasoline and no pollution.

In 1970 an Oregon highway engineer calculated that every student who could be switched from bus to bike would save the school system $20 per year. That figure has almost tripled in ten years. If commuting up to five miles each way makes economic sense, then requiring able-bodied school children to ride bicycles similar or shorter distances to school could help slow the rising cost of education. Safe bikeways and strict enforcement can protect these kids during round trips between school and home.

The burgeoning energy crisis can be expected to have an effect on both car owners and bicyclists. Current predictions are that heating oil and gasoline will remain in short supply for years. What happens when goods remain in short supply? Prices hike upward—and quickly. While you can counter the increasing price of gasoline by buying a smaller car, driving less, or walking, consider the alternative of bicycling. An easy-to-ride two-wheeler can be your partial answer to the energy crisis.

In summary, all of these factors—ecology, energy crisis, cost of living, and everybody's need for regular exercise to head off cardio-vascular deterioration—point to one solution: the bicycle or adult tricycle. Cycling truly is for everyone. The bicycle solves these problems at the personal level; it also eases problems at the business, city, state, and Federal level. No longer must the state and Federal governments pour billions of dollars into more and more freeways. A fraction of the highway construction budget would provide bikeways throughout the country's cities and towns with a two-way effect—fewer cars as people take to bicycles and 1/26th the cost of building freeways. Encouraging bicycling would conserve oil stocks and lessen pollution. Business would benefit through a healthier work force. The number of men incapacitated or killed by heart disease in their forties and fifties could be sharply reduced through sensible exercise programs.

Cycling can also be lots of fun as proved by the Cyclemates—groups of junior-high youngsters I led during the summers of the last decade, across the United States and Canada and all around the Pacific Northwest. We proved that kids 13 to 16 years old could pedal their bicycles up and down mountains, across seemingly endless plains, through cities, and over distances few people thought possible. On our first tour, Cyclemates I pedaled from the parking lot of North Mercer Junior High School (near Seattle, Washington) to New York City. I was the only adult along with eight boys and seven girls, and we pedaled the whole distance without benefit of a sag wagon.

The following summer Cyclemates II pedaled across the plains of middle America from Mercer Island to Washington, D.C. We spent a full hour briefing President Nixon on our trip when he received us at the White House (Fig. 1).

Fig. 1—Cyclemates' leader, Fran Call, briefs President Nixon on the group's bicycle trip from Mercer Island, Washington (a suburb of Seattle), cross country to Washington, D.C. Two stripes on jackets denote that the group is Cyclemates II.

Cyclemates III extended the mileage and pedaled from Mercer Island to Halifax via the Gaspé Peninsula of Quebec Province. We were self-sufficient, carrying all of our equipment and clothes in our panniers and saddle bags. During one day we pedaled 189 miles.

On Cyclemates IV in 1976 we broke that record by riding 194.7 miles across eastern Kansas in one day. The trip ended in Colonial Williamsburg, Virginia. Other trips have spanned scenic areas of the Pacific Northwest. I am proud to report that not one of the 165 kids on the tours failed to travel the full distance.

You can follow the Cyclemates' tracks through the training and planning stages for long-distance touring in Chapters Ten, Eleven, and Twelve. The Cyclemates are truly unique in that no other group of kids that young has traveled so far strictly on its own. These girls and boys accepted a monumental challenge, met every adversity, and developed a stick-to-it attitude that will benefit them all through their lives. I think their performance proves the greatness and quality inherent in youngsters in this country.

You too can enjoy bicycling just for the fun of it. When you drive a car, few really important or interesting stimuli impinge on your consciousness, whether you are hurtling along an Interstate at 70 mph or dodging traffic in town. If you choose to walk around the waterfront, a university campus, a park, or the old, interesting parts of your city, you add a whole new dimension to your perceptions —but you spend hours at it. Bicycling combines the best of walking and driving. You can observe and ponder the little-known sights of your environs at speeds close to walking, while covering much more territory than is open to you as a stroller.

If you want to really see our national parks, tour by bike instead of being hustled around on a bus or driving yourself. Trails open up on all sides, inviting you to see sights not accessible to the car traveler. The Cyclemates and I took time on our trips to immerse ourselves in the scenic splendors of Glacier and Yellowstone National Parks in the United States and of Banff in Canada. Whether you bike along with your family or join one of the organized touring societies, you'll get more from your vacation via bicycling—as detailed in Chapters Ten and Eleven.

I've been particularly pleased to see historic and scenic trails or routes being preserved by other bicycle enthusiasts in every state. Old canal routes, abandoned railway rights-of-way, publicly owned waterways, and parkways offer land on which bikeways are being constructed or are being considered for construction. Motorized vehicles are excluded from bikeways and trails to preserve quiet and enhance the environment. A Federal program to expedite further construction of bikeways awaits financing, a split-off from the highway trust fund.

Every individual sport spawns competition—and bicycling is no exception. This book does not consider bicycle racing, as that is a complete and specialized subject all its own. Numerous bicycling tabloids report on events scheduled and the results of races run; they are noted in the Appendix.

Finally, a word on costs. Few activities offer the value or benefits available through bicycling with so little expense. Once you buy a bicycle—and good ones are available in the $150 to $300 range— there's little additional expense. Front tires made it cross-country on Cyclemates' bikes with tread to spare. Rear tires, subject to extra weight and traction wear, either were replaced near the end or worn out at the finish of all three trips—still a minor expense for 3,000-4,000 travel miles. With no fuel cost, minimum expense for occasional do-it-yourself lubrications, and a long life of five to ten years, the bicycle costs peanuts compared to a car, motorcycle, or boat. And, if you buy your bicycle used, as discussed in Chapter Five, you can cut even these minuscule costs in half.

Bicycling really is for everyone. But get involved. Learn about gears and changers. Practice correct form and develop your skills. Gain the health benefits that can be yours through regular bicycling exercise. Finally, leave your car in the garage and tour by bicycle for a different vacation—one you'll always remember.

# 2.

# Fitting You to a Bicycle

Learning about bicycles, discovering what separates the fun bike or the exquisitely machined touring bicycle from the also-rans can be almost as much fun as riding. Like boat-owners who spend more time scraping, calking, and varnishing than skippering their boats in the water, appreciating the differences that small parts make in bicycle performance can be a joy itself. But since this is a practical book, let's look first at some of the basic factors involved in selecting a bike:

WEIGHT. Like airplane design, every ounce that's not there improves performance. One rule you can count on—the lighter the bike, the more it costs. Parts made of aluminum alloy instead of steel, and tubular (sew-up) tires instead of clinchers, all cost more when precision engineered for light weight. Yet for long tours and for riding responsiveness, the ultimate in performance and enjoyment comes with a lightweight bike.

RIDER AGE. Not only frame and wheel size but ruggedness are important considerations for youngsters' bikes. You can't expect the same respect for lightweight performance from a child as from an adult—so you buy a heavier bike that can take punishment, possibly one without multiple gears. If a youngster uses a bike to haul newspapers, he will need a different bike than the youngster who goofs around with a highrise or stinger type bike.

COST. Along with weight reduction, precision engineering and other features important to the serious bicyclist increase cost. Value rather than cost remains the key consideration; that is, maximum benefit from minimum cost. As in most products, value increases rapidly from the lowest-cost bikes to the moderately expensive, then gradually drops off, with extra dollars buying successively smaller increments of value at the high price end.

MECHANICAL ABILITY. If you are all thumbs and scarcely recognize a wrench from a screwdriver, opt for a simple reliable machine. Give up some of the ultimate performance possible with lightweight gear-changers and sensitive moving parts likely to require frequent adjustment and maintenance. Bikes do work themselves out of adjustment. If you must haul it to the local cycle shop for minor adjustments, you'll soon tire of the trouble, find your wallet flat, and leave the bike in the garage or basement because it caused too many problems.

INTENDED USE. Bicycles used for general utility—riding to the store in good weather, pedaling a few miles for exercise, or getting from home to school, a friend's house, or tennis court—call for different attributes than a bicycle to be used regularly for commuting or touring.

(This book does not cover racing, as it is a unique field of its own. By the time a youngster or adult becomes interested in racing, his know-how about bicycles, his own preferences and prejudices based on experience, and money available dictate specific selections that are beyond the scope of these pages.)

There is no all-purpose bicycle. You may be tempted to cut costs and buy a heavy or medium-weight bike. Chances are, you'll soon be frustrated with such a bike's lack of responsiveness and tire of pushing so much dead weight around. Look ahead and benefit from the experience of others by buying "up." Grow into a bike that really suits your needs as you improve your skills.

Rather than buy a new inexpensive bicycle devoid of many of the features you would like to have, consider buying a used bike. Chapter Five details where and how to buy a used bicycle to suit your needs—at a cash saving. Several years ago, when the first wave of the bike boom hit, used bikes were impossible to find—except those stolen and sold at big discounts. Deliveries of new bikes were months behind orders. New bicycle enthusiasts were scrambling for high-performance, derailleur 10- and 15-speed bicycles. Now, suppliers in Japan, Europe, and the United States have caught up with the big demand. Cyclists who bought bicycles early—one, two, or three years ago—are trading up; that is, they recognize the benefits of newly designed lightweight, high-performance components and are willingly paying the higher price to buy what they want. These advanced bicyclists are now trading in their used bicycles or selling them to friends or through classified ads. If cash is a problem, a high-quality used bicycle can be a better buy than an inexpensive new bike—for the same dollar price.

The *Bicycle Selector Guide* (Fig. 2) will help to separate some of the confusing variables to be considered in selecting a bike. You'll note the broad categories for bicycles according to age and intended use. Many different brands of bicycles are available, and each brand offers several series you can identify with price, construction, and selection of components. Children's bikes in both the 6-to-9 and 10-to-14 age categories emphasize rugged construction because children will not care for their bikes. Due to the fragile design of derailleurs, I recommend that for children's bikes you choose one-speed hubs in the 6 to 9 group and protected internal hub changers for the 10 to 14 group.

In the middle teens and later, a 5-speed derailleur affords a first step up from the heavy, rugged children's bike. All major manufacturers supply a 5-speed with up (or flat) handlebars, wide saddle, fenders, and a rack over the rear wheel. This series weighs about 35 pounds and costs less than $150. Some manufacturers make an internal-hub 5-speed gear changer rather than an external derailleur with a single chainwheel and 5-gear rear cluster.

The next step up is to the 10-speed bike with turned-down handlebars, narrow saddle, steel rims, lightweight-steel tubing frame equipped with one-piece hubs and clincher tires. Typical bikes in this class weigh about 30 pounds and cost about $100 to $250.

You can spend a little more and get these added benefits: a high-carbon or chromolly seamless straight-gauge steel tubing frame, alloy rims for either clincher or sew-up tires, quick-release hubs, chrome-plated stays, and higher-quality chainwheels, freewheels, and derailleurs. This improved model will weigh in at about 25–28 pounds and cost in the range of $200–$350.

For a really fine long-distance touring bicycle (Fig. 3), step up once more to the 10-speed with a wide range of gears (38 to 52 tooth chainwheels and 30 to 14 tooth freewheels, for example), cotterless crank, *Reynolds 531* double-butted tubing throughout frame, stays,

| Item | Young Children 6-9 | Children 10-14 | Utility, Exercise, Shopping | Commuting, Short Touring | Extensive Touring |
|---|---|---|---|---|---|
| Frame—Size | 16 | 16-24 | 19½-25½ | 19½-25½ | 19½-25½ |
| —Construction | conventional | conventional | conventional | lightweight seamless tubing | lightweight double-butted |
| Wheels—Diameter | 18-24 | 24-26 | 26-27 | 27 | 27 |
| Tire Size | 1⅜-1.75 | 1¼-1⅜ | 1¼-1⅜ | 1¼ | 1¼ |
| Rims | steel | steel | steel | steel | alloy |
| Crank | cottered or one-piece | cottered or one-piece | cottered | cottered or cotterless | cotterless |
| Gears | None—single Speed | 3- or 5-speed internal hub | 5-speed internal hub or derailleur | 10-speed derailleur | 10- or 15-speed derailleur |
| Brakes | coaster | coaster or caliper | caliper | caliper | caliper |
| Handlebars | **flat or low BMX** | turned down | flat | turned down | turned down |
| Saddle | spring | spring, narrow | spring | narrow | narrow |
| Weight Range | 35-45 lbs. | 35-45 lbs. | 32-42 lbs. | 25-35 lbs. | 21-28 lbs. |
| Price Range | **$50-$150** | **$75-$200** | **$75-$200** | **$100-$250** | **$200-$700** |

Fig. 2—Bicycle Selector Guide

and fork, alloy rims, and precision-machined components throughout. The derailleur should be capable of handling the wide range of gears, respond quickly and smoothly to shift changes, and keep the chain on the gears selected. Bicycles in this class weigh about 23 pounds and cost upward from $400.

One word about brand names for components—French, Italian, and English makers of bicycle hubs, cranks, headsets, pedals, gear wheels, derailleurs, and frames acquired early on a deserved reputation for quality design and construction. As the bicycle boom gathered momentum, these old-line makers fell far behind in filling orders and they increased prices in quantum jumps. As a result, other manufacturers, principally the Japanese, applied their engineering and manufacturing know-how to the production of bicycle components. The results are now in the marketplace with many excellent components comparable to European models at considerably lower prices. Any specific model of bicycle may be equipped with varied components. Instead of buying by brand name only, look for the quality differences you can recognize from the following data.

Fig. 3—A lightweight responsive touring bicycle can be a joy to ride. Size, selection of components, and overall weight combine to fit a bicycle to your specific requirements.

POINTS TO PONDER

Selecting a bicycle requires fitting the size and features desired into a given price range. As an aid in picking the right bicycle for you or your children, consider these factors while using the *Selector Guide* chart.

FRAME. The right size frame fits you as precisely as a pair of pants. Of course you can adjust the height of the saddle post, but why settle for a make-do? Frame size is measured in inches from the top of the seat tube to the pedal bracket hub (see Fig. 4). Frame sizes vary from about 18 to 26 inches. Selecting a frame size according to body height has been one system, but it may fail to fit when a person happens to have longer or shorter legs than average. A better way fits frame size to inseam measurement. For starters select a frame size that measures about 10 inches less than your inseam. But check the frame size on the spot in a bicycle shop by standing over the frame with both feet flat on the floor (Fig. 5). Allow ½- to 1-inch space between your crotch and the top tube. You should be able to straddle the top tube member when you are at rest without tipping the bicycle to one side or the other. Without this crotch clearance, you will find riding uncomfortable—and possibly injurious.

Fig. 4—Bicycle frame size is measured on the slant between the center of the bottom bracket and the top of the seat tube.

Fig. 5—When a bicycle frame size fits you exactly, you can straddle the top tube with both feet flat on the ground—with ½ to 1 inch to spare.

FRAME CONSTRUCTION. Cost reflects the type of metal in the frame and the joining mechanics. The best all-around frames are built with double-butted tubing made of high carbon manganese-molybdenum or chrome molybdenum alloy steel (see Fig. 6). Note the extra metal thickness at the ends where joints are brazed. The special alloys of steel combine high strength, fatigue resistance, and a tensile quality that provides flexibility and resilience for added comfort in riding. Note in the various decals attached to bicycles the differences in frame construction (Fig. 7). High quality tubing comes in plain gauge—that is, without added thickness at the ends and, hence, less strength than the butted design. Note also that the fine butted tubing may not be used for all parts of the frame. You can figure an added cost for each increment of quality—lowest for plain gauge tubing, medium for butted tubing on the main diamond tubes (seat tube, top tube, and down tube as noted in Fig. 4) and the highest for tubing such as *Reynolds* butted *531* used in all the frame members and the fork as well. Close scrutiny of the decal wording, as stated in the decals (Fig. 7), will help you appraise quality. *Columbus, Tange,* and *Falk t*ubes can be in the same range of quality of *Reynolds,* and they also come in different grades.

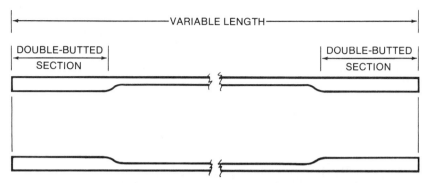

Fig. 6—Double-butted high-strength alloy seamless-steel tubing combine maximum strength with minimum weight. Double thick end sections add extra metal for strength at joints. Long sections in the middle are thin-walled to minimize weight.

Cheap bicycles are built with frames electrically welded from ordinary steel rolled into a tubular shape and seam welded. High temperatures during welding weaken the metal locally at the joints—precisely where extra strength is needed. Low-temperature brazing limited to 850° F retains the heat-treated strength of the alloy-steel drawn to shape in a seamless design for the *Reynolds 531* tubing.

Fig. 7—Note decals on frame to determine whether tubes are constant thickness or double butted. If you see no decals, you can be assured the frame tubing is either ordinary steel or one of the superlight nonsteel alloys.

Reinforcing lugs strengthen the joints on better frames. Note the lugged design in Fig. 8. A plain joint without reinforcing lugs is shown in Fig. 9. Long-life frames are dependent on quality construction as evidenced by lugs and the use of high quality alloy-steel tubing.

Fig. 8—Since weakest sections of frame assembly are at the welded or brazed joints, better bikes include shaped lugs to reinforce the joint.

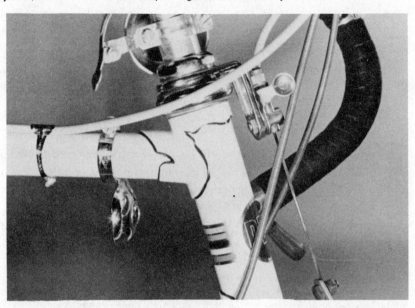

Fig. 9—Less expensive bike frames are joined without lugs and tend to break apart.

WHEELS. Assemblies of rims, spokes, hubs, and tires make up another important element. Frame size and wheel diameter are closely related, although you can sometimes fit 25-, 26-, or 27-inch wheels on an adult frame to vary size. Tires will be considered separately later. Rims for the best lightweight bicycles will be an alloy of aluminum. Steel rims, on the other hand, are rugged and will absorb more punishment than lightweight alloy rims. So, for children's bikes and utility adult bikes likely to be ridden over rough terrain, steel rims are preferred. For long-distance touring and possibly commuting, look for aluminum rims. Either type of rim can be made for clincher or tubular (sew-up) tires.

SPOKES. *Robergel, DT,* and other top spokes are made from chrome nickel stainless steel to remain rust-free. Like high quality frame tubes, the best spokes are butted at both the hooked end and the nipple end for extra strength. If you should need to replace one or more spokes, rather than attempt to relate spoke length to wheel size, remove a good spoke and order or pick up exact replacements.

HUBS. The central wheel unit holds the hook ends of the spokes plus the machined bearing surfaces for the axle. Most new hubs use the wide flange to provide a soft ride with little performance loss. The best hubs for touring bikes are forged from aluminum. For a quick-release, hubs are hollow, permitting the skewer to pass through the center (Fig. 10). Quick-release hubs allow you to remove the wheel in seconds in case of a flat tire or to stow a bike in a car trunk.

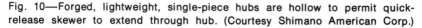

Fig. 10—Forged, lightweight, single-piece hubs are hollow to permit quick-release skewer to extend through hub. (Courtesy Shimano American Corp.)

CRANK. Pedals fit at the ends of the crank arms that rotate in the bottom bracket. For light weight, the best cranks are forged aluminum alloy and come in three pieces—center and two crank arms. The best designs are assembled without tapered cotter pins. The cottered arms are easier to manufacture, but they tend to wear and become loose with use. Some cranks are one-piece and may be slipped through the bracket without disassembly. (The chainwheel attached to the crank will be considered in Chapter Three along with gears and chains for speed changers.)

PEDALS. Rubber tread pedals (Fig. 11-A) may be okay for children's and adult bicycles used for short trips, but steel rat-traps are preferred for touring. The lightweight metal pedals (Fig. 13-B) include serrated edges for better grip on shoes—particularly wet sneakers. Rubber tread pedals weigh more than the rat-traps and individual rubber treads turn on their mounting axles when worn. Pedal spindles have either a $\frac{9}{16}$-inch thread to screw into European cranks or ½-inch thread to fit American cranks.

Fig. 11—Rubber-tread pedals (A) are heavy and slippery when wet. Rat-trap pedals (B) come in various sizes with serrated metal edges. Toe-clips fitted to rat-traps improve bicycling efficiency.

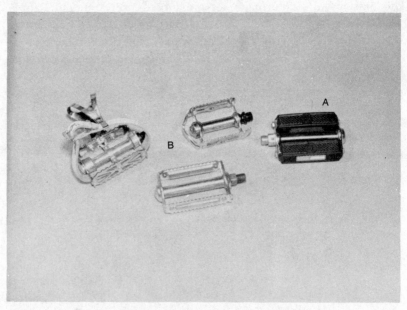

HANDLEBARS. Two parts make up the handlebars for a bicycle and both can be selected for individual fit. Flat or conventional handlebars extend back with the handles at the end (Fig. 12). Touring and racing handlebars turn down and sometimes outboard, depending on the maker (Fig. 13). Flat handlebars permit an upright riding position and may be satisfactory for short rides, particularly where a primary objective is to view one's surroundings. However, for touring, the drop or turned-down bars offer three major advantages: (1) The body when leaning forward operates more efficiently, as the lungs

Fig. 12—Flat or up handlebars permit upright stance for short trips.

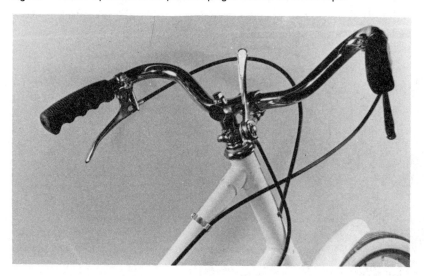

Fig. 13—With turned-down handlebars, rider assumes efficient pedaling posture and distributes weight equitably between handlebars, pedals, and saddle.

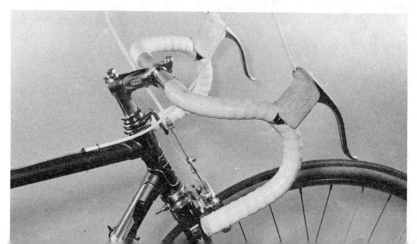

and diaphragm hang from the backbone in a natural position; long trips will be much less tiring. (2) Body weight is more evenly distributed—about a third on the handlebars, a third on the pedals, and a third on the saddle. (3) Turned-down bars offer a greater variety of hand positions. Changing hand and body positions during a long tour reduces fatigue. At least four and as many as six hand positions are available with the drop handlebars (Figs. 14-18). Note that the uphill and "work" positions cause the body to be bent farther forward to reduce wind resistance and to increase pedaling efficiency. Various manufacturers offer handlebars with varied shapes, but those with the "maes" bend offer one of the best combinations of curvature with a straight section directly out from the stem—a handy place for hands during easy cycling or when you should be keeping your head up to watch for city traffic during commuting.

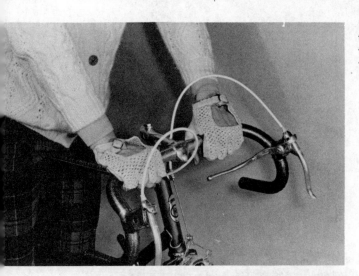

Fig. 14—Hands in position close to stem offer alternative position to relieve back or neck strain or for casual riding.

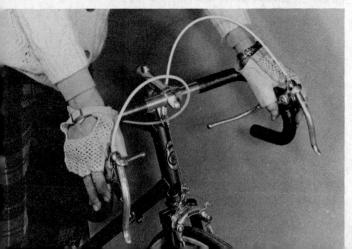

Fig. 15—Hands at beginning of handlebar curve effectively control balance.

Fig. 16—Hands far around curve permit maximum pedaling efficiency and pulling up with arms when climbing hills.

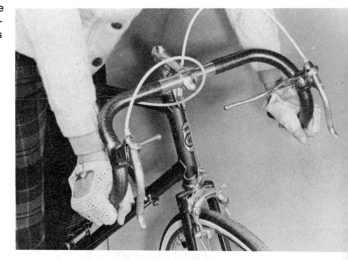

Fig. 17—Hands just below brake attachment permit keeping two fingers at the ready over brake handle when riding in traffic.

Fig. 18—Alternative hand position near stem with hands on auxiliary brake handles are for coasting at moderate speeds.

When fitting the handlebar to a specific rider, note the measurements in Fig. 19. Just as you find a frame size uniquely fitted to your inseam and leg length, so must you find that combination of handlebar and stem length that suits your specific arm length. The stem affords two adjustments—height and distance between steering head and the crosswise portion of the handlebars. Rather than try various stem lengths at random, buy or borrow an adjustable stem to try. To find the most comfortable stem length for you, mount the handlebars of your choice in an adjustable stem and ride it for several hours or days at different positions.

As a starting point for finding a comfortable stem length, measure the distance from your elbow to your fingertips. Select a stem length that equates this elbow-fingertip distance between the forward tip of the saddle to the centerline of the crosswire position of the handlebars. Refer to Fig. 19. You will note that both ends of this span are adjustable within certain limits. A quick way to measure this distance is to lay your arm with outstretched fingers parallel to the top tube between saddle and handlebars (Fig. 20). Various stem lengths are available, or you can adjust the position of the saddle fore and aft on its mount. However, most cyclists find the best position for the saddle to be slightly behind a vertical line from the crank bracket centerline (see Fig. 19). About 1¾ to 2½ inches aft provides optimum riding efficiency. Handlebars should feel comfortable and natural after a long ride—say two or more hours. Therefore, set the adjustable stem for the elbow-to-fingertip distance and try it. If this distance doesn't feel "right" for you, adjust the saddle or stem distance until you do feel comfortable after extensive riding. A small difference in stem distance can make a big difference in your enjoyment of cycling. Remember, there is nothing standard about stem lengths. Those that may come on a particular bike may fit average riders, but few people are average, particularly you. So spend some time and effort to fit handlebars and stem to your personal dimensions. Chapter Three tells how to position brake handles on both flat and turned-down handlebars for efficiency and comfort.

SADDLES. Seats for bicycles are appropriately called saddles because you're mounting a mechanical steed for riding. Saddles come in three basic styles, as shown in Fig. 21.

1. Mattress or bedspring saddles (Fig. 21-A) afford less comfort than you might suspect. Mattress saddles may be fine for sitting and

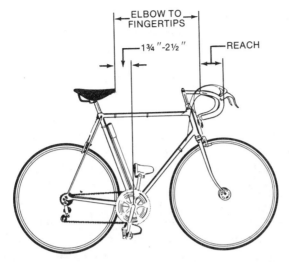

Fig. 19—Two important dimensions in fitting a bicycle. Forward end of saddle should be from 1¾ to 2½ inches aft of a line extended vertically above bottom bracket. Both stem length and saddle position can be adjusted to elbow-to-fingertip distance shown.

Fig. 20—Quick check on desired handlebar position is to measure distance from saddle to handlebars with arm and fingers extended.

chatting or casual riding, primarily for youngsters. But the width of mattress saddles induces inner leg chafing on long rides, and the springs absorb much of the pedaling energy expended without providing forward locomotion.

2. Touring saddles (Fig. 21-B) are long and narrow with less posterior support than the mattress saddle but more than the racing saddle. Riding with turned-down handlebars shifts about a third of one's body weight to the saddle. The narrow forward section provides support without chafing during pedaling.

3. Racing saddles (Fig. 21-C) are narrower and lighter to improve pedaling efficiency.

Saddles are built with a metal or fiberglass base and a vinyl, leather, or nylon seat. The best saddles are built with thick butt leather, as leather absorbs moisture and feels better underseat. Nylon and vinyl can get slick and slippery in hot weather or in the rain. Saddles may be adjusted three ways—up and down with the seat post, fore and aft (most saddles) under the seat, and tipped by rotating around the seat-post attach fitting. Already noted and shown in Fig. 19 is the preferred fore-and-aft position of the saddle. For most riding, the saddle should also be horizontal, although a slight tip upward at the forward end may improve comfort in riding. If a tipped saddle feels better, then tip it. Most riders find a level position better over long hauls.

Fig. 21—Three saddle types—(A) bedspring or mattress, (B) touring, and (C) modified racing. Some racing saddles are much narrower.

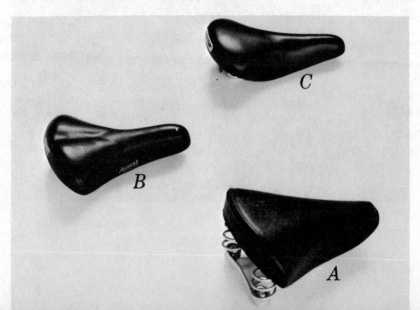

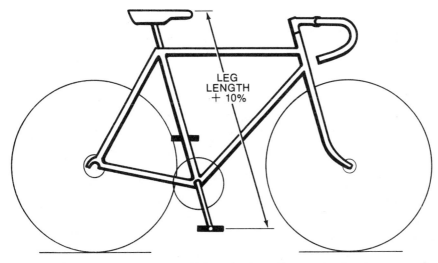

LEG
LENGTH
+ 10%

Fig. 22—Saddle height most efficient for long-distance touring is measured
from bottom pedal when crank is in line with seat tube.

Saddle height is something else again—and one of the most critical
fits of cycle to rider. If the frame size is correct, then the saddle will
sit several inches above the top tube. Many beginning riders set
saddles too low for efficient pedaling. One saddle-height system calls
for the knee to be only slightly bent when the leg is extended to
the lowest pedal position. In this position the saddle may appear
to be awkwardly high at first. But try riding several miles before
making a final decision. You'll find pedaling easier if the knees rise
to a minimum height when the pedal reaches its highest position.

Another system developed from a series of scientific experiments
at Loughborough University in England calls for the saddle to be
set about 10 percent higher than the leg measured from floor to
crotch (Fig. 22). The added 10 percent over your leg measurement
permits a slight crook at the knee with the pedal at its bottom position.
The added distance also permits effective ankling (see Chapter Six).
However, like many other averages, the 10 percent figure might
not suit you or feel comfortable over a long ride. If you have been
used to riding with a saddle much lower, you may feel comfortable
at that position because you are used to it. Try riding with the
saddle at the position shown in Fig. 22 over a period of several

days, possibly working up to the full height by increments. The most efficient, comfortable saddle height will put you ahead of other pedalers in speed and endurance on tours or fitness jaunts. Medical scientists who have studied muscle efficiency explain that muscles in their extended position can apply more force and power than when shortened—hence the need to avoid sharply bent knees. But the saddle should not be so high that the legs cannot complete the full crank revolution with a smooth, fluid motion uninterrupted by a snap or jolt as the leg reaches its straight or fully extended position. Saddle height as diagrammed in Fig. 22 has proved to be a good, consistent guide for measuring and setting the saddle.

Once the saddle height is established, the stem supporting handlebars should be adjusted to match the height of the saddle. At these positions weight is most efficiently distributed between front and rear wheels and between arms and legs.

## TIRES

On the Cyclemates' trip from Mercer Island to Halifax, only rear tires required replacement for wear. You too can get a surprising number of miles from bicycle tires if you pay attention to inflation pressure, mount them correctly, and keep away from thorns, glass, and road junk that causes punctures. When it comes to selecting tires, you should remember these tips:

TYPE. Tubular (sew-ups) and clincher (wire-ons) are the two types of tires used on bicycles. Tubulars include a sewn-in tube and are very flexible and light. They are used for racing and for some touring, although they are more perishable than clinchers; that is, they are more prone to puncture. But for riding response and comfort you can't beat tubulars. Tubulars cost more—from two or four times more than clinchers. The price for a tubular tire varies inversely according to weight—the lighter they are, the more they cost. A silk, smooth-tread weighing 5.98 ounces costs $50, while a common cotton cord tubular weighing 15.8 ounces costs about $18, at the time of this writing. Prices will certainly go up, but the ratio of price to weight will likely remain. For touring, select only the tubulars with thick rubber tread, as a guard against excessive punctures.

Clincher tires offer advantages of their own—greater resistance to punctures and quicker repairs to a tube if a puncture does occur.

But you pay a small price in added weight. On the three Cyclemate cross-country tours, all bikes were equipped with clincher tires. In case of a puncture, the tire may be pried off the rim to get at the tube with a tire wrench (see Chapter Fourteen). A rubber patch kit easily closes the hole, and you're on your way in five or six minutes.

Sizes. Tubular and clincher tires require their own rims, as one type will not fit the other. If you use your bike for different kinds of riding, you might keep two pairs of wheels—one equipped with tubulars and one fitted with clinchers. Balloon tires in 24- and 26-inch diameters measure 2¼ inches—a full inch wider than the lightweight 1¼-inch sizes fitted to touring and racing bicycles. Common sizes are 1¼, 1⅜, and 1¾ inch to fit 20-, 24-, 26-, and 27-inch wheels.

Inflation. Each of these tire sizes requires its own inflation pressure, as noted in Table N on page 189. You'll find that tubulars and some lightweight clinchers come with *Presta* air valves. Most clinchers are fitted with *Schrader* valves, like those on automobile tires. To inflate the tubulars, you need a *Schrader*-to-*Presta* adapter or a pump designed for *Presta* valves. *Presta* valves are hand opened by screwing counterclockwise and closed by screwing clockwise after filling with air. Proper inflation will reduce pedaling effort and prevent blowouts.

Tread. Rolling resistance increases as blocks of rubber meet the road. Racing tires exhibit very little tread, usually in a multiple ribbed design to prevent sidewise skids but little resistance to rolling. For touring, however, you need more of a tread, such as the diagonal or herringbone designs for traction. These and other tread designs are shown in Fig. 23. Only the balloon tires exhibit a deep, block-type tread, and that is one reason for their rolling resistance.

## SPECIAL BICYCLES

Two-wheel, one-person bicycles dominate the market, but other designs and styles are available to satisfy specific requirements. Among them are:

Tandems. Bicycles built for two or more persons to ride on one frame in tandem are fitted with a crank and pedals at each position for one good reason—everybody aboard is expected to pedal. No free rides! When two people ride a tandem and both pedal with the same efficiency as they would if riding alone, tandem cycling can be fun and relatively easy. Good tandems weigh less per person

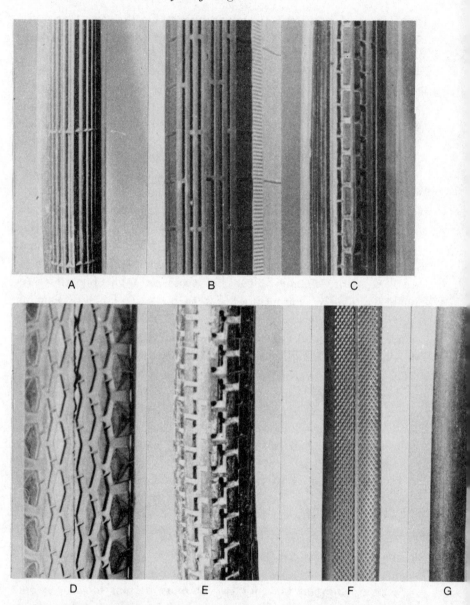

Fig. 23—Tire tread designs. Designs (A) and (B) offer low rolling resistance with grooves for sidewise traction. Additional blocks of rubber at center of design (C) increase rolling resistance slightly but afford greater traction. Tread designs (D) and (E) include blocks too big for efficient touring—okay for short trips. Tread designs (F) and (G) are typical of superlightweight sew-ups.

accommodated than similar quality single-person bikes. A well-built tandem—that is, one built with *Reynolds 531* tubing, alloy cranks, double-walled rims, and other quality components—may weigh only 44 to 46 pounds. When you divide that in half, the weight per person amounts to 22 or 23 pounds—the equivalent of the very best lightweight touring bikes. *Gitane* makes a tandem that weighs less than 50 pounds. Toy tandems can weigh twice as much, as they are built from thick-walled tubing, heavy wheels, and clumsy components. These tandems are frequently rented to couples for a fun tour at a resort area rather than for serious cycling. If you are thinking about a tandem, consider each of the components as carefully as you would in buying a single-person bicycle. Such tandems designed for touring can be expensive—$600 and up. Also, make sure your intended biking partner is committed to pedal his or her share of the way. Rather than buy one expensive tandem, consider buying two well-built, lightweight touring bicycles. The cost will be about the same.

TRICYCLES (ADULT). Three-wheel cycles appear primarily for riders at the extreme ends of the age scale—very young children unable to master the intricacies of a bicycle and elderly persons who desire the assurance three wheels provide. Elderly riders tend to pedal much more slowly than bicyclists and find the tricycle easy to manage when stopped for traffic and other hazards. But tricycles are finding another popular use—as a substitute for a second car for shopping. Most tricycles come equipped with wire baskets capable of hauling several grocery bags full of food. Tricycles are characterized by small wheels (20-inch diameter wheels work best), coaster brakes for the rear wheels and caliper brakes for the single front wheel, three or five-speed gears, and a frame designed mainly for women. A fair to good quality tricycle should weigh less than 60 pounds to rate as reasonably efficient. Tricycles won't do for extensive touring, but serve admirably for short trips of two or three miles. As a substitute for a second car, the $200 to $400 spent for a tricycle could be a good investment to reduce costs and improve the homemaker's exercise and health regimen.

FOLDING BICYCLES. About the only good reason to have a folding bicycle is to carry it along on a boat or airplane for ground transportation. Folding bikes are seldom useful for traveling any distance beyond a few miles. Except for boat or airplane use, you can forget the folding bike because a normal bicycle with the front wheel removed can be stowed just as well in a car trunk. If storage space is limited in an apartment, a fixed-wheel bike will require very little more space than a folding design and weigh about half as much as a folding or take-apart bike. Our advice: forget the folding bike; it's more trouble than it's worth—and seldom practical.

UNICYCLE. One-wheel cycles can be fun and challenging to ride, but they are essentially toys. Unicycles are available in 20- and 24-inch wheel sizes. Examine your motives before investing in what is a vehicle with very limited use.

# 3.

# Mechanics of Bicycles: Gears and Brakes

For years the only type of bicycle sold had a single-speed hub with a coaster brake for the rear wheel. Then, multi-speed hubs, 5-, 10-, and 15-speed derailleurs, and front and back wheel caliper rim brakes literally revolutionized bicycling. Much of the fun of bicycling comes from being able to pedal up hills without straining or to zip over flat country at a comfortable cadence. Front and rear power brakes afford greater safety when used with even a modicum of common sense. Since these mechanical features play such a big part in bicycling today, you owe it to yourself to learn the intricacies of gearing and braking. Don't back off from the mathematics, numbers, and charts. They're not difficult to understand. You'll benefit from the know-how packed in these charts when you select a bike. Use these data to get the most out of your bicycle under all cycling conditions.

*Single-Speed Hubs* with an easy-to-use coaster brake still make sense for youngsters riding around the block, to school, or on short trips in the neighborhood. They are simple to use and to maintain. Kids instinctively backpedal for braking. Further, small hands cannot generate the force needed to apply caliper brakes effectively compared to the backpedal force they can generate with leg muscles. With only back-wheel braking, kids will not apply front-wheel braking only—and tumble over handlebars.

*Multi-speed Hubs* (Fig. 24) change gears internally in response to a cable control. Two, three, or five speeds are available in multi-

THREE-SPEED HUB WITH COASTER BRAKE

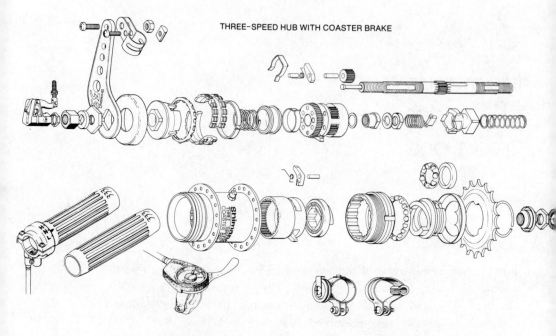

Fig. 24—Three-speed rear hub with coaster brake. This drawing is not intended to guide you through the workings of the system but is intended to show the complexity of internal hub gear changers. If something goes wrong internally, take it to a trained mechanic. (Courtesy, Shimano American Corp.)

speed hubs. For youngsters, if they absolutely insist on more than a single speed, internal speed changers are preferable. The reasons are:

• Multi-speed hubs are fully enclosed. Gear changers are protected from damage through carelessness, abuse, or lack of maintenance attention. These gears are within the metal hub with dust seals at each end. Lubrication is fully contained in the hub package or may be added through a fitting in the hub shell. In contrast, derailleurs for external gears hang out in the open to collect dirt, pants legs, and the flotsam common to youngsters. Derailleur arms extend downward from the gear cluster, usually on lightweight supports (kids' bikes do include heavier roller supports) that are easily bent when bikes fall to the ground or hit rocks, curbs, and bike stands.

• Multi-speed hubs can be more easily shifted than derailleurs. Shift levers are marked for gear positions or click into detents to help youngsters find the right gear. Youngsters may not be tuned to the "ker-chunking" of a misaligned chain on a gear cluster. A front derailleur cage may continue to rub on a chain and wear through. Since derailleurs operate only when the chain is moving, shifting to the right gear without damaging the gears or chain requires skill—more than youngsters can manage at times.

• Many of the 5- or 10-speed bicycles available with derailleur gear changers offer far too many speeds for casual riding. More than two or three speeds can be used efficiently only for touring or racing. A 10-speed derailleur on a kid's bike is a gimmick—one that is likely to cause more trouble than it's worth.

• Multi-speed hubs combine gear-changers with a coaster brake (Fig. 24). Backpedal brakes afford greater reliability and safety for young riders than do caliper rim brakes. Many caliper rim brakes are installed on bicycles with multi-speed hubs, but youngsters under age 11 should not be expected to use them. Children in the 11- to 13-age bracket may learn the intricacies of caliper brakes in preparation for graduating to a 10-speed derailleur-equipped bicycle where coaster brakes are not available.

• Finally—if a youngster aged 10 or under rides a 10-speed bike, what does he have to look forward to? Encourage him to work up the scale of mechanical equipment as his interests and skills mature.

Bicycles equipped with multi-speed hubs offer a good middle range of gear ratios, as detailed in Table A. Check the specifications on any bike equipped with multi-speed hubs against the gear-inch or distance-traveled charts in Fig. 29. You can compare their gearing with external derailleur gear ratios in Table B. If you live in a hilly area, make sure the gears available include a low gear in the range of 1.2 to 1.35 or stated as gear-inches in the range of 37 to 44. Also, see Chapter Two for more information on picking the "right" bike.

*Multi-Speed Derailleur-Equipped Bicycles* rate tops for serious cyclists. First, they offer an almost unlimited range of gear ratios, as detailed in Tables B and C. Second, they operate much more simply than the internal-hub gearing, and the parts are out in the open. Third, they weigh very little relative to their efficiency. All in all, 5-, 10-, or 15-speed bikes have been the biggest single factor behind the booming interest in bicycling.

Basic elements of the derailleur bicycles are shown in Fig. 25. Variations are available for each of the elements. For example, the

FREEWHEEL
CLUSTER

CHAIN

FRONT
DERAILLEUR

REAR
DERAILLEUR

SMALL
CHAINWHEEL

LARGE
CHAINWHEEL

Fig. 25 — Major components of a 10-speed derailleur power train.

rear freewheel cluster may include four, five, or six gears with the number of teeth on each sprocket ranging from twelve to thirty-two. The rear cluster operates free wheeling through an internal design that permits coasting. Internal-hub coaster brakes cannot be used with derailleurs due to their complex roller and spring arrangements for keeping the chain taut.

Chainwheels are available with teeth varying from 24 to 56 and can be grouped in twos or threes or used singly. Chainwheels come in various qualities too—the main difference being weight and durability.

Derailleurs front and back operate simply—they push or pull the chain from one gear wheel to another and function only when the chain is moving. Derailleurs for back clusters make use of a pantagraph principle for positioning the chain on one of the four, five, or six freewheels of the rear cluster. Front derailleurs are even simpler—they brush the sides of the chain to move it in or out to the chainwheel selected.

Control cables run from a lever device mounted on the frame (Fig. 26) or at the end of the handlebars (Fig. 27). Cables operate against spring tension to move the derailleur mechanisms in one direction. The control lever thus moves the derailleur mechanism in toward the wheel and compresses a spring. Moving the control lever back permits the spring to draw the derailleur mechanism away from the wheel toward the small freewheel. Rollers operate automatically through another spring to take up slack in the chain as it moves from larger to smaller gears both at the front and rear. Thin teeth on the gear wheels permit the chain to move from one to the other with a minimum of interference. However, the thin teeth (compared to single-speed bikes) call for extra attention to keep them lubricated and free of wear-producing grit and dirt. See Chapter Thirteen for maintenance and adjustment procedures to keep the chain and gears functioning smoothly. Like most mechanisms, gears, chain, and gear changers respond beautifully to even a minimum of care.

Fig. 26—Two derailleur shift levers, one for the front and one for the rear, mounted on down tube. A less desirable location is near the stem where ends of levers could hurt a person thrown forward in a collision.

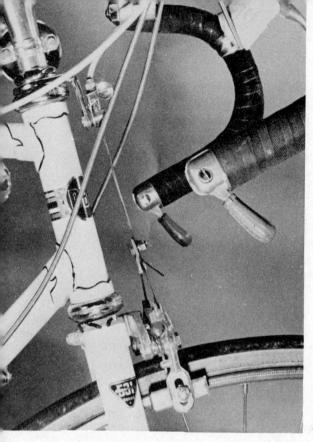

Fig. 27—Gear shift levers at ends of handlebars permit shifting without removing hands from handlebars. Because handlebar-end shift levers are short, they are usable only with high-quality responsive derailleurs.

When you examine the rear gear cluster and the chainwheels, note their arrangement. The rear cluster positions the largest of the freewheels next to the wheel hub. The smallest of the freewheels will be farthest outboard—away from the wheel hub. To prevent the gear cluster plus the rear derailleur mechanism from sticking too far out in the breeze (thereby exposing it to the greater probability of damage), the rear wheel spokes and rim will be "dished." That is, the rim of the wheel will not be centered over the hub. Instead, the rim will be shifted toward the derailleur. Dishing is accomplished by loosening the spokes on the left side of the wheel and tightening those on the right side. The wheel continues to run true, but the plane of the rim is shifted axially relative to the hub.

Chainwheels, in contrast, will be assembled to the crank arm on the right side with the largest chainwheel outboard. One or two smaller chainwheels may be assembled between the large chainwheel and the bottom bracket. With this arrangement, the larger chainwheel aligns with the second smallest freewheel of the rear cluster. By running at a slight angle, the chain runs easily with either the smallest or middle freewheel of the rear cluster. The smaller chainwheel aligns with the second largest of the freewheels in the rear cluster —again to minimize the angle made by the chain as it engages a freewheel to the left or right of a plane directly aft of the chainwheel. On a 5-speed bike, the chainwheel is aligned with the center freewheel of the rear cluster. The derailleur shifts the chain two wheels to the left or two wheels to the right of the center gear. A full-range derailleur with limit stops set correctly (see Chapter Thirteen) will have no difficulty shifting the chain to high and low gears.

One of the benefits of a 10-speed over a 5-speed chainwheel-freewheel combination is the smoother alignment possible for the chain. Although technically either chainwheel of a 10-speed machine can mesh with any of the five freewheels of the rear cluster, those combinations resulting in large angular deflections will not run as smoothly as chainwheel-freewheel combinations more nearly in alignment.

## GEARING

The chains on modern 10-speeds are linked with cross pieces at ½-inch pitch. That is, the center of one chain rivet is ½ inch from the center of the next chain rivet. Due to the light, precision construction of the chains, no take-apart links are used. To change chain length, the rivets must be forced out with a special tool (see Chapter Fourteen). After links are added or removed, the chain is rejoined with rivets using the same tool.

Each tooth on a chainwheel or rear gear wheel engages one link of the chain. Therefore, gear ratios may be easily computed using the number of teeth as the variables. Obviously, the same number of links must pass over both the chainwheel and the rear gear wheel in any combination. A chainwheel with 40 teeth drives a rear freewheel with 20 teeth through two full revolutions for every full revolution of the pedals. The gear ratio for these two gears would then be 2.00. Table B details the gear ratios available for chainwheels with 24 through 56 teeth in combination with freewheels ranging from 12 to 30 teeth. This range of chainwheel and rear gear wheel teeth covers most of the popular sizes found on 5-, 10-, and 15-speed bicycles.

Rather than use straight gear ratios, which would be comparable to rear axle ratios on cars, you're more likely to find whole numbers like 65 or 70 referred to as gear ratios. More properly these numbers are called gear-inch ratios. The formula for figuring gear-inch ratios is:

$$\frac{\text{Teeth on chainwheel}}{\text{Teeth on freewheel}} \text{ (gear ratio) x diameter or rear wheel} = \text{gear inches}$$
(round number to nearest whole number)

An example of this formula would be:

$$\frac{\text{Teeth on chainwheel}}{\text{Teeth on freewheel}} \quad \frac{48}{20} \text{ x 27 (dia. of rear wheel)} = 65 \text{ gear inches}$$
(rounded from 64.8)

From Table B you can find the gear ratio resulting from combinations of chainwheel and freewheel. Simply mutliply this gear ratio by the diameter of the rear wheel—usually 27 inches for lightweight touring or commuting bikes—to derive the gear-inch number. More effort is required to pedal a bicycle with the same gear ratio equipped with 27-inch wheels than with 26-inch wheels because the bicycle travels $\pi$ or 3.14 inches farther with each wheel revolution. Hence, the diameter of the rear wheel becomes a factor in pedaling effort along with the combination of gears. Table C computes the gear-inch number for the range of gear ratios shown in Table B for both 26- and 27-inch wheels.

One other useful device for selecting and using various combinations of chainwheel and freewheel sizes is the distance traveled during one full revolution of the pedals. Multiplying the gear-inch number by $\pi$ (3.14 or 3 1/7) yields the distance traveled in inches for every 360-degree revolution of the pedal crank. Using the same gears (48-tooth chainwheel mated with a 20-tooth freewheel) with a gear-inch number of 65 multiplied by $\pi$ yields a distance traveled of 203 inches or just under 17 feet for each full pedal revolution. The chart in Fig. 28 shows the distance traveled in inches for each combination of chainwheel and freewheel teeth during one pedal revolution. A second scale relates the distance traveled in feet.

The chart in Fig. 28 simplifies picking a combination of chainwheel and freewheel sizes to suit the terrain you'll be traveling over. Moving

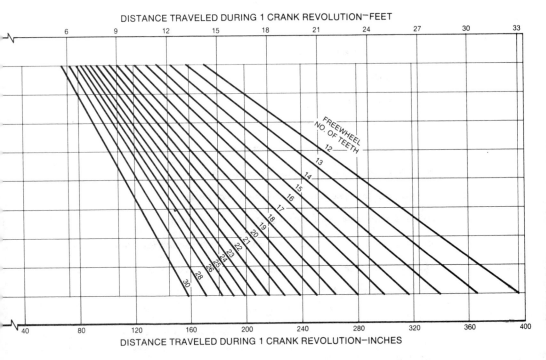

DISTANCE TRAVELED DURING 1 CRANK REVOLUTION–FEET

DISTANCE TRAVELED DURING 1 CRANK REVOLUTION–INCHES

Fig. 28—Chart of travel distances for full range chainwheel-freewheel combinations.

vertically up the chart from a specific distance traveled in one revolution of the chainwheel (360 degrees of pedal crank motion), you will note that several chainwheel-freewheel combinations yield the same or nearly the same gear ratio or gear-inch number. Avoid selecting chainwheels and rear clusters where different combinations yield the same gear-inch number or traverse the same distance during one pedal revolution; there's little point in buying a 10-speed bike that provides only seven different gear combinations.

Alpine gearing calls for widely spaced chainwheels and regular spacing of freewheels in the rear cluster. For example, a 52-36 double chainwheel in combination with a rear cluster of 14-16-19-22-26-tooth freewheels permits relatively easy pedaling up steep hills with good speed available over flat, level distances. Fig. 29 charts the full range of gear and distance-traveled combinations available with one alpine-gearing chainwheel-rear cluster combination. This is the combination

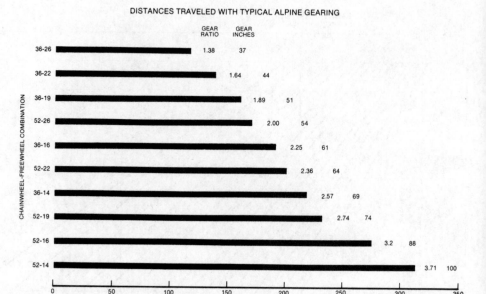

Fig. 29—Distance traveled with each chainwheel-freewheel combination for Alpine gearing. Note smooth progression of distances covered with curves at both low and high ends.

I used on Cyclemates III. The 36–26 low gear (all combinations are noted with number of teeth on the chainwheel first and teeth on the freewheel second) provides a gear ratio of 1.38 and a gear-inch number of 37. High gear is 3.71 and 100. Note the even progression of distances traveled for each combination of chainwheel and freewheel from low to high gear. No close gear ratios occur near the center where easiest shifting occurs. Also, note the spread between distances traveled at both the low and high ends of the gear combinations. Plotting a similar chart before you buy a 10-speed combination simplifies checking the progression of gear ratios through all combinations. Simply pick off the distances traveled with each gear combination from Tables B and C and scale them off on common graph paper.

## BRAKES

The gears that make you go rate equally in importance with the brakes that bring you to a stop. You wouldn't think of driving a car without effective, well-adjusted brakes. Don't consider biking out of your back yard without good brakes on your bicycle—and knowing how to use them. Three types of brakes are in general use on bicycles —coaster brakes inside the rear hub, caliper rim brakes, and the new caliper disc brakes.

COASTER BRAKES. *Bendix, Shimano,* and the older *New Departure* hub brakes offer the simplest method for braking. What is more natural than backpedaling if you want to apply brakes? Children, particularly, can learn to use coaster brakes quickly and effectively. The coaster brake rear hub permits three modes of operation—forward with single or multiple gears as pedals rotate forward, coasting with the rear wheel hub disengaged and pedals stopped, and braking with pedal pressure applied backwards or counterclockwise (when viewed from the right).

Braking force is generated by friction between stacked plates or serrated half-cylinders inside the hub. A backward rotation of the pedals engages a pawl that forces plates or cylindrical brake pads together. One set of plates is keyed to remain motionless. The other set is keyed to turn with the wheel. Friction between the contacting surfaces supplies the braking force to slow the bicycle or bring it to a stop.

CALIPER RIM BRAKES. Nearly all adult bicycles and many youngsters' bicycles are equipped with caliper brakes on both front and rear wheels. Caliper rim brakes offer many advantages over the rear-hub coaster brake—plus a number of disadvantages. Caliper brakes permit braking on both wheels rather than just one. By bearing on both sides of the rim at a greater distance from the axle, less rubbing pressure generates considerably more braking force than the friction between brake pads inside the hub at the axle.

Two mechanisms are in general use for applying braking at the rims—center-pull and side-pull calipers. Both work well when properly adjusted, but the center-pull (Fig. 30) includes a self-centering cable pull that equitably divides the cable force from the handle. Excellent side-pull brakes (Fig. 31) are available, particularly the *Campagnolo*. Less expensive bicycles are frequently fitted with side-pull calipers. With side-pulls, one brake arm exerts less lever action on the brake pads than the other. Unless the rim is truly round with a minimum of side wobble, and the individual pads are precisely adjusted for equal distances from the rim, more friction force will be applied to one side than the other, lessening the total braking available.

Fig. 30—Center-pull caliper brakes automatically divide braking force through triangular cable sling.

Caliper brake handles are mounted on the handlebars and can be individually adjusted for comfort and ready accessibility to your hands. Handles are mounted under the handle grips on flat handlebars. Due to their mechanical action, brake handles on down-turned handlebars afford more leverage and, thereby, more braking force than handles mounted under the grips of flat handlebars.

Secondary brake handles permit partial braking with handles located immediately to each side of the stem (Fig. 18). Due to their position and the leverage available, these secondary brake handles are useful mainly for controlling speeds while coasting down hills. When riding in traffic or when frequent full stops can be anticipated, don't depend on the secondary handles for braking.

Maintenance and precise adjustment of brake elements are essential

Fig. 31—Side-pull calipers require more precise adjustment to equalize braking force on both sides of wheel.

for good, reliable braking with caliper brakes. Brake handles must be securely attached to the handlebars. The length of the brake-actuating cables must be adjusted precisely to get maximum power from the handles. Brakes must be fitted with fresh pads close enough for quick, effective braking but not so close as to develop drag. All of these adjustments are detailed in Chapter Thirteen.

CALIPER DISC BRAKES. Relatively new, caliper disc brakes are a fall-out from the disc brakes that replaced drum brakes on automobiles (Fig. 32). A separate, flat braking disc attached to the hub avoids the recurring problem of out-of-round and wobbly wheel rims. Except for the disc, the caliper braking action is the same as for caliper rim brakes. Greater friction force between pads and disc surfaces is required because the disc is close to the axle.

Fig. 32—Caliper disc brakes eliminate problem of wobbly rims for even braking. (Courtesy, Bendix.)

Caliper rim brakes will continue to find favor on lightweight touring and racing bicycles because of their low weight. Reliability and resistance to damage and poor maintenance are likely to favor the caliper disc brake for bicycles below the high performance class, namely those for youngsters.

## TABLE A: Gear Ratios Available with Multi-Speed Rear Hubs

### SHIMANO 3-SPEED HUB

| Number of Teeth | | Gear Ratios | | |
|---|---|---|---|---|
| Chainwheel | Rear Sprocket | High | Normal | Low |
| 28 | 16 | 1.31 | 1.75 | 2.34 |
|  | 18 | 1.17 | 1.56 | 2.08 |
|  | 20 | 1.05 | 1.40 | 1.86 |
| 30 | 16 | 1.41 | 1.88 | 2.50 |
|  | 18 | 1.25 | 1.67 | 2.22 |
|  | 20 | 1.12 | 1.50 | 2.00 |
| 32 | 16 | 1.50 | 2.00 | 2.67 |
|  | 18 | 1.33 | 1.78 | 2.37 |
|  | 20 | 1.20 | 1.60 | 2.13 |
| 34 | 16 | 1.60 | 2.13 | 2.84 |
|  | 18 | 1.42 | 1.89 | 2.52 |
|  | 20 | 1.28 | 1.70 | 2.26 |
| 36 | 16 | 1.69 | 2.25 | 3.00 |
|  | 18 | 1.50 | 2.00 | 2.67 |
|  | 20 | 1.35 | 1.80 | 2.40 |
| 38 | 16 | 1.79 | 2.38 | 3.18 |
|  | 18 | 1.58 | 2.11 | 2.81 |
|  | 20 | 1.43 | 1.90 | 2.53 |
| 40 | 16 | 1.88 | 2.50 | 3.33 |
|  | 18 | 1.67 | 2.22 | 2.96 |
|  | 20 | 1.50 | 2.00 | 2.67 |
| 42 | 16 | 1.98 | 2.63 | 3.50 |
|  | 18 | 1.75 | 2.33 | 3.10 |
|  | 20 | 1.58 | 2.10 | 2.80 |
| 44 | 16 | 2.06 | 2.75 | 3.66 |
|  | 18 | 1.83 | 2.44 | 3.25 |
|  | 20 | 1.65 | 2.20 | 2.96 |
| 46 | 16 | 2.16 | 2.88 | 3.84 |
|  | 18 | 1.92 | 2.56 | 3.42 |
|  | 20 | 1.72 | 2.30 | 3.06 |
| 48 | 16 | 2.25 | 3.00 | 4.00 |
|  | 18 | 2.00 | 2.67 | 3.56 |
|  | 20 | 1.80 | 2.40 | 3.20 |
| 50 | 16 | 2.35 | 3.13 | 4.17 |
|  | 18 | 2.08 | 2.78 | 3.70 |
|  | 20 | 1.88 | 2.50 | 3.33 |

| No. of Teeth on Chain-wheel | 12 | 13 | 14 | 15 | 16 | 17 | 18 | 19 | No. of Teeth 20 |
|---|---|---|---|---|---|---|---|---|---|
| 24 | 2.00 | 1.85 | 1.71 | 1.60 | 1.50 | 1.41 | 1.33 | 1.26 | 1.20 |
| 25 | 2.08 | 1.92 | 1.79 | 1.67 | 1.56 | 1.47 | 1.39 | 1.32 | 1.25 |
| 26 | 2.17 | 2.00 | 1.86 | 1.73 | 1.63 | 1.53 | 1.44 | 1.37 | 1.30 |
| 27 | 2.25 | 2.07 | 1.93 | 1.80 | 1.69 | 1.59 | 1.50 | 1.42 | 1.35 |
| 28 | 2.33 | 2.15 | 2.00 | 1.87 | 1.75 | 1.65 | 1.56 | 1.47 | 1.40 |
| 29 | 2.42 | 2.23 | 2.07 | 1.93 | 1.81 | 1.71 | 1.61 | 1.53 | 1.45 |
| 30 | 2.50 | 2.31 | 2.14 | 2.00 | 1.88 | 1.76 | 1.67 | 1.58 | 1.50 |
| 31 | 2.58 | 2.38 | 2.21 | 2.07 | 1.94 | 1.82 | 1.72 | 1.63 | 1.55 |
| 32 | 2.67 | 2.46 | 2.29 | 2.13 | 2.00 | 1.88 | 1.78 | 1.68 | 1.60 |
| 33 | 2.75 | 2.54 | 2.36 | 2.20 | 2.06 | 1.94 | 1.83 | 1.74 | 1.65 |
| 34 | 2.83 | 2.62 | 2.43 | 2.27 | 2.13 | 2.00 | 1.89 | 1.79 | 1.70 |
| 35 | 2.92 | 2.69 | 2.50 | 2.33 | 2.19 | 2.06 | 1.94 | 1.84 | 1.75 |
| 36 | 3.00 | 2.77 | 2.57 | 2.40 | 2.25 | 2.12 | 2.00 | 1.89 | 1.80 |
| 37 | 3.08 | 2.85 | 2.64 | 2.47 | 2.31 | 2.18 | 2.06 | 1.95 | 1.85 |
| 38 | 3.17 | 2.92 | 2.71 | 2.53 | 2.38 | 2.24 | 2.11 | 2.00 | 1.90 |
| 39 | 3.25 | 3.00 | 2.79 | 2.60 | 2.44 | 2.29 | 2.17 | 2.05 | 1.95 |
| 40 | 3.33 | 3.08 | 2.86 | 2.67 | 2.50 | 2.35 | 2.22 | 2.11 | 2.00 |
| 41 | 3.42 | 3.15 | 2.93 | 2.73 | 2.56 | 2.41 | 2.28 | 2.16 | 2.05 |
| 42 | 3.50 | 3.23 | 3.00 | 2.80 | 2.63 | 2.47 | 2.33 | 2.21 | 2.10 |
| 43 | 3.58 | 3.31 | 3.07 | 2.87 | 2.69 | 2.53 | 2.39 | 2.26 | 2.15 |
| 44 | 3.67 | 3.38 | 3.14 | 2.93 | 2.75 | 2.59 | 2.44 | 2.32 | 2.20 |
| 45 | 3.75 | 3.46 | 3.21 | 3.00 | 2.81 | 2.65 | 2.50 | 2.37 | 2.25 |
| 46 | 3.83 | 3.54 | 3.29 | 3.07 | 2.88 | 2.71 | 2.56 | 2.42 | 2.30 |
| 47 | 3.92 | 3.62 | 3.36 | 3.13 | 2.94 | 2.76 | 2.61 | 2.47 | 2.35 |
| 48 | 4.00 | 3.69 | 3.43 | 3.20 | 3.00 | 2.82 | 2.67 | 2.53 | 2.40 |
| 49 | 4.08 | 3.77 | 3.50 | 3.27 | 3.06 | 2.88 | 2.72 | 2.58 | 2.45 |
| 50 | 4.17 | 3.85 | 3.57 | 3.33 | 3.13 | 2.94 | 2.78 | 2.63 | 2.50 |
| 51 | 4.25 | 3.92 | 3.64 | 3.40 | 3.19 | 3.00 | 2.83 | 2.68 | 2.55 |
| 52 | 4.33 | 4.00 | 3.71 | 3.47 | 3.25 | 3.06 | 2.89 | 2.74 | 2.60 |
| 53 | 4.42 | 4.08 | 3.79 | 3.53 | 3.31 | 3.12 | 2.94 | 2.79 | 2.65 |
| 54 | 4.50 | 4.15 | 3.86 | 3.60 | 3.38 | 3.18 | 3.00 | 2.84 | 2.70 |
| 55 | 4.58 | 4.23 | 3.93 | 3.67 | 3.44 | 3.24 | 3.06 | 2.89 | 2.75 |
| 56 | 4.67 | 4.31 | 4.00 | 3.73 | 3.50 | 3.29 | 3.11 | 2.95 | 2.80 |

# Gear Ratios

| 21 | 22 | 23 | 24 | 25 | 26 | 27 | 28 | 29 | 30 | No. of Teeth on Chain-wheel |
|---|---|---|---|---|---|---|---|---|---|---|
| 1.14 | 1.09 | 1.04 | 1.00 | .96 | .92 | .89 | .86 | .83 | .80 | 24 |
| 1.19 | 1.14 | 1.09 | 1.04 | 1.00 | .96 | .93 | .89 | .86 | .83 | 25 |
| 1.24 | 1.18 | 1.13 | 1.08 | 1.04 | 1.00 | .96 | .93 | .90 | .87 | 26 |
| 1.29 | 1.23 | 1.17 | 1.13 | 1.08 | 1.04 | 1.00 | .96 | .93 | .90 | 27 |
| 1.33 | 1.27 | 1.22 | 1.17 | 1.12 | 1.08 | 1.04 | 1.00 | .97 | .93 | 28 |
| 1.38 | 1.32 | 1.26 | 1.21 | 1.16 | 1.12 | 1.07 | 1.04 | 1.00 | .97 | 29 |
| 1.43 | 1.36 | 1.30 | 1.25 | 1.20 | 1.15 | 1.11 | 1.07 | 1.03 | 1.00 | 30 |
| 1.48 | 1.41 | 1.35 | 1.29 | 1.24 | 1.19 | 1.15 | 1.11 | 1.07 | 1.03 | 31 |
| 1.52 | 1.45 | 1.39 | 1.33 | 1.28 | 1.23 | 1.19 | 1.14 | 1.10 | 1.07 | 32 |
| 1.57 | 1.50 | 1.43 | 1.38 | 1.32 | 1.27 | 1.22 | 1.18 | 1.14 | 1.10 | 33 |
| 1.62 | 1.55 | 1.48 | 1.42 | 1.36 | 1.31 | 1.26 | 1.21 | 1.17 | 1.13 | 34 |
| 1.67 | 1.59 | 1.52 | 1.46 | 1.40 | 1.35 | 1.30 | 1.25 | 1.21 | 1.17 | 35 |
| 1.71 | 1.64 | 1.57 | 1.50 | 1.44 | 1.38 | 1.33 | 1.29 | 1.24 | 1.20 | 36 |
| 1.76 | 1.68 | 1.61 | 1.54 | 1.48 | 1.42 | 1.37 | 1.32 | 1.28 | 1.23 | 37 |
| 1.81 | 1.73 | 1.65 | 1.58 | 1.52 | 1.46 | 1.41 | 1.36 | 1.31 | 1.27 | 38 |
| 1.86 | 1.77 | 1.70 | 1.63 | 1.56 | 1.50 | 1.44 | 1.39 | 1.34 | 1.30 | 39 |
| 1.90 | 1.82 | 1.74 | 1.67 | 1.60 | 1.54 | 1.48 | 1.43 | 1.38 | 1.33 | 40 |
| 1.95 | 1.86 | 1.78 | 1.71 | 1.64 | 1.58 | 1.52 | 1.46 | 1.41 | 1.37 | 41 |
| 2.00 | 1.91 | 1.83 | 1.75 | 1.68 | 1.62 | 1.56 | 1.50 | 1.45 | 1.40 | 42 |
| 2.05 | 1.95 | 1.87 | 1.79 | 1.72 | 1.65 | 1.59 | 1.54 | 1.48 | 1.43 | 43 |
| 2.10 | 2.00 | 1.91 | 1.83 | 1.76 | 1.69 | 1.63 | 1.57 | 1.52 | 1.47 | 44 |
| 2.14 | 2.05 | 1.96 | 1.88 | 1.80 | 1.73 | 1.67 | 1.61 | 1.55 | 1.50 | 45 |
| 2.19 | 2.09 | 2.00 | 1.92 | 1.84 | 1.77 | 1.70 | 1.64 | 1.59 | 1.53 | 46 |
| 2.24 | 2.14 | 2.04 | 1.96 | 1.88 | 1.81 | 1.74 | 1.68 | 1.62 | 1.57 | 47 |
| 2.29 | 2.18 | 2.09 | 2.00 | 1.92 | 1.85 | 1.78 | 1.71 | 1.66 | 1.60 | 48 |
| 2.33 | 2.23 | 2.13 | 2.04 | 1.96 | 1.88 | 1.81 | 1.75 | 1.69 | 1.63 | 49 |
| 2.38 | 2.27 | 2.17 | 2.08 | 2.00 | 1.92 | 1.85 | 1.79 | 1.72 | 1.67 | 50 |
| 2.43 | 2.32 | 2.22 | 2.13 | 2.04 | 1.96 | 1.89 | 1.82 | 1.76 | 1.70 | 51 |
| 2.48 | 2.36 | 2.26 | 2.17 | 2.08 | 2.00 | 1.93 | 1.86 | 1.79 | 1.73 | 52 |
| 2.52 | 2.41 | 2.30 | 2.21 | 2.12 | 2.04 | 1.96 | 1.89 | 1.83 | 1.77 | 53 |
| 2.57 | 2.45 | 2.35 | 2.25 | 2.16 | 2.08 | 2.00 | 1.93 | 1.86 | 1.80 | 54 |
| 2.62 | 2.50 | 2.39 | 2.29 | 2.20 | 2.12 | 2.04 | 1.96 | 1.89 | 1.83 | 55 |
| 2.67 | 2.55 | 2.43 | 2.33 | 2.24 | 2.15 | 2.07 | 2.00 | 1.93 | 1.87 | 56 |

# TABLE C: Selected Inch-Wheel Numbers for Gear Ratios

| Gear Ratio | Inch-Wheel Number 26-Inch | 27-Inch | Gear Ratio | Inch-Wheel Number 26-Inch | 27-Inch |
|---|---|---|---|---|---|
| .80 | (21) 20.8 | (22) 21.6 | 1.73 | (45) 45.0 | 46.7 |
| .86 | (22) 22.4 | (23) 23.2 | 1.74 | 45.2 | (47) 46.9 |
| .89 | (23) 23.2 | (24) 24.0 | 1.77 | (46) 46.0 | 47.7 |
| .92 | (24) 23.9 | (25) 24.8 | 1.78 | 46.3 | (48) 48.0 |
| .96 | (25) 25.0 | (26) 25.9 | 1.81 | (47) 47.0 | 48.8 |
| 1.00 | (26) 26.0 | (27) 27.0 | 1.82 | 47.3 | (49) 49.0 |
| 1.04 | (27) 27.0 | (28) 28.1 | 1.85 | (48) 48.1 | (50) 49.9 |
| 1.07 | (28) 27.8 | (29) 28.9 | 1.89 | (49) 49.2 | (51) 51.0 |
| 1.11 | (29) 28.9 | (30) 30.0 | 1.93 | (50) 50.2 | (52) 52.0 |
| 1.15 | (30) 29.9 | (31) 31.1 | 1.96 | (51) 51.0 | (53) 52.9 |
| 1.19 | (31) 31.0 | (32) 32.1 | 2.00 | (52) 52.0 | (54) 54.0 |
| 1.23 | (32) 32.0 | (33) 33.2 | 2.04 | (53) 53.1 | (55) 55.0 |
| 1.26 | (33) 32.8 | (34) 34.0 | 2.08 | (54) 54.1 | (56) 56.1 |
| 1.30 | (34) 33.8 | (35) 35.1 | 2.11 | (55) 54.9 | (57) 56.9 |
| 1.33 | (35) 34.6 | (36) 35.9 | 2.15 | (56) 55.9 | (58) 58.0 |
| 1.37 | (36) 35.6 | (37) 37.0 | 2.19 | (57) 57.0 | (59) 59.1 |
| 1.41 | (37) 36.6 | (38) 38.1 | 2.23 | (58) 58.0 | (60) 60.2 |
| 1.46 | (38) 38.0 | (39) 39.4 | 2.26 | 58.8 | (61) 61.0 |
| 1.48 | (39) 38.5 | (40) 40.0 | 2.27 | (59) 59.0 | 61.3 |
| 1.52 | 39.6 | (41) 41.0 | 2.30 | (60) 59.9 | (62) 62.0 |
| 1.54 | (40) 40.0 | 41.5 | 2.33 | 60.6 | (63) 62.8 |
| 1.56 | 40.6 | (42) 42.1 | 2.35 | (61) 61.1 | 63.4 |
| 1.58 | (41) 41.1 | 42.6 | 2.37 | 61.6 | (64) 63.9 |
| 1.59 | 41.3 | (43) 42.9 | 2.38 | (62) 61.9 | 64.2 |
| 1.60 | (42) 41.6 | (43) 43.1 | 2.41 | 62.7 | (65) 65.0 |
| 1.63 | 42.4 | (44) 44.0 | 2.42 | (63) 63.0 | 65.3 |
| 1.66 | (43) 43.1 | 44.8 | 2.45 | 63.7 | (66) 66.1 |
| 1.67 | 43.4 | (45) 45.1 | 2.46 | (64) 64.0 | 66.4 |
| 1.69 | (44) 44.0 | 45.6 | 2.48 | 64.5 | (67) 66.9 |
| 1.70 | 44.2 | (46) 45.9 | 2.50 | (65) 65.0 | 67.4 |
| 2.52 | 65.5 | (68) 68.0 | 3.50 | (91) 91.0 | (94) 94.4 |
| 2.54 | (66) 66.0 | 68.5 | 3.53 | 91.8 | (95) 95.3 |
| 2.56 | 66.5 | (69) 69.0 | 3.54 | (92) 92.0 | 95.6 |

TABLE C: Selected Inch-Wheel Numbers for Gear Ratios (Continued)

| Gear Ratio | Inch-Wheel Number | | Gear Ratio | Inch-Wheel Number | |
| | 26-Inch | 27-Inch | | 26-Inch | 27-Inch |
| --- | --- | --- | --- | --- | --- |
| 2.58 | (67) 67.0 | 69.5 | 3.57 | 92.8 | (96) 96.2 |
| 2.60 | 67.5 | (70) 70.1 | 3.58 | (93) 93.0 | 96.5 |
| 2.62 | (68) 68.1 | 70.6 | 3.60 | 93.5 | (97) 97.0 |
| 2.63 | 68.4 | (71) 70.9 | 3.62 | (94) 94.0 | 97.6 |
| 2.67 | (69) 69.4 | (72) 72.0 | 3.64 | (95) 94.6 | (98) 98.2 |
| 2.69 | (70) 70.0 | 72.5 | 3.67 | 95.5 | (99) 99.0 |
| 2.71 | 70.5 | (73) 73.0 | 3.69 | (96) 96.0 | 99.5 |
| 2.73 | (71) 71.0 | 73.6 | 3.71 | 96.5 | (100) 100.0 |
| 2.75 | 71.5 | (74) 74.1 | 3.73 | (97) 97.0 | 100.5 |
| 2.77 | (72) 72.0 | 74.7 | 3.75 | 97.5 | (101) 101.2 |
| 2.78 | 72.3 | (75) 75.0 | 3.77 | (98) 98.0 | 101.9 |
| 2.81 | (73) 73.0 | 75.7 | 3.79 | (99) 98.5 | (102) 102.4 |
| 2.82 | 73.3 | (76) 76.0 | 3.85 | (100) 100.0 | (104) 104.0 |
| 2.84 | (74) 73.9 | 76.5 | 3.92 | (102) 102.0 | (106) 106.0 |
| 2.86 | 74.4 | (77) 77.0 | 4.00 | (104) 104.0 | (108) 108.0 |
| 2.89 | (75) 75.1 | (78) 77.9 | 4.08 | (106) 106.0 | (110) 110.1 |
| 2.92 | (76) 76.0 | 78.8 | 4.15 | (108) 108.0 | (112) 112.0 |
| 2.93 | 76.2 | (79) 79.0 | 4.17 | (109) 108.5 | (113) 112.7 |
| 2.95 | (77) 76.7 | (80) 79.6 | 4.23 | (110) 110.0 | (114) 114.1 |
| 3.00 | (78) 78.0 | (81) 81.0 | 4.25 | 110.4 | (115) 115.0 |
| 3.06 | (79) 79.5 | (82) 82.5 | 4.31 | (112) 112.5 | (116) 116.4 |
| 3.08 | (80) 80.0 | (83) 83.0 | 4.33 | (113) 113.0 | (117) 117.0 |
| 3.11 | (81) 80.9 | (84) 83.9 | 4.42 | (115) 115.2 | (119) 119.2 |
| 3.15 | (82) 82.0 | (85) 85.0 | 4.50 | (117) 117.0 | (122) 121.5 |
| 3.19 | (83) 83.0 | (86) 86.0 | 4.58 | (119) 119.0 | (124) 123.7 |
| 3.23 | (84) 84.0 | (87) 87.1 | 4.67 | (122) 122.0 | (126) 126.0 |
| 3.27 | (85) 85.0 | (88) 88.1 | | | |
| 3.31 | (86) 86.0 | 88.2 | | | |
| 3.33 | (87) 86.5 | (89) 88.7 | | | |
| 3.38 | (88) 87.9 | (91) 91.1 | | | |
| 3.42 | (89) 89.0 | (92) 92.2 | | | |
| 3.46 | (90) 90.0 | (93) 93.3 | | | |

NOTE: Inch-wheel numbers in () are rounded to whole numbers.

# 4.

# Accessories
# That Tailor
# Bike to Function

Unreliable and short-lived lights, reflectors, and saddlebags of various kinds plagued the serious touring cyclist for years. Now, new products made for endurance and safety are finding their way into bicycle shops. Many of these new accessories are imported. You can expect to pay more for these high-styled and uniquely designed accessories, but they are worth it. Although you may not find a full line of accessories at local bicycle shops, several mail-order sources carry full lines (see Appendix).

## PANNIERS, BAGS, AND BASKETS

Panniers (French for basket or bag) are double bags supported by a metal frame directly over the rear wheel. They may be constructed of coated nylon, cotton duck, or metal. For touring, lightweight nylon bags carry clothing, personal items, spare parts, tools, and other gear. The double panniers balance weight and provide surprising capacity. The panniers (Fig. 33) are made from 8-oz. waterproof nylon, and include ten compartments including six zippered outside pockets to organize clothes, tools, maps, etc. A rear pocket holds two sew-up tires, for example. The main compartment measures 4 x 11 x 12 inches. Two bags weigh 2 pounds 6 ounces.

A day-trip bag rides on top of a rear carrier (Fig. 34). The "Day-tripper" snaps into place with its own stretch cord and fits nearly all rear carriers. The small pack carries raingear, tools, spare tire, and other parts. The compartment measures 11 x 4½ x 4½ inches and includes four inside pockets over a stiffened bottom. The "Daytripper" is made from tough waterproof 6-ounce nylon with a zipper running around three sides.

Smaller and less-expensive double panniers are also available. Several companies make superlightweight touring packs of nylon that weigh 20 ounces or less (they are available from the catalogues listed in the Appendix). One superlightweight pair of panniers weighs only 19 ounces; that means each one weighs less than ten ounces, even though it offers a 10 x 10 x 4-inch compartment. Some double panniers use short bags on the side with a large bay riding on top of

Fig. 33—TC panniers neatly organize touring gear in six zippered pockets around main bag. Touring panniers should carry load astraddle the rear wheel to keep center of gravity low for good balance.

Fig. 34—"Daytripper" short-tour bag rides atop rear carrier. The "Daytripper" may be used alone or in combination with TC panniers.

the rear carrier; this arrangement can be a disadvantage, as it means toting much of the load high above the wheels. As much of the load as possible should be carried low, near the wheel hubs for better balance. Therefore, when you have a choice, select a bag with deep side pockets, and plan to stow heavy tools and spare parts at the bottom to keep the center of gravity low.

Double front panniers for a front wheel are offered by a few touring sources. The double front panniers are V-shaped, 8 inches at the top tapering to 4 inches at the bottom and 3½ inches across. Total weight is 18 ounces. While we have never used the front double panniers, the front-mounted weight, although carried on a frame that bolts to the front axle on each side, would appear to affect steering. A small handlebar bag, such as the *T.A.* Canvas model or the nylon Nomad from *Eclipse* (see Appendix for catalogues), provides ample carrying capacity for candy bars, camera, and often-needed personal items.

A great variety of sturdy cotton bags is available from surplus stores. Cyclemates adopted these because of their cost—$9 a pair. Also, straps and flaps accommodate excess bulk easier than zippered pockets.

Metal panniers can be constructed from ten-quart oil cans at a cost of about $6 a pair, according to an article in *Bicycling* magazine for December 1972. The writer toured hundreds of miles with the roomy panniers attached to a metal pack frame on his bicycle. With an elastic shower cap at the top, the metal panniers are fully waterproof.

Roll-shaped bags can be fitted to the rear of the bike's saddle. *Karrimor* saddle bags from England come in a variety of sizes. *Brooks* and *Bikecology* saddle bags pack a large capacity with only a minor demand for saddle height. Rather than carry touring gear in a saddle bag, where it extends beyond the width of the saddle and raises the center of gravity, I recommend double panniers with much of the weight low. A small tool bag hung behind the saddle can keep a tube patch kit and tire irons available for ready use. These small lightweight bags would not heighten the center of gravity appreciably.

Touring bag racks for either rear or front wheels serve two functions: (1) The rack supports the weight of the double panniers or top-only bags with bars that attach to the axle hub. Since all bicycle, rider, and bag weight is supported through the two bearings in

Fig. 35—Lightweight handlebar bag
includes three pockets for stowing
sunglasses, dog repellent, candy
bars, and other items needed while
riding.

Fig. 36—Chrome-plated TC carrier
fits 26- or 27-inch wheels and provides two vertical support bars to
keep panniers from rubbing wheel.

each wheel, bringing this load directly to the axles reduces frame
strain. (2) Side support bars should prevent the bags from rubbing
any part of the wheel. Obviously, if a fabric bag rubs a wheel for
long, a hole soon appears. Also, the rubbing friction increases pedaling
force. Single-rod supports for racks in combination with large cross-
country touring panniers may require a light strip of wood near
the bottom of the bags to keep corners out of the wheel.

One sturdy pannier carrier is an imported English design in a
chrome finish (Fig. 36, from Touring Cyclist Shop). The TC carrier
weighs 28 ounces. Cast alloy carriers come with and without a
spring-leaf to hold packages securely. Two problems with this
carrier: (1) The attachment at the forward end of the carrier fits
around the two rear wheel stays. On one Cyclemates trip, while

this attachment secured the frame fore and aft, it kept slipping down on the stays due to the weight of the panniers. To correct this, I got a "T" shaped metal support that holds the front of the rack securely above the rear brake bolt, as shown in Fig. 37. (2) Inexpensive carriers often have only one brace down to the bike frame on each side; it is necessary to fasten a thin wood strip horizontally above the axle to prevent the bags from rubbing on the wheel.

A child carrier can also be fitted to the rear wheel behind the bicycle saddle. A child seat should include leg shields to keep the child's legs out of the spokes. A strap restrains the child in the seat. A child's seat should be easily detachable, to permit quick removal when not needed. While a seat behind the saddle packs the child's weight at a high center of gravity, such a position is preferable to a papoose-type sling that carries the child on the back of the cyclist. Either position requires expert cycling for the child's safety.

Front wheel bag frames may be supported with a rod to the front axle on each side. The double front panniers ride on a metal rack. A smaller TA handlebar bag carrier cantilevers forward from center-pull brakes. Only light bags should be used with this rack.

Water bottles may be carried in wire racks that clamp to either the down tube or the seat tube. Water bottles are not as convenient if carried in saddle bags. Either metal or plastic water bottles are lightweight and can be sterilized as needed. A wire rack is also available for carrying a water bottle forward of the handlebars in

Fig. 37—"T" support prevents forward end of carrier from slipping down on wheel stays.

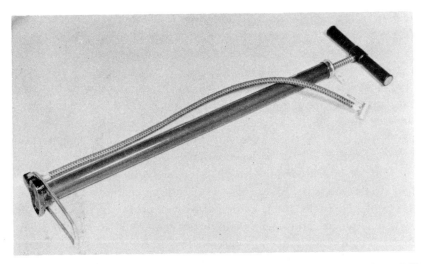

Fig. 38—Heavy-duty stand-on tire pump was carried by Cyclemates II and III because lightweight pumps wore out often and were slow. Note the snap-off end fitting that preserves tire pressure as pump is disengaged.

line with the stem, but this position interferes with a handlebar bag.

Lightweight metal or plastic tire pumps are easily carried directly on the seat or down tube. While these lightweight pumps can be used occasionally, the Cyclemates II and III carried a heavy-duty stand-on pump with a snap fitting for *Schrader* valves (Fig. 38). The lightweight pumps didn't stand up to the frequent use.

Gaily decorated straw baskets hung from the handlebars of ladies' bikes proclaim the femininity of the owner. Otherwise, they are of little use. Since they are not supported by rods attached to the axle, they can carry very little weight. Also, they include no lid, and the attachment at the handlebars interferes with hand positions near the stem. But they're pretty even if they're impractical.

## LIGHTS

Safety regulations require that a cyclist riding at night equip his bicycle with a front white light visible from 500 feet ahead and a red light or reflector on the rear capable of being seen 200 to 300 feet away. Local regulations may vary somewhat, but front and rear lights are vital if the cyclist is to be seen by motorists at night.

Further, safety engineers are agitating for lights that will define the bicycle and help motorists recognize the bicyclist. Three types of bicycle lights are shown in Fig. 39, and they represent most of the variations available.

Self-contained battery-operated lights for fixed mounting on bicycles suffer many of the same problems that plague ordinary flashlights. Batteries must be replaced regularly, switches are often unreliable, and they are heavy (due mainly to the batteries) for the light they produce. Further, they are subject to theft.

Two types of self-contained but removable lights aid the occasional night rider. One is the square-case model in the center of Fig. 39. The case carries two cells and is equipped with a spring clip that fastens it to the handlebars. To prevent theft, unclip it and take it with you. The other self-contained light (not illustrated) is a tube-case flashlight with white and red lenses facing opposite directions. A fabric strap fastens this light to the left arm or, preferably, the left leg for riding at night. The up and down motion of the leg attracts attention and helps to identify the cyclist.

Fig. 39—Three light systems for bicycles: Left, self-contained battery-powered light for fixed mounting. Center, self-contained battery light with clip for quick mounting on bicycle. Right, generator-drive system with white front light and red rear light. Knurled wheel on generator is friction-driven from front tire.

Generator-driven lights reduce the cost of batteries for cyclists riding consistently at night. The generator set at the right in Fig. 39 includes a forward-directed white beam, a smaller red taillight, and the generator for mounting on the fork. The knurled wheel at the lower end bears against the tire which drives the generator rotor inside the case. The drive wheel may be disengaged for daytime riding to eliminate the drag. When selecting a generator light, insist on at least a 6-volt system. Single and double beams for high and low visibility and safety are available.

All generator light systems share two problems: (1) Light output varies with speed. If you plan leisurely trips at night, forget a generator system, because the current output falls below levels needed to meet safety regulations when pedaling slowly. (2) Installation can be tricky. The drive wheel must bear against the tire with enough force to drive the rotor but not enough to damage the tire. Also, wires must be taped to the frame and connected between generator and lights. One of the most reliable (and most expensive) systems builds the generator into the hub of the front wheel. The Sturmey-Archer *Dynohub* front wheel unit offers one big advantage—it is not easily stolen.

Generally, unless you ride often and for long periods at night, I recommend a battery-operated light easily removable to prevent theft. The leg-mounted two-way light is a good choice. When you buy any battery or generator-driven light system for your bicycle, spend enough to get a good one. A lighting system that fails can be a hazard. Whatever type of electric light system you opt for, install a big red reflector where it can be viewed from the rear, or install two, one on each side. And polish them with a cloth before each night ride.

## ALARM SYSTEMS

Letting pedestrians know you're around can help prevent accidents. Tinkly bells or one of the bulb air horns (Fig. 40) will do nicely; they're inexpensive and look impressive. But you can shout with equal effectiveness, so, why buy a horn? An electric horn amounts to a useless and troublesome nuisance that offers little not available from a bulb-powered horn.

To attract motorists' attention, you need more than a bulb horn. The answer is a Freon-powered horn that blasts out a warning with authority. Freon is one of the propellants in aerosol cans. Bike horns powered by Freon are adaptations of the boat horns that can be heard for a mile or more across open water. *Supersound* "Safety Horn" powered by Freon contains enough propellant for about 100 blasts at around $4.75. For riding in traffic, Freon horns command attention, but don't blast a pedestrian with one.

## MISCELLANEOUS

Two major groups of accessories—security chains and locks, and bicycle carriers—are treated in Chapter Nine. Numerous other gadgets and safety accessories are available to satisfy special needs.

Speedometers and cyclometers (Fig. 41) can be useful additions to a touring bike. The speedometer drives off a wheel hub through a cable and must be keyed to a specific wheel size. The *VDO* speedometer (from Wheel Goods Corp.) even includes a bulb that can be wired to a generator for visibility while riding at night. *Huret* and *Stewart-Warner* also make bicycle speedometers.

Cyclometers or odometers operate on a different principle to record mileage. The small unit at the right in Fig. 41 is strictly mechanical, with a gear arrangement that advances each time a striker mounted on the front wheel turns one revolution. Each cyclometer must be purchased for a specific wheel size.

A pacing device called a *Mininome* sounds a beat at variable times through an earphone while you ride to help you build or control cadence. The *Mininome* (from Touring Cyclist Shop) and how it is used are discussed in Chapter Six.

Bike flags fly high behind the cyclist on fiberglass whip masts. One triangular 8 x 10-inch flat is cut from fluorescent nylon. Flags are intended to help the cyclist be seen from front and rear by motorists. Their darting motion can't help but attract attention.

Dog repellent in aerosol cans direct a stinging but safe stream at challenging dogs. One problem has been to pack the "dog bomb" where it is handy and readily available at an instant's notice. "Halt" is one brand of dog repellent that comes in two sizes. Both fit a spring mount that keeps the can near at hand. You can also devise your own ammonia spray, as noted in Chapter Ten.

Tire savers (Fig. 42) rub lightly on the tire tread to brush off glass or sharp stones. Tire savers mount behind the fork and behind the seat tube. The curved wire that actually sweeps the tire tread is lightly

Fig. 40—Bulb horns for mounting on handlebars come in all sizes and shapes. This one is a "bugle" horn.

Fig. 41—Speedometer (left) records speed through cable drive from front wheel hub. A cyclometer records distance covered on the center array. A click-type cyclometer (right) records distance traveled when a striker on the front wheel advances the mechanism one click for each revolution.

Fig. 42—Tire-saver lightly brushes away glass shards, sharp sand, or metal bits to head off punctures as you ride.

spring-loaded by being inserted in tough plastic sleeves. For touring with sew-up tires, tire savers work effectively to reduce punctures. The friction induced by the rubbing wire causes insignificant drag.

Fenders or mudguards add both weight and wind resistance, but on wet, dirty streets or roads, they can reduce splatters. The full-length metal fender requires at least one and preferably two stays to maintain alignment. The added weight makes it impractical for touring. Light plastic fenders keep most of the splatters off the rider. Because they are nearly straight, they can be packed in a bag between rains and snapped on and off quickly. A pair will fit both front and back wheels, although the panniers catch most of the splatters from the rear wheel. A lightweight aluminum fender mounts with one bolt for easy installation and removal. Fenders are a matter of personal choice. On Cyclemates tours we found fenders unnecessary. They're just one more part to get loose or to rub on the tire. When dry, splatters brush off easily.

Two-wheel trailers appear to be a great innovative idea for touring, but having tried one of the more popular models, we recommend against using them for anything more than short trips. Even though they trail straight and true down hills and around curves, they are heavy, about 25 pounds, and add far too much drag for 60- to 100-mile days. Since the trailers hook on to a touring bicycle behind the seat post, they cannot be used with double panniers that rise above the rack. At $100 to $200 you're better off to buy big panniers—and save the weight and drag of two more wheels. For bulky food shopping or for hauling newspapers, golf bags, or other gear too heavy or bulky for a bicycle, a trailer might pay off. But for touring—NO!

Biking clothes are becoming available in a wide variety to suit special needs—from high-visibility knitted watch caps to electrically heated socks and shirts. Since these accessories fall outside the usual items affixed to a bike and because clothing changes so rapidly from season to season and year to year, you should investigate late issues of *Bicycling* magazine and the catalogs of the major mail-order suppliers noted in the Appendix.

# 5.
# Where
# and How
# to Buy
# a Used Bicycle

For years few used bicycles turned up on the market. When a cyclist replaced an older bicycle, the used bike was sold to a friend. You had to know someone to find a used bike because of their scarcity. Or you had to battle the crowds at police auctions and take pot luck; and the prices paid for some used bicycles at auctions rivaled the prices paid for new ones—mainly because of the six- to nine-month wait for hot new 10-speeds.

Now things are different. Used bicycles are again available at reasonable prices because booming demands for 10-speeds have largely been filled. New bikes are still selling in the millions. But, more and more, cyclists are trading in or selling used bikes. The classic "trading up" pattern is showing up in the bicycle market as it has in cars, houses, and boats for years. Once a confirmed bicyclist tastes the thrills of pedaling and piloting a light, responsive bicycle up and down hills with an effective gear changer, he begins thinking of an even better bike. Sometimes, trading-up occurs long before the old bicycle shows signs of wear. The desire to ride the latest is making more and more used bicycles available.

Stolen bikes still appear in the used market. But reports from metropolitan police units and campus security patrols indicate that fewer bikes are being stolen for sale. Increased awareness of security by owners (see Chapter Nine) reduces opportunities for organized theft. Registration and positive identification measures are returning more stolen bikes to their owners.

## WHERE TO LOOK

Newspaper classified ads offer the first logical market. Before beginning your search, read and study Chapter Two to determine the type of bicycle you want. Determine which brands, wheel size, frame size, and other features are important to you. Depending on how long you are willing to wait, you may need to compromise, but don't compromise on anything as basic as frame size. Pick several alternative brands and check the prices of new models. If you know what you want before you begin looking, first, you will not be deluded by price since you will know what bikes of the type you prefer sell for new. Second, by knowing the features important to you, much of your search can be conducted over the telephone. Third, by knowing the new performance, you can better appraise the performance of used bicycles. By asking knowledgeable questions, you will impress the seller that you are no neophyte to be conned into buying a piece of junk.

Examine newspaper classifieds on the weekend, as these papers carry the biggest selection. Sunday editions are best. Don't wait until your home edition is delivered—buy one at a newsstand on Saturday. Get the jump on other shoppers; there's little point in locating a bike that suits your needs only to find it was sold the day before. Search for leads in the paper that carries the biggest volume of advertising. Sellers recognize when a newspaper is doing a good job, and the more ads, the better your choice. A second good source of leads are the neighborhood shoppers, the newspapers that appear on Wednesday or Thursday filled with grocery store ads. Look too at the "nickel papers" —those found on supermarket checkout stands for free.

Bulletin boards or swap boards at a store, factory, or business concern offer other leads to bicycles. Take down the telephone numbers and begin calling immediately. People hang notices on community or plant bulletin boards to avoid paying for a classified ad. Swap boards at community colleges or universities are good sources of leads because of the high bicycle population on campuses.

Use your telephone to narrow the possibilities in a preliminary search. Develop a checklist of those features you consider most important—frame size, wheel and tire size and type, brand, components, and price. Offered price should not be a deterrent at first. During telephone screening, you're more interested in finding the bicycle that suits you. Use a checklist to compare possibilities on a point-for-point basis by telephone. When you locate a bike that comes close to your specifications, travel to the location and check it out quickly. Others may find such a bike attractive too. Asking an owner to hold it for your inspection seldom works. So many callers fail to show that the bike will likely go to the first reasonable offer.

Police auctions offer another opportunity to buy used bicycles once or twice a year. Auctions are publicized in the newspapers, but you could miss the inside-page small-space notice. Instead of waiting, call the police office and ask. Bicycles that show up at police auctions have been abandoned or were picked up for one reason or another. If a bicycle cannot be positively identified by serial number or other mark, the police will not return it (see Chapter Nine). It isn't enough to point out the brand name and list accessory equipment because other bikes may be similarly equipped. So a bike may be confiscated and end up in a warehouse for sale.

Auction bikes may be damaged, rusty, or missing important pieces. Usually a bike will be sold "as is." Unless you examine a specific bike before bidding on it, you could be buying a two-wheeled problem. Read the notice carefully to see when bicycles may be inspected ahead of the actual auction. Take advantage of that time to find one or more bikes that fit your needs.

During the bidding, don't get carried away and bid more than a specific bike is worth. If you have done your homework, you will know the new price of comparable bikes and, possibly, the price of similar used bikes in a bicycle shop. During the inspection you will have determined any parts that must be replaced. *Before bidding begins,* decide on your maximum bid. Any time the bidding goes higher, drop out. People at auctions become excited, and emotional fervor sometimes affects bidding. But if you have developed your notes, you won't be drawn into bidding and paying more than a bike is worth.

Bicycle shops take used bikes in trade on new bicycles. Therefore, you can call several shops by telephone to see if a bike you want happens to be available. You'll pay a higher price than you might from a private seller through a classified ad, but the dealer bike may be reconditioned. It will certainly be thoroughly checked and adjusted, ready for immediate use, if the shop values return business. Further, a knowledgeable shop owner will not take junk bikes in trade. Cheapie heavyweight specials turned out *en masse* in Taiwan and similar spots seldom bring enough for the shop owner to bother with. He can make a better profit by buying new cheapies than by taking junkers in trade.

## SELECTING THE USED BICYCLE

Before spending time checking the condition of a used bicycle, determine if it is one you would want regardless of its condition. There's little point in spending your valuable time examining bearings and the power train on a bike that is too small or generally the wrong type.

First, look at the whole bike. Is it the type of bicycle you will be happy with? Examine the criteria for bicycle selection in Chapter Two. Even if someone gave you a used bicycle, you wouldn't accept a balloon-tired monster for long-distance touring. An extreme example, perhaps, but the point is—don't waste time with a bike that fails to meet your basic needs. Part of your homework before venturing into the used bike market will be to single out those features you consider important. You probably would not select a bicycle with flat handle-bars if you plan extensive touring. Neither would you want an extremely lightweight racing vehicle to haul groceries from the supermarket.

You'll find certain features together. *Maes*-type turned-down handle-bars will usually be associated with a narrow saddle, while flat handle-bars will be matched with a bedspring seat. Even balloon-tired, 16-inch-wheel kids' bikes are equipped with 10-speed derailleurs, so external gear changers no longer connote a lightweight bike suitable for racing or touring. But light weight *is* associated with the better (more expensive) derailleurs—*Campagnolo* or *Sun Tour*—and the lightweights will show a slim, lean look all over.

Check frame fit before getting into the nitty-gritty of checking the condition of individual parts. You'll want a frame that permits you to straddle the top tube with both feet on the floor and a ½ to 1-inch clearance under the crotch. The exact frame dimension is less important than the fit you can test. (See Chapter Two for further details on frame size and fit.)

Handlebar and stem length, although important for comfortable riding, are less important than frame size. You can replace a stem, but you're stuck with a frame. For preliminary screening by telephone, you should know the frame size you're looking for. If the owner doesn't know the frame size, ask him to measure the distance from floor to top tube, then add another ½ inch. The total should equal the distance from floor to crotch while you stand errct.

## CHECKING THE USED BICYCLE

The time to check over a used bicycle is before you buy it—not after. Since bikes are usually sold "as is," you're the one stuck if you must replace a fouled-up derailleur or cone bearings chewed up with sand. Few bicycles are equipped with an odometer, so you can't check mileage the way you would for a used car. Instead, you should check out each part and working mechanism as follows:

WHEELS. Spin the wheels with the bike off the ground. Look at the wheels first from the side. From that view you can check for an uneven rim or flat spots where the wheel might have been bent in a collision with a curb. A wheel that's out of round will cause the bike to ride rough and the brake pads to bear unevenly around the rim—possibly even touching the tire for a quick blow-out.

Spin the wheel again and look down parallel to the fork toward the axle to check for wobble. Wheels may ride smoothly but still wobble from side to side as a result of minor damage or unevenly tightened spokes. Wheel wobble causes problems in adjusting brake pads for even pressure and consistent stopping. (See page 74 for brake check.) Locate the wobble portions of the rim and check spoke tension by pinching two spokes together on the side away from the wobble. Possibly a simple spoke adjustment will correct the out-of-plane condition. A sharp bulge is more likely to be the result of a bent rim. Check both front and rear rims. On the rear check the dishing of the rim that allows room for the gear cluster.

Wheel bearings are checked by ear and touch. With someone holding the bike in the air again, spin the wheels and listen with your ear close to the bearing hub. You can hear any grinding or gnashing of bearings when even a small amount of sand or dirt is trapped inside. Also with a finger on a nut close to the hub, you can feel slight vibrations that result from grit or dirt in the balls of the bearing. Dirt enters bearings when bearing cones are allowed to run loose.

Check the wheel axles for looseness too. Hold the fork and wheel off the ground and attempt to move the wheel up and down on the axle. Any detectable movement indicates that the cones are improperly adjusted and may have been ridden out of adjustment for long enough to damage the bearings. Repeat the inspection of rear wheel bearings.

Finally, examine the tires for wear on both sides and the tread. Rub spots around the sides of the tire will be easily visible. Check rub spots for possible fracture of the cords. On the tread, check spot wearing due to braking skids. Bulges or spot wear around either of the tires could be a result of previous punctures.

Pick at spokes near their center and twang them like a guitar string. Each spoke should sound a similar note if evenly tensioned. You can quickly locate loose or bent spokes. Straight loose spokes can be tighened if the nipples are not corroded. Although most spokes are made from stainless steel, corrosion can freeze nipples at the rim. With a spoke wrench, you can check whether the nipples are free for retensioning.

FRAME. Look over each of the tubes for possible bends or cracks. You can usually tell whether a frame has been repainted because the coverage will be uneven or show tiny runs. Also, there will likely be fewer stripes or accent colors on a repainted frame. Any time a frame has been repainted, look with extra care for bends or other structural damage. Look carefully at each of the joints—lugged or not. A clue to a poor frame will be a heavy lug, possibly with gaps between the tube and the inside of the lug. Good quality lightweight bikes will be fitted with lugs trimmed away from the unstressed attach point in a graceful design to reduce weight. Further, brazing will be continuous around the full surface where lugs meet tubes. Any sign that the frame has been bent indicates the bike has probably been in an accident. Unless there is absolutely no alternative, we suggest passing up any bike with a bent frame—even one that has been straightened with little sign of former damage.

Look for rust, hardened grease, or caked dirt as an indication that the bike may have been in storage. While not riding a bicycle seldom damages it, rust from storage in a damp environment can freeze nuts or pit bearings and make maintenance or replacement either difficult or expensive.

Examine each of the bolt heads or nuts that may be adjusted or removed during maintenance. If the corners of the flats are rounded, and nicks and scratches cover the nut, you can figure some amateur without proper tools and probably with little knowledge of what he was doing worked on the bike. Damaged bolts and nuts indicate a lack of respect for a well-made vehicle. You can guess what may have happened to bearings inside and out of view.

Check the pedals in the same way you checked wheel hubs—by listening and by touch. Pedals should turn easily and keep on turning with little friction evident. With an ear close, you can hear grit and dirt in the pedal bearings. Also, examine the screw threads exposed on the crank opposite pedals for rust. A frozen pedal thread can make the pedal extremely difficult to remove.

Two bearings support the front fork—one at the top and one at the bottom. Hold the front wheel off the ground, and with one hand on the handlebar stem, attempt to move the front fork axially in the headset bearings. Headset bearings must take rotating loads and axial thrust loads; therefore, they are subject to double wear. Check for looseness and sideplay by attempting to move the stem fore and aft or from side to side. Some looseness in bearings can be adjusted out, much like adjusting wheel bearing combs as long as all of the balls in the bearing are in place and the threads of the nuts have not rusted unduly.

One bolt head frequently subject to abuse is the stem bolt. Considerable torque is required to expand the tapered wedge bolt that prevents the stem from turning in the fork tube. If you should be carrying a wrench, try the stem bolt to see if it can be turned; otherwise, maintaining or repairing the whole headset can be a problem. Much the same can be said for the binder bolt that clamps the handlebars in position. Try the handlebars to see if they are the least bit loose in the clamp that is tightened by the binder bolt.

Cranks are fitted to their axle with square or other shaped opening or with a cotter pin. You'll find cotterless cranks on the better bikes. A cottered crank costs less to make—so you find it on less expensive bicycles. That's one visible clue. Check for looseness by holding one crank while attempting to move the other crank backward or forward. The fit between pin face and axle can wear to develop slop. Operate the cranks much as you did the wheels and the headset. Listen for grit or an occasional catch that could mean one or more balls from the race are missing. In its position close to the ground, bottom bracket bearings tend to pick up more dirt than any others except pedals unless bearings are kept tight.

Try to move the cranks in the bottom bracket bearings from side to side to check for end play. As you turn the crank slowly (rear wheel in the air if the chain cannot be easily disengaged), look for the fit between the end plate of the axle and the shell of the bottom bracket. The fit should be so close, you can barely see a space to move—the closer the better, as long as the axle rotates freely. A wide opening or one with gaps admits dirt that leads to bearing problems.

As you are examining the crank and chain wheel, look for loose bolts attaching the crank spider and the inside chainwheel. Also, look for missing spacers that separate the two or three chainwheels. Chainwheel attach bolts are subject to considerable force as each pedal thrust is transmitted to the chain. They can and do work loose with time and riding. A missing bolt can lead to a fall or to a bent chainwheel. Look along the plane of the chainwheel to check for flatness and to detect any previous bends.

HANDLEBARS. Aside from their basic shape (turned down or flat), look for signs of rust at the attach sleeve and whether the binder bolt appears frozen in rust. You will probably want to adjust the position of handlebars from time to time or replace the stem if the handlebar-saddle distance proves to be uncomfortable. The condition of tape on the handlebars (if any) is not important, as most riders prefer to tape them to suit themselves in color and material (see Chapter Fourteen). In your preliminary look, you will have checked stem length. If the stem is too short or too long, figure on spending from $10 to $20 and a lot of hard work to replace it with one that fits your arm length. Figure that addition into the total price of the bike.

SADDLE. Narrow saddles generally go along with lightweight bikes. Chapter Two details the difference in saddle types. During your condition check, examine the adjusting nuts under the saddle for freedom from rust. You'll need to adjust the saddle to suit your individual comfort three ways—fore and aft, tipping up and down, and possibly twisting the saddle into alignment with the frame. A clamp bolt at the top of the seat tube can be loosened to slide the seat post up or down in the seat tube. Check to make sure this bolt is free of rust, as you will surely want to adjust seat height.

BRAKES. Caliper brakes controlled by handlebar levers can be checked without actually riding the bike. Coaster brakes, since they are inside the rear hub, can only be checked by riding the bike and applying the brakes. A poor second choice for checking coaster brakes is to hold the bike in the air while hand pedaling to start the back wheel in motion before braking. If there is no space to ride, as might be the case in a loft or basement full of bikes to be auctioned, at least check brake action with the wheel in the air.

Caliper brakes can be checked at several places. First, try to move the brake handles to assure they are firmly attached to the handlebars. Unless threads of the attachment screw are stripped, handles can be tightened. Next, depress and quickly release handles to see if they snap back to their rest position. Quick action signifies the mechanism, and particularly the cable, is not sticky and likely to hang up in use.

Squeeze the handles as tightly as possible to check brake pad action at both front and rear wheels. The handles should not reach or bear on the handlebar, otherwise brake action will be limited. A minimum of a ½-inch space should remain between the brake handle and the handlebar with the brake fully engaged. Check the front brake pads to ·see that both pads contact the wheel rim; then let off on the handle slightly to check if one pad lets loose before the other. Both pads should move together, although this action can be adjusted easily if the wheel is relatively flat and true. Repeat the check of brake pad action on the rear wheels. Examine the brake pads themselves to see if they are worn to the point where replacement is imminent (see Chapter Fourteen).

POWER TRAIN. Chainwheel, chain, rear cluster, and front and rear derailleurs comprise the key power units for any exterior gear-changing bike. Later, we'll consider the speed changers that fit in the rear hub.

Chain condition offers another good clue to the maintenance the bike may have experienced. A well-cared-for bike will include a chain free of rust and recently oiled. One thing to look for are stiff links— those which do not rotate around the rivet easily. Stiff links lead to skipping and can cause hard gear shifting. With the rear wheel off the ground, turn the crank slowly and look at each link as it moves over the derailleur rollers. If you notice one or more links that appear to remain off the rollers, move them to the lower loop where there is a normal sag. Move the links in your fingers to test for free movement. If the links are merely stiff and not frozen with rust, you can usually work them free by adding penetrating oil and working the link back and forth around the pivot.

Check gear changing action by supporting the rear wheel off the ground. For a bike that has two or three chainwheels, rotate the crank, then move the gear shift lever for the front derailleur first. The chain should move smoothly from high to low chainwheel. Note how much effort is required to move the levers. An unusual amount of force indicates a hangup in the system, or a sticky cable operation. However, if the derailleur itself shifts the chain from one chainwheel to the other with no problems, stiff cable operation can be cured rather easily.

Next, check rear derailleur operation by moving the gear changing lever through its full travel. The cable should shift from one gear to the other smoothly as the wheel turns and the chain continues to move. Don't attempt to change gears or check the operation of the derailleur system except when the crank and rear wheel are in motion. If at all possible, check derailleur operation during a short test ride.

A derailleur that is not working properly will fail to shift the chain onto the extreme high- or low-gear freewheel of the rear cluster. Derailleurs can be adjusted to correct such problems, but you may not be permitted to tinker with the mechanism. Look for such obvious defects as loose adjusting or limit screws, bent derailleur hangers, sticky cable operation, and rusty or dirty parts. A thorough knowledge of derailleur operation may also permit you to pick out the problem that prevents a gear changer from shifting the cable onto the extreme high and low freewheel. (See Chapters Thirteen and Fourteen.)

Gear changers inside the rear hub, such as the *Shimano* or *Sturmey-Archer* hubs with or without a coaster brake included, use a planetary gear system for changing ratios. A cable and handle control operates like a gear-shift to move the gears from one range to another. You can check their operation by holding the rear wheel off the ground. Crank the rear wheel while you shift gears with the handle control. Check the difference in rear wheel rotational speed relative to crank rotation to see if the gears inside the hub are actually changing. With help you can listen with an ear close to the hub for clashing of gears or rough running as a result of dirt or worn gears. Note the gear indicator at the entry to the hub and on the handle to see if they agree. The shifter should cycle through all three or five gears without a hitch. If the gear changer will not move into a low or high gear, it may be due to dirt or hardened grease. You have no way of recognizing the problem short of disassembling the hub—something you shouldn't attempt unless you are an experienced bicycle mechanic. While *Sturmey-Archer* hubs are generally reliable, you may be stuck for the cost of repair. Consider that possible extra cost as part of the price when considering a particular bicycle.

Coaster brakes on one-speed bikes, generally *Bendix*, should stop a bicycle quickly. If the brake doesn't stop the wheel held in the air when you back the pedals, it will not stop the bike during riding. As with the *Sturmey-Archer* hubs, disassembling, cleaning, lubricating, and then reassembling coaster brakes shouldn't be attempted by the home mechanic. Before deciding on a bike with a coaster brake, test it by riding. Sometimes it is simpler and less expensive to replace the hub than to repair it. Again—if you find a problem with the coaster brake of a one-speed bike, allow for the cost of repair or replacement of the hub in your final price.

Finally, if at all possible, you should ride the bicycle you're considering buying before you decide. You wouldn't consider buying a used car without at least driving it around the block. Take a used bike out for a spin on the same basis. You needn't go far, around the parking lot in front of a bike shop, or up and down a driveway. The owner may be wary of your taking it far. On your trial ride, check off the following concerns:

How is the ride? Do you feel a thump or bump in either wheel? You can feel a side-to-side wobble if cones are loose in one of the wheels.

Do the brakes function properly? A coaster brake should be able to lock the wheel into a skid on smooth pavement, so give it a hard back pedal and be prepared for a skid to one side. Caliper brakes should also stop the bike quickly. Try both brakes together first. Then activate each brake separately to check individual braking action. You will already have checked for sticky operation of handles and cable.

Do the gears change smoothly? You will need to change gears while pedaling, but note how quickly the derailleur responds and how far you must move the change levers to initiate a gear change. Be sure to check both chainwheel and rear cluster derailleurs. Listen closely after changing into each gear for any sign of "ker-chunking." Such noises indicate the chain is not properly centered on the gear. This may be a problem with the derailleur or in your own shifting technique. Check the smoothness of pedaling, as your inspection of the bike at rest may not have disclosed stiff links in the chain. You may also notice an unevenness in pedaling that could signal balls missing from bearings in the bottom bracket or one of the wheels.

## NEGOTIATING A PRICE AND DELIVERY

Agreeing on a price for a used bicycle requires a bit of horse trading and homework on your part. You won't find a "blue book" of prices for used bicycles similar to those for used cars. Therefore, investigate the current prices of similar or identical new bicycles as a starting point. A used bike should not be priced much above half the price of an identical new bike equipped with the same accessories. Therefore, you know where to start negotiating if you know the price of the same bike new. While shopping around, note the prices of various bicycles. They tend to fall into specific price classes—under $100, around $200, and on up, with the higher priced lines thinning quickly. Therefore, you need not develop a complete list of new bicycles and their prices. If you can identify the price class of a bicycle, you're close.

Components help to categorize a specific bicycle within a price range. *Campagnolo* parts and components will generally be found on the expensive bikes. A *Reynolds 531* double-butted decal on the frame puts it into the over $500 class new. *Shimano* 3-speed rear hubs and 5-speed rear cluster derailleurs are used on a number of American and foreign bicycles and connotes quality at a lesser price than *Campagnolo*. You will perceive these differences after compiling only a short list of new bike prices as part of your homework.

Condition of a specific bicycle also affects price. A used bike in mint condition that was obviously treated with care will be priced higher and be worth more than a bike with rust on the chain and dirt around the wheel and bottom bracket bearings. You must judge condition yourself after examining the bike as noted above.

Where you buy also affects price. Buying a used bicycle from a shop offers the advantage of an implied if not a specific guarantee. The bicycle shop will also know exactly the price the used bike sold for when it was new. Expect to pay somewhat more for a bicycle you find used in a bicycle shop. The bike will probably have been cleaned and reconditioned—another reason for paying more. If the bicycle was reconditioned, that is, bearings replaced or inoperative equipment rebuilt or replaced, the bicycle could be the operating equal of a new bike although it will obviously not look new. Don't count on haggling much on the price set by the dealer.

Negotiating a price with a private party does involve a bit of haggling if you're after the bottom price. A bicycle advertised in the classified ads will usually be priced higher than the intended selling price. Therefore, if you pay the asking price, you will be paying more than you need to pay. There's much to be gained and little to be lost by offering a lower price. Suppose you find a bicycle that meets your needs

—frame size okay, condition good to excellent, features you consider important—and the price is $120. From your homework, you know the bicycle originally sold in the $200 price range. Instead of agreeing immediately to the $120 price, offer $100—*cash*. Emphasize the cash and be prepared to hand over currency or perhaps write a check. The seller may sell you the bike for $100, particularly if you indicate that you've looked at other bikes and $120 is definitely out of line.

More likely, the seller will refuse your first offer. You come back with, "Well, how much will you take?" By haggling a bit, you can probably compromise on a price around $110. On a bike that sold new for around $200, go easy on paying much more than $110 unless the bike is obviously near new, in top condition, and ridden very little.

Fig. 43—Typical Bill of Sale.

BILL OF SALE

Date_____

I, _____ , of _____ ,
      (name of seller)                 (address of seller)

_____ sell to
          (city and state)

_____ the following described bicycle
      (name of buyer)

which I own free and clear of any liens or other encumbrances:

Manufacturer      _____

Wheel size        _____

Serial No.        _____

for the sum of $_____ .

                _____
                (signature of seller)

When you agree on a price, you need a Bill of Sale to convey title. Fig. 43 details a Bill of Sale blank that you can copy. The important elements are:

• An exact description of the bicycle, including brand, wheel size, accessories to accompany the bike, and the serial number.

• Date.

• Name of the seller.

• Your name as buyer.

• Price.

• Conditions of sale—usually "as is" when a private party rather than a bicycle shop is involved.

You need the Bill of Sale to protect your interest in case the bicycle should be identified by police as one that may have been stolen. Getting a Bill of Sale for any piece of used equipment assures title transfer on a business-like basis.

# 6.
# Riding Effectiveness: Techniques and Tips

Experienced cyclists ride with an effortless grace that melds smoothness and power into one continuous fluid motion. You'll find that good form pays off when riding a bicycle, as in any other sport or physical activity. An accomplished cyclist makes bicycle riding look deceptively simple, like watching an accomplished skier as he turns and glides swiftly down a slope without jerky motions and with skis close together and parallel—or like watching advanced tennis players stroke and shift positions with a deftness of footwork that makes it all look so easy. Advanced skiers and tennis players display their enviable form only after practice and lessons in the proper techniques. Practice alone won't work. You must practice correct form and techniques to advance your bicycling skills just as skiers and tennis players practice good form and technique.

Understand the "right" way and practice until you too can ride smoothly and powerfully with ease and confidence. Some of the techniques important in effective riding are posture, balance, breathing, ankling, cadence, shifting, and braking.

## POSTURE

Cyclists new at riding a lightweight bicycle with turned-down handlebars frequently complain of neck and back aches. With turned-down handlebars, the leaning forward position develops efficiency and distributes body weight among handlebars, saddle, and pedals. But holding the head up to see from a leaning forward position strains neck muscles unused to such activities, and an ache develops. Muscles in the neck are simply not accustomed to holding the head up when the body trunk is close to horizontal. Sun bathers who read while lying on their stomachs experience the same strain and neck ache if they maintain the position too long.

For best cycling, the saddle should be slightly higher than the handlebars. Slightly may mean a half inch or an inch for a tall person. But don't start riding with the seat in its best position; work up to the correct and efficient posture gradually to avoid painful neck and back aches. You will barely touch the ground even with your toes while straddling a saddle at its most efficient position. So begin with the seat low; it's adjustable by loosening the seat-post clamp at the top end of the seat tube. While learning to ride, keep your hands on the high part of the handlebars as far apart as possible for steering-control leverage. See the four basic hand positions shown in Figs. 14-17. Build up to the preferred seat position a step at a time. Muscles in the back of your neck will strengthen to hold your head up in the same way as the muscles in your legs toughen and strengthen from the pedaling you'll be doing at the same time.

Backache can be prevented by selecting handlebars that are comfortably distant from the saddle but don't make you stretch. Women who ride men's bikes will probably find the saddle-handlebar distance too long. They should exchange the long stem for a short stem. The cross portion of the handlebars should be about equal to the distance from your elbow to extended fingertips, as shown in Fig. 20.

Backaches usually result from holding one position too long. You can shift hand positions to relieve strain. Occasionally, remove your hands completely from the handlebars and stretch your arms back or skyward. But ride without hands only along those stretches where traffic is not a problem and road conditions are level. A skill you should learn is balancing the bicycle and keeping it headed straight and true without hand control.

Whether you crouch far forward or sit upright depends on wind conditions. When heading into a wind, lean down close to the handlebars to cut resistance. When coasting downhill at a 30-mph clip, you create your own headwind. Try this test to judge for yourself the effect of body posture on wind resistance while coasting down a steep hill, preferably one with little traffic: Start rolling with the body forward, crouched over the handlebars to minimize wind resistance; then raise up to expose chest and shoulders to the wind. You can feel the difference in speed immediately. Or if you can find a friend with essentially the same type of bicycle, test the effect of body posture on wind resistance together. Start off at the same speed with both of your bodies crouched forward. Then, raise your body upright while your friend continues with body forward and head down. Your friend will immediately shoot ahead and leave you behind. You must make up for wind resistance with extra pedaling effort. On short trips, the difference may not be noticeable. But on day-long grips, you'll be significantly more tired at the end of the day if you ride upright and expend extra effort overcoming wind resistance. Any headwind exaggerates the difference.

When you're riding with a tailwind, use your body like a sail. Pedal with the body trunk as nearly upright as comfortable. The added area of your back and shoulders intercepts more of the wind's force and helps push you along.

## BALANCE

The truly expert cyclist exhibits sure balance during all kinds of riding. When practicing balance, place your hands far apart on the handlebars for greater control leverage. Try bringing your hands close in to the stem and you'll notice a tendency of the bike to wobble.

To practice and learn correct balance, find a straight line marked on the surface of a parking lot or a centerline of a deserted street. A road cut off at a dead end by a freeway makes a good practice location. The line will ordinarily measure about 4 inches wide. As you ride, try keeping both tires within the line. You'll find this skill test noted in Chapter Eight. Being able to ride straight within a narrow band while confidently balanced aids safety.

Maintaining balance is easier while pedaling in low gear. The more times your legs move up and down and the crank moves around, the easier you'll find it to keep your balance. Practice shifting into a low gear as you pedal up to a stop sign or traffic light. Faster pedaling helps you retain balance while slowing down and allows you to accelerate faster when the red light turns to green. When riding in a crosswind, shift to at least one gear lower than you might otherwise select, and increase cadence. Gusty crosswinds can throw you off balance, but rapid pedaling permits you to react more quickly and maintain or regain balance. Maintaining balance in winds becomes a major safety factor in traffic. Wobbling the front wheel for balance may cause you to slip off the edge of a pavement slab or confuse the motorist behind you. The Cyclemates found out about balance while pedaling in fierce crosswinds in the mountains and on the plains of Canada.

Your goal in developing balance should be to ride in a perfectly straight line with barely perceptible deviations while your body remains practically motionless from the waist up. Your legs will move smoothly up and down in a perfectly rhythmical motion. Avoid, particularly, any side-to-side motion of the body trunk. This sideways motion not only imperils balance but wastes energy.

## BREATHING

Like other strenuous exercise, how you breathe affects endurance and the benefits you gain from bicycling. Most important is to avoid rapid, shallow breathing or panting. Instead, develop the habit of breathing in deeply and holding your lungs full momentarily, then expelling the air slowly. During average speed bicycling, learn to breathe deeply and regularly.

Developing a "second wind" results from an equalization of bodily metabolic and respiratory functions to maintain a stable acid-base balance in the blood. Dr. Stanley J. Stamm, of the Cardiopulmonary Research Laboratory of the Children's Orthopedic Hospital and Medical Center in Seattle, explains that initially in muscular exercise the acidity of the blood increases. Lactic acid resulting from muscle activity due to pedaling (or any other strenuous activity) enters the bloodstream from working cells. The body compensates by increasing the breathing rate to remove carbon dioxide. When the lungs rid the body of carbon dioxide from the blood at the same rate as the lactic acid is being generated, the acid-base equilibrium is reestablished—and we get our second wind.

One way to equalize the acid-base status more quickly is to breathe out against some resistance—as through pursed lips. Or breathe in through your mouth when breathing heavily and exhale through the nose. Breathing out against resistance has the effect of reducing the velocity of air passing out through the thin neck of the air sacs in the lung. When exhaling with a whoosh, the air rushes through the tiny passages with such velocity that the walls collapse. A venturi effect reduces inside pressure and the outside pressure collapses the tubes momentarily. However, by breathing out against some restriction, the passages remain open while air flows out more slowly and smoothly. Under these conditions the carbon dioxide transferred from blood to the air in the lungs flows out with the exhaled air more easily. Restoring the acid-base balance quickly gets you over the hump and into your "second wind" sooner than if you breathe out with a quick whoosh. The effectiveness of breathing out against a resistance was discovered accidentally when researchers observed emphysema victims exhaling through tightly pursed lips. They had discovered the effect from experience and were exhaling against the resistance to improve their breathing effectiveness. Try it yourself next time you're pedaling fast or climbing a long hill.

## ANKLING

Efficiency in bicycling absolutely demands good form in ankling—the up-and-down action of the ankle while pedaling. Ankling brings into play the muscles of the ankle and permits full use of leg muscles pulling up on one pedal while pushing down on the opposite pedal. (Pulling up, of course, requires toe-clips on pedals, and toe-clips are also fundamental in ankling.) Instead of drawing propulsion power only from the leg muscles used in pushing down on pedals, ankling distributes muscle activity among three sets of muscles, thereby increasing power and endurance.

Ankling calls for moving the foot at the ankle from a tipped-up position (relative to the leg bone) to a tipped-down position while the pedal moves from its 12 o'clock position to its 6 o'clock position, as viewed from the right side of the bicycle. From the far-down toe position, the ankle then swings the foot up to the toes-up position while the pedal moves between the 6 and 12 o'clock. Both the leg and ankle muscles pull up on the pedal during the last half of the cycle. Figure 44 diagrams these positions for one 360-degree revolution of one pedal. The opposite leg, foot, and ankle follow the same sequence—but alternately. Now, look at what happens at the different positions.

As the pedal reaches 12 o'clock, the foot with toes tipped up is in position to push forward and apply power immediately, rather than hesitate until the pedal moves to a position where the foot can push downward. As the ankle moves from toes-up to flat during the first

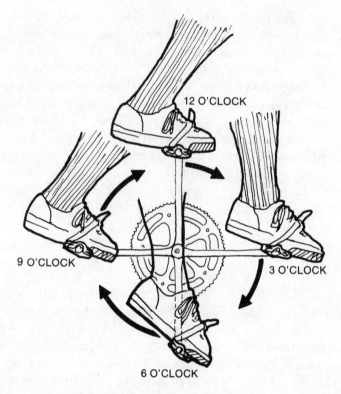

12 O'CLOCK

9 O'CLOCK

3 O'CLOCK

6 O'CLOCK

ANKLING POSITIONS "BY THE CLOCK"

Fig. 44—Ankling can be learned and practiced by clock positions. Beginning at the top or 12 o'clock position (as viewed from the right side of the bicycle), the foot with the ball centered over the axle of the pedal should be tipped up relative to the leg and pushing forward on the pedal. As the pedal approaches the 3 o'clock position, the foot approaches a flat or square position and force is straight down. At 6 o'clock, toes are almost curled under, tipped down relative to the leg and pushing backward. As the pedal rotates through 6 o'clock, the toes begin pulling up on the toe-clips as the foot again approaches the flat position at 9 o'clock. Approaching the 12 o'clock position, toes are tipped up and getting ready to push forward as the pedal rotates through 12 o'clock. Ankle action results from tipping the toes up to tipping them down and back again through the 360-degree motion of the pedal.

quarter of the pedal revolution, the foot switches from pushing forward to pushing down. As the pedal moves through 3 o'clock, toes reverse and begin pullling up against the toe-clips until the foot reaches neutral as the pedal passes through 9 o'clock. During the last quarter of the circle, the ankle moves the foot to a toes-up position and draws the pedal with it, applying power all the way.

Proper ankling can increase propulsion efficiency by 30 to 40 percent compared to pedaling with minimum ankling and without toe-clips. Practice ankling by pedaling with one foot. Notice how you can maintain power throughout the full 360-degree pedal travel by alternately pushing down and pulling up. Practice full ankling until you can continue for long stretches automatically—without any conscious thought. Ankling should become as natural and unthinking on a bicycle as putting one foot in front of the other is in walking.

## TOE-CLIPS

As noted above, toe-clips are absolutely essential for effective ankling. Since toe-clips come in small, medium, and large sizes, check to be sure the toe-clips on your bicycle pedals fit your shoes. While purists, and particularly racers, swear by special bicycling shoes that fix the foot in precise position, Cyclemates and many others use only thick-soled tennis oxfords. The plate on the bottom of cycling shoes can be adjusted to keep the ball of the foot directly over the center of the pedal. The stiff soles on cycling shoes provide more support and comfort for long-distance cycling—another advantage. While special cycling shoes improve efficiency, they are seldom practical for touring or casual biking. You can't easily walk around in cycling shoes. On a tour, as on a Cyclemates trip, you don't spend all of your time on your bicycle. Tennis oxfords are light and easy to walk in while setting up camp, shopping, or sightseeing. Boat shoes with their wriggle-tread sole make good all-purpose shoes for bike touring too. An extra pair of shoes adds excess weight on a long trip. So unless you are a purist, fit toe-clips to your rat-trap pedals that can be tightened around the toe of thick-soled tennis oxfords (Fig. 45). There is one shoe that's a compromise between a cycling shoe and a tennis shoe. It is called the Bata Biker, and while it doesn't look as stylish as a good tennis shoe, it is good for walking and excellent for cycling.

Another thing you will notice about expert bicyclists is that they are forever adjusting the straps on their toe-clips. Here's why. When riding in city traffic, you must be prepared for quick stops. If you brake to an emergency stop and can't slip your foot out of the toe-clips, you're likely to fall into a car or onto a curb.

You can afford to give up some efficiency and ride with loose toe-clips anywhere quick stops may occur with little warning. When approaching such places, reach down and pull the buckle of the toe-clip strap to loosen it. You can do this while you're riding. Then, when you move into a long stretch or approach a hill, you want all the power you can muster. Reach down again and pull on the strap to tighten the toe-clips again. Learn to adjust the strap quickly and easily without looking down at the pedals. You can loosen or tighten straps by feel with only the barest break in your rhythm.

How tight should toe-clips be for maximum efficiency? If the strap on your toe-clips cuts off circulation, the strap is much too tight. However, your shoe should not slide around or move up and down in the toe-clips. Toe-clips should be tight enough to change from pushing down to pulling up without jerking as the pedal moves through the 6 o'clock position. Adjusting straps to suit travel conditions is the key to achieving that extra 30 to 40 percent efficiency you can expect from

Fig. 45—Thick-soled tennis oxfords or boat shoes when properly fitted into toe-clips can be almost as effective as cycling shoes.

correct ankling. When the strap is loose to permit quick, safe foot action in case of a stop, you can expect about 10 to 15 percent efficiency. The metal cage around the toe still permits considerable upward force to be exerted while ankling.

When beginners practice ankling for the first time, particularly if pedaling up a hill, they may notice a pulled or stretched Achilles' tendon—right above the heel. That important tendon can get very sore when ankling over a number of miles the first time. Like building up neck and back muscles, approach ankling in easy stages; work at it until you can feel the stretching of the Achilles' tendon. It may be sore, but work on it again the next day to build up the strength. Once conditioned, it will not continue to bother your efficient cycling. You are more likely to notice sore muscles and tendons when pedaling in cold weather.

## CADENCE

Smooth, rhythmic pedaling at a constant rotational speed, or revolutions per minute (RPM), of the crank mark the expert cyclist. These are the cyclists who exhibit good cadence. Two factors are involved in good cadence—a constancy of rotational speed and a brisk pace of around 65 to 80 RPM. For casual cycling around town, a slower cadence between 50 and 65 may be more appropriate.

With the 10-speed bike, you can adjust gearing to terrain and wind conditions to maintain your cadence. Formerly, a cyclist was forced to change cadence—slowing on uphill stretches or against the wind, and pedaling faster with the wind or on downhill slopes too flat to coast. Learning to be an expert cyclist calls for an understanding of cadence and for developing a rhythmic feel for the rate or pace of cadence.

Associated with cadence is over-the-road speed. If you are turning at a constant 70 RPM, how fast will you be traveling? Obviously, your over-the-road speed depends on your gear ratio and wheel diameter. Two charts will help you figure road speed. Figure 46 relates gear ratios and cadence to speed in terms of miles per hour. Figure 47 displays much of the same information in graph form. This information will be useful, however, only if you can check cadence with some accuracy. Two methods are available:

Use a stop watch. When a cyclist establishes a cadence that feels comfortable on a level stretch of road, he will count the number of

CADENCE CHART

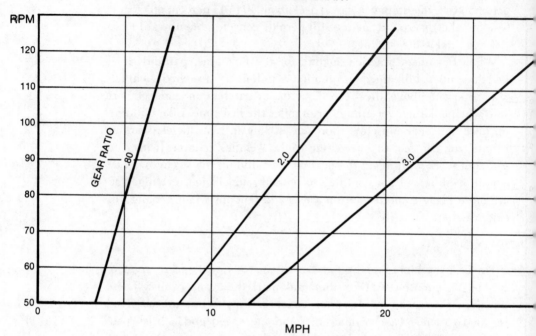

Fig. 46—Cadence table relates RPM of pedal rotation to distance traveled over the road at varied gear ratios and gear-inch numbers.

times the right leg makes a complete revolution in one minute. Accuracy in this method depends on maintaining a constant cadence during the timing run. A wrist watch with a sweep second hand can also be used to gain a rough idea of cadence during a short stretch.

Use a *Mininome*. This new device electronically adjusts timing to provide a regular "beep" through an earphone. The *Mininome* is an adaptation of the metronome used by musicians. You can use the *Mininome* two ways: (1) As you maintain a constant cadence, adjust the beeping rate until it matches your cadence; then read your cadence directly. (2) You can decide on a cadence goal and adjust the beeping rate to that cadence; as you ride, adjust your pedaling rate until your right foot reaches the same position each time you hear the beep in your ear.

Maintaining a constant cadence improves efficiency in the same way that driving at a constant speed improves gasoline mileage. How-

CADENCE AND OVER-THE-ROAD SPEED

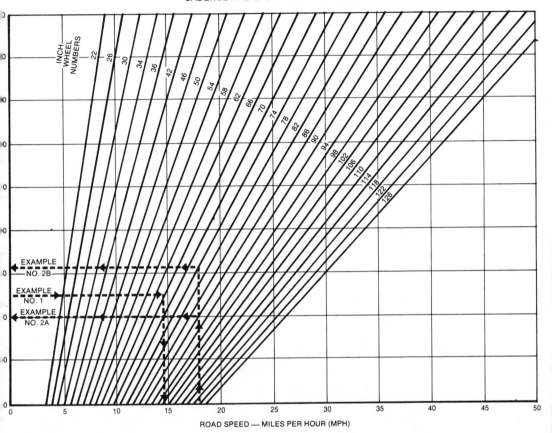

Fig. 47—Cadence and over-the-road speed in miles per hour (MPH). This chart works two ways. If you know your cadence and inch-wheel number, you can find MPH, as in Example No. 1. Enter from left at 75 RPM and follow across to inch-wheel No. 66, then read downward to find road speed at 14.8 MPH. Or, if you are aiming at a specific speed, read up and find the inch-wheel-cadence combination that yields your desired speed. In Example No. 2A, read upward from 18 MPH to inch-wheel No. 86 and read across left to 70 RPM. Or, if you would prefer a lower inch-wheel number and a higher cadence, continue reading up to inch-wheel No. 74 and read left to cadence at 81.5 RPM.

ever, keeping warm on a cold, windy day may mean more than cycling efficiency—so you pedal at a higher cadence to keep warm. Racers generally pedal at a higher cadence because they are more interested in sprint speeds than in long-distance endurance. But, generally, find the cadence that's best for you by experimenting, then stick to it, changing gears as necessary to maintain the cadence without straining leg muscles.

Developing a constant cadence calls for practice. If you are beginning to cycle seriously, find the cadence at which you are now cycling most of the time. If it is 50, plan to increase cadence to 55 for a while until that becomes comfortable, then bump the rate to 60. At some speed between 60 and 80, you will find your most effective cadence. Riding at your best cadence should become as automatic as ankling. It requires smooth operation of the derailleur or hub changer for adjusting gear ratio.

## GEAR CHANGING

As you ride up and down hills, into and out of the wind, pedal forces can change radically unless you change gears. Plan to use all of your gears. What is the point of buying a bicycle with ten speeds and then using only three or four of the middle-range gears?

Practice until you become familiar with the full range of gears, preferably in a school parking lot or other area where traffic and distractions won't interfere. Gear positions on a derailleur-equipped bicycle are not fixed. You won't find easy detents that mark each gear front and back. You can shift 4-on-the-floor gears in a car by feel; you should be able to do the same with a bicycle. But, while you are learning, you will need to watch the shift lever and check its position against the gear driven by the chain. While you are looking down or back, you don't want to run into something or wander into a car's path, so pick a deserted parking lot and shift gears up and down until you are thoroughly familiar with each ratio. Practice shifting from one gear to the next without jumping a gear. And don't shift the chain on both chainwheels and rear cluster at the same time. Of course, you will only shift while actually pedaling, because derailleurs function just as the name implies. The derailleur actually derails the chain, moves it off the gear and allows it to catch on the adjacent gear. Develop a feel for how much movement of the gear shift handle is necessary to derail the chain up or down one gear. Unless the chain is perfectly aligned, you will hear "ker-chunking" noises as the teeth rub or bear against the side links of the chain as well as on the cross links.

Shifting gears in traffic and while touring calls for a skill developed with practice to keep from breaking cadence. Timing is all important. For example, you look ahead and see the road changing to a slight upgrade with a gradual increase in steepness. If you wait too late to shift, you will either slow your cadence or find yourself working harder than you might prefer. On the other hand, you may shift too soon and find yourself pedaling at an uncomfortably fast cadence to keep up with others in a group. Experienced cyclists change gears frequently. They can tell from the feel of pedaling force whether to shift up or down while maintaining a steady cadence. Try relating shift timing to driving a 4-speed manual shift car. If you attempt to drive up a steep hill in high, the engine lugs and labors. But if you shift down to third or second too soon, the engine revs up and runs faster than necessary, using extra gasoline and wearing itself out early.

As you ride, study the road ahead and anticipate gear changes. Experience will help you judge whether a hill can be taken in fifth or third gear. Shift through a series of gears rather than suddenly shifting from tenth to third. Instead, shift down to fifth, then fourth, then third. You can shift easily from tenth to fifth on most bikes by shifting the chain with the front derailleur from the large to small chainwheel. For an even progression through the high middle range of gears, you may need to shift back and forth between the high and low chainwheel. Otherwise, plan to shift from seventh to fifth, if shifting to sixth requires shifting the front derailleur. How closely you follow each gear will depend on how expertly you change gears. When you are preparing for touring, spend the time necessary to develop confidence and ease in shifting gears—it pays off.

## BRAKING

Caliper brakes on front and rear wheels provide for excellent control when the brake systems are properly adjusted. Chapter Thirteen discusses checks and adjustments for various braking systems. Handlebar brake handles provide high leverage for applying rim pressure through double brake pads on both front and rear wheels.

With so much braking power available, you should apply brakes cautiously during casual cycling and learn the most effective braking practices for emergencies.

When applying brakes, squeeze the handle controlling rear brakes first, as the rear wheel usually carries more weight. While touring with panniers, the added weight on the rear wheel will generate more braking force through the added traction without skidding. A heavily loaded wheel retains traction and resists skidding more than a lightly loaded wheel. Therefore, develop the habit of braking first with the rear brakes and follow up with the front wheel brakes.

Experienced cyclists use both front and rear wheel brakes about equally, but they have trained themselves to apply rear wheel brakes first. If you were to clamp hard on a front wheel brake only in an emergency stop, you could be tossed over the handlebars. In traffic you can appreciate the hazards of such a maneuver. Some youngsters' bikes mount a brake lever on each handlebar, but both sets of calipers function on the rear wheel. Without brakes on the front wheel, a child cannot lock the front wheel only and cause a spill.

Properly adjusted brakes should be capable of skidding either a front or rear tire on dry pavement. But once a tire begins to skid, you lose control. For most effective braking, learn to recognize a skid the instant it begins and let up on the brake handle. Allow the wheel to begin rolling again before reapplying brakes.

Auxiliary brake levers permit braking from hand positions close to the handlebar stem. These auxiliaries, however, do not provide as much leverage as primary handles. Auxiliary levers are good for controlling speed while coasting down a long hill but will seldom stop your bike quickly, particularly if you are headed down a fairly steep grade.

When coasting down a long steep hill, apply brakes in stages rather than continuously. Brake with considerable force to slow your rate, then allow the wheels to roll freely before braking again. Continuous braking will tend to glaze the brake pads and reduce braking effectiveness. When braking on long downhill runs, equalize the braking as closely as possible between front and rear wheels. If there is a difference, be sure the rear wheel is braking more than the front. One other tip—don't wait too long to begin braking when coasting downhill. Anticipate possible stops or sharp turns at the bottom of a hill and slow your pace before reaching the bottom. Braking early on long downhill runs becomes particularly important when touring with extra weight in panniers and handlebar bags.

## LEARN BY RIDING

Combine practice with theory to improve your skills in bicycling. Continue to practice good form in learning balance, cadence, and gear shifting. Plan to learn as much as possible about your relationship with your bicycle through riding. You learn by doing, as long as you practice the principles proved through experience.

# TABLE D: Cadence and Speed—Miles Per Hour (MPH)

| Inch-Wheel Number | Revolutions/Minute (RPM) | | | | | | | | | |
|---|---|---|---|---|---|---|---|---|---|---|
| | 50 | 60 | 70 | 80 | 90 | 100 | 110 | 120 | 130 | 140 |
| 22 | 3.27 | 3.93 | 4.57 | 5.24 | 5.89 | 6.55 | 7.20 | 7.85 | 8.50 | 9.15 |
| 24 | 3.56 | 4.28 | 4.99 | 5.70 | 6.43 | 7.14 | 7.85 | 8.56 | 9.27 | 10.0 |
| 26 | 3.28 | 4.65 | 5.41 | 6.19 | 6.95 | 7.73 | 8.50 | 9.29 | 10.0 | 10.8 |
| 28 | 4.16 | 5.00 | 5.82 | 6.65 | 7.50 | 8.32 | 9.15 | 10.0 | 10.8 | 11.7 |
| 30 | 4.45 | 5.35 | 6.24 | 7.14 | 8.03 | 8.90 | 9.81 | 10.7 | 11.6 | 12.5 |
| 32 | 4.75 | 5.71 | 6.65 | 7.62 | 8.56 | 9.50 | 10.5 | 11.4 | 12.4 | 13.3 |
| 34 | 5.05 | 6.07 | 7.08 | 8.19 | 10.1 | 11.1 | 12.1 | 13.1 | 14.2 | |
| 36 | 5.35 | 6.43 | 7.48 | 8.56 | 9.64 | 10.7 | 11.8 | 12.8 | 13.9 | 15.0 |
| 38 | 5.65 | 6.68 | 7.90 | 9.05 | 10.2 | 11.3 | 12.4 | 13.5 | 14.7 | 15.8 |
| 40 | 5.95 | 7.15 | 8.32 | 9.51 | 10.7 | 11.9 | 13.1 | 14.3 | 15.5 | 16.7 |
| 42 | 6.24 | 7.50 | 8.74 | 9.99 | 11.2 | 12.5 | 13.7 | 15.0 | 16.2 | 17.5 |
| 44 | 6.54 | 7.85 | 9.15 | 10.5 | 11.8 | 13.1 | 14.4 | 15.7 | 17.0 | 18.3 |
| 46 | 6.84 | 8.20 | 9.56 | 11.0 | 12.3 | 13.7 | 15.1 | 16.4 | 17.8 | 19.2 |
| 48 | 7.14 | 8.56 | 9.98 | 11.4 | 12.9 | 14.3 | 15.7 | 17.1 | 18.5 | 20.0 |
| 50 | 7.43 | 8.92 | 10.0 | 11.9 | 13.4 | 14.9 | 16.4 | 17.8 | 19.3 | 20.8 |
| 52 | 7.73 | 9.26 | 10.8 | 12.4 | 13.9 | 15.4 | 17.0 | 18.5 | 20.1 | 21.6 |
| 54 | 8.03 | 9.63 | 11.2 | 12.9 | 14.5 | 16.0 | 17.7 | 19.3 | 20.9 | 22.5 |
| 56 | 8.32 | 10.0 | 11.7 | 13.4 | 13.4 | 15.0 | 16.6 | 18.3 | 20.0 | 21.6 |
| 58 | 8.62 | 10.3 | 12.1 | 13.8 | 15.5 | 17.2 | 19.0 | 20.7 | 22.4 | 24.2 |
| 60 | 8.91 | 10.7 | 12.5 | 14.3 | 16.1 | 17.8 | 19.7 | 21.4 | 23.2 | 25.0 |
| 62 | 9.20 | 11.1 | 12.9 | 14.8 | 16.6 | 18.4 | 20.3 | 22.1 | 25.0 | 25.8 |
| 64 | 9.50 | 11.4 | 13.3 | 15.3 | 17.1 | 19.0 | 21.0 | 22.8 | 24.7 | 26.6 |
| 66 | 9.80 | 11.8 | 13.7 | 15.7 | 17.7 | 19.6 | 21.6 | 23.6 | 25.5 | 27.5 |
| 68 | 10.1 | 12.1 | 14.1 | 16.2 | 18.2 | 20.2 | 22.3 | 24.2 | 26.3 | 28.3 |
| 70 | 10.4 | 12.5 | 14.6 | 16.7 | 18.7 | 20.8 | 22.9 | 25.0 | 27.0 | 29.2 |
| 72 | 10.7 | 12.9 | 14.9 | 17.1 | 19.3 | 21.4 | 23.6 | 25.7 | 27.8 | 30.0 |
| 74 | 11.0 | 13.2 | 15.4 | 17.6 | 19.8 | 22.0 | 24.2 | 26.4 | 28.6 | 30.8 |

# TABLE D: Cadence and Speed—Miles Per Hour (MPH) Continued

| Inch-Wheel Number | Revolutions/Minute (RPM) | | | | | | | | | |
|---|---|---|---|---|---|---|---|---|---|---|
| | 50 | 60 | 70 | 80 | 90 | 100 | 110 | 120 | 130 | 140 |
| 76 | 11.3 | 13.6 | 15.8 | 18.1 | 20.3 | 22.6 | 24.9 | 27.1 | 29.4 | 31.6 |
| 78 | 11.6 | 13.9 | 16.2 | 18.5 | 20.9 | 23.2 | 25.6 | 27.8 | 30.1 | 32.4 |
| 80 | 11.9 | 14.3 | 16.6 | 19.0 | 21.4 | 23.8 | 26.2 | 28.4 | 30.9 | 33.2 |
| 82 | 12.2 | 14.6 | 17.0 | 19.4 | 21.9 | 24.4 | 26.8 | 29.3 | 31.7 | 34.1 |
| 84 | 12.5 | 15.0 | 17.4 | 19.9 | 22.4 | 25.0 | 27.5 | 30.0 | 32.4 | 35.0 |
| 86 | 12.8 | 15.4 | 17.8 | 20.4 | 23.0 | 25.6 | 28.2 | 30.7 | 33.2 | 25.8 |
| 88 | 13.1 | 15.7 | 18.3 | 20.9 | 23.6 | 26.2 | 28.8 | 31.4 | 34.0 | 36.6 |
| 90 | 13.4 | 16.1 | 18.7 | 21.4 | 24.1 | 26.8 | 29.5 | 32.2 | 34.7 | 37.4 |
| 92 | 13.7 | 16.4 | 19.1 | 21.8 | 24.6 | 27.4 | 30.2 | 32.8 | 35.5 | 38.3 |
| 94 | 14.0 | 16.8 | 19.5 | 22.3 | 25.2 | 27.9 | 30.8 | 33.6 | 36.3 | 39.2 |
| 96 | 14.2 | 17.1 | 19.9 | 22.8 | 25.7 | 28.5 | 31.4 | 34.2 | 37.1 | 40.0 |
| 98 | 14.5 | 17.5 | 20.4 | 23.2 | 26.2 | 29.2 | 32.1 | 35.0 | 37.8 | 40.8 |
| 100 | 14.8 | 17.9 | 20.8 | 23.8 | 26.8 | 29.8 | 32.8 | 35.7 | 38.6 | 41.6 |
| 102 | 15.1 | 18.2 | 21.1 | 24.2 | 27.3 | 30.3 | 33.4 | 36.4 | 39.4 | 42.5 |
| 104 | 15.4 | 18.6 | 21.6 | 24.7 | 27.8 | 30.9 | 34.1 | 37.1 | 40.2 | 43.3 |
| 106 | 15.7 | 18.9 | 22.0 | 25.2 | 28.4 | 31.5 | 34.7 | 37.8 | 40.9 | 44.1 |
| 108 | 16.0 | 19.3 | 22.4 | 25.6 | 28.9 | 32.1 | 35.4 | 38.6 | 41.7 | 45.0 |
| 110 | 16.3 | 19.6 | 22.8 | 26.1· | 29.4 | 32.7 | 36.0 | 39.3 | 42.5 | 45.8 |
| 112 | 16.6 | 20.0 | 23.2 | 26.6 | 30.0 | 33.3 | 36.7 | 40.0 | 43.2 | 46.6 |
| 114 | 16.9 | 20.4 | 23.6 | 27.1 | 30.5 | 33.9 | 37.3 | 40.7 | 44.0 | 47.5 |
| 116 | 17.2 | 20.7 | 24.0 | 27.6 | 31.0 | 34.5 | 38.0 | 41.5 | 44.8 | 48.3 |
| 118 | 17.5 | 21.1 | 24.4 | 28.0 | 31.6 | 35.1 | 38.7 | 42.2 | 45.5 | 49.1 |
| 120 | 17.8 | 21.4 | 24.9 | 28.5 | 32.1 | 35.7 | 39.3 | 42.9 | 46.3 | 50.0 |
| 122 | 18.1 | 21.8 | 25.3 | 29.0 | 32.6 | 36.3 | 40.0 | 43.5 | 47.1 | 50.8 |
| 124 | 18.4 | 22.2 | 25.7 | 29.4 | 33.2 | 36.9 | 40.7 | 44.3 | 47.9 | 51.6 |
| 126 | 18.7 | 22.5 | 26.1 | 29.9 | 33.7 | 37.5 | 41.3 | 45.0 | 48.6 | 52.5 |

# 7.

# Fitness:
# Your Bonus
# from Bicycling

Thinness and agility, quickness of step, a slow heartbeat while at rest but with extra capacity there if you need it, steady nerves and easy relaxation, the ability to work, run, bicycle, swim, or walk briskly without undue fatigue—they're all yours when you are physically fit. Fitness revolves around a free-flowing vascular system with a healthy heart that distributes oxygen from lungs to cells and returns carbon dioxide. Feeling fit really means feeling good!

Exercise has been studied from so many different angles that repetition of the benefits may be a cliché. For review, however, exercise can help you to—

● Attack your daily work or fun activities with more energy. The fit person gets more done in a day because he is able to spend more energy. The fit person doesn't get drowsy after lunch, and needs fewer hours of sleep to remain alert. Energy reserves are built up through exercise over time. In effect, the fit person works with greater capacity both mentally and physically.

● Extend your productive years by reducing the rate of aging. Sedentary work fails to provide for muscle activity and to tax the heart and vascular system. The human body responds to a challenge, but it deteriorates when not used. The whole aging process is accelerated by excess weight and reduced activity levels. Dr. Paul Dudley White, President Dwight Eisenhower's consulting physician when Ike suffered heart attacks, has been quoted many times on the need for regular exercise to reduce the rate of aging. A fully conditioned man can turn the physiological clock back ten years or more through continued exercise.

• Keep well and avoid sickness. Exercise for children and adults alike reduces the number and severity of illnesses. Let's take one common example—the role of exercise in the prevention and treatment of back problems. When back muscles fail to support the spine, slipped discs or pinched nerves can make life miserable. Swimming, walking, jogging, and bicycling all relieve the tensions and increase the suppleness of the back muscles. Or, take heart disease. The role of regular exercise in preventing or relieving heart disease and in rebuilding heart capacity is no longer questioned. In Seattle, the Cardiac Pulmonary Research Institute (CAPRI) conducts medically supervised rehabilitation programs that recondition bodies and rebuild damaged hearts through regular exercise that begins with walking and progresses to jogging or pedaling a stationary bicycle. Slowly, the damaged heart is taxed in graduated steps until it achieves the capacity for pumping blood equal to its work potential. In some cases this capacity is greater than what was present prior to the heart problem.

Presently, coronary artery disease is the leading cause of death. Recently the death rate from coronary artery disease was 364.5 per hundred thousand, about 39 percent of deaths from all causes. If strokes and other arterial diseases are added, the death rate approaches 50 percent—a staggering wastage of human potential. Compared to the half who died from cardiovascular disease, only 1/6 died of cancer, the second leading cause, and 1/16 died from accidents, the third leading cause of death.

Preventive heart exercise may head off or defer cardiovascular complications. Exercise helps keep blood vessels stretchy and pliable, making it easier for the heart to pump larger quantities of blood to every cell. Following a regimen of prescribed exercise, adults usually notice a slower pulse rate at rest and a less rapid rise in pulse with exercising. Regular exercise increases the heart's overall capacity, thereby providing a greater reserve for handling emergencies.

• Control weight and retain a look of youth. As both men and women grow older, the basal metabolism rate declines along with normal physical activity. You see the result in extra weight around the middle, wrinkles, and a lack of vitality that reduces activity and leads to further debilitation. Exercise breaks this vicious circle by burning off excess calories (see Table G) and maintaining a higher basal metabolism. With less weight to haul around and a higher rate of body activity, you look and feel younger.

• Calm tension-jangled nerves and promote psychological well-being. Physical activity helps to loosen the tension one picks up during the day from a fast-paced job. Rather than attempting to relieve tensions with a double martini before dinner, substitute aggressive exercise and note the difference. Few people get the exercise they need to counteract the aggravation and tension picked up during daily confrontations with life's frustrations. The good feeling of fatigue that results from exercise brings on healthful sleep without drugs, so you benefit both ways.

• Improve your self-image—how you feel about yourself. Researchers report a healthy reduction in negative thinking and a much more positive outlook following extended exercise programs. A man naturally feels better about himself when he feels better physically. And how a man feels about himself is reflected in his self-image, the confidence he exudes, and his positive dealings with others. Bicycling offers you the increasingly rare opportunity to enjoy "blessed aloneness," to think privately and to contemplate your options.

• Increase the efficiency of body functions. Regular exercise develops what athletes recognize as a "training effect." That is, after running or bicycling for a few days or weeks, the body adapts to the increased requirements and begins functioning more efficiently. By efficiently, physiologists mean that the same energy output is attained from few input calories. Instead of working at 20 percent efficiency, the body may work up to 25 percent efficiency. The effect is much like a car's engine that gets only twelve miles per gallon because it is out of tune and functioning sluggishly. But when the engine is tuned up, the same engine turns out fifteen miles per gallon. Your body when conditioned by exercise works more efficiently; that is, it converts more of the food energy it ingests into useful output.

## WHAT KIND OF EXERCISE?

The term "regular" appears often in the above recital of benefits from exercise. Regular means repetitive over a period—daily, preferably. Regular can also mean three or four times a week. A once-a-week golf game fails to qualify as regular exercise because bodily benefits wear off between times. Regular exercise need not be overly taxing. The repetitive aspect rather than the time spent each day is what is most important.

Two kinds of exercise are recognized—isotonic (muscle contraction with movement, such as cycling, running, swimming or calisthenics), and isometric (muscle contraction without movement). The late Charles Atlas developed a body-building program on isometrics— pushing one hand against another, for example. These two exercises increase strength and sometimes improve muscle tone and flexibility. Isometric exercises do little for the cardiovascular system or for the development of endurance. Many calisthenic exercising can be useful for slimming one's waist, thighs, or other body parts. Calisthenics can loosen stiff muscles and improve body tone. But few calisthentics tax the heart, lung, and blood distribution system enough to develop the training effect noted earlier.

To build endurance and benefit from a regular exercise program, consider these two facts about exercise:

1. Tennis, handball, skiing, and such team sports as volleyball call for start-and-stop activity. In tennis you run for a ball, swing, and relax for a few seconds before you react to another return—or retrieve a ball. These sports demand very short peak energy spurts. In contrast, walking, swimming, jogging, and bicycling call for continuous action at a relatively level rate. Of course, the rate changes between types of exercise. Jogging is more strenuous than walking, for example. Also, walking at three miles per hour requires less energy than walking at four and a half miles per hour. Even greater variations of energy expenditure occur in bicycling.

2. To build endurance and expand your physical capacity, exercise should be strenuous enough to cause you to huff and puff, to work up a sweat, and to feel your heart rate increase. Many muscles should participate in exercise activity to extend benefits throughout the body. Bicycling affords this wide-range body-building exercise to a greater degree than any of the other exercise media except swimming. Walking and jogging exercise the legs and heart. Jogging, particularly, calls for energy expenditures that quickly increase heart rate and breathing; it provides excellent exercise, but provides little work for the back and arm muscles. Swimming uses more of the muscles equitably than other exercises and also calls for a high rate of energy

expenditure. But swimming requires an indoor pool or an outside body of water—and compatible weather. Bicycling exercises legs and back muscles normally plus arm muscles when climbing hills. You can disregard the weather when cycling either by wearing protective clothing outside or by using an indoor cycling exerciser.

Two factors relate in determining how much exercise is enough to build endurance through a progressive exercise program: (1) Rate of energy expended; and (2) time over which a specific rate of energy is expended. Dr. Cooper's studies with Air Force personnel in their twenties and thirties primarily indicated that the pulse rate should reach 150 per minute for a period of at least five minutes. Participants in the very successful CAPRI program measure pulse rate regularly during exercise.

The training effect from sustained high levels of exercise builds endurance and expands the total capacity of your heart-lung-vascular system. At high levels of energy expenditure, as in swimming and running, the training effect begins after about five minutes and continues for as long as the exercise continues. For bicycling, this threshold occurs at speeds above 10 mph on the average. To reach the training effect threshold at low levels of energy expenditure, more time at the sustained low level is required. To reach the training effect threshold in walking requires covering about two miles in forty minutes or less.

Bicycling affords exercise that falls between the strenuous extremes of swimming or running and easy but time-consuming walking. For some people swimming and running can be hard work and boring. Both have one big attribute, however; they get your exercise for the day over in a hurry. When exercise degenerates into work, the shorter the time the better. Bicycling provides more than exercise. As noted elsewhere, bicycling permits quiet and privacy for contemplation when you bicycle alone; it also affords pleasant companionship on group rides. In either case, the cyclist can observe the environment and the changing scenery while exercising and, thereby, relieve the boredom that quickly sets in while circling a track or churning back and forth between ends of a pool.

If you are over the age of 35, before beginning any exercise program you should determine your maximum work capacity through an exercise stress test. During the closely monitored stress tests, you increase the work rate in stages until you reach your maximum work capacity. You will be thoroughly examined before starting. During the test you are wired into an electrocardiograph, and a physician with emergency equipment is present for safety and to interpret test results. Either a treadmill or a bicycle ergometer is used to build up the work load. As the speed and grade increase on the treadmill, your heart rate will increase until it reaches a maximum rate. Shortly thereafter, you will call a halt because of lack of breath, rubbery legs, or both.

Your recorded maximum pulse rate becomes a key factor. During later exercise periods, your heart should not exceed 70 or 85 percent of that recorded maximum. Rather than say you should bicycle so many miles in X minutes, you can set your own limits—*after* taking the maximum stress test. You simply monitor your pulse rate and adjust the rate of exercise to remain within 70 to 85 percent of the maximum rate. You can read your own pulse rate by placing a finger on the cardioartery under your jawbone to either side of the Adam's apple, or by pressing on the radial artery that runs along the inner forearm bone. Count the heart beats for fifteen seconds, multiply by four, and you quickly determine your work rate. If you have ever had any symptoms of heart or vascular distress, by all means avoid a self-administered exercise program.

Attempting to prescribe a bicycling exercise program for everyone —or even anyone—without knowing the individual's medical history and present condition remains practically impossible. However, to be on the safe side, work less than an easy average program rather than more. An easy progression for cycling begins by pedaling one mile in 6 to 10 minutes four or five days out of the first week. During the second week, bicycle two miles in 10 to 15 minutes. Third week, three miles in 15 to 17 minutes. Fourth week, four miles in 20 to 22 minutes. Fifth week, five miles in 26 to 30 minutes. Beyond the fifth week you may continue to build up distances at a rate that will keep pulse rate within the 70 to 85 percent of maximum.

You can measure training effect by recording pulse rates for the same amount and exertion level of exercise. At the fifth level, for example, determine your pulse rate after riding five miles in 26 minutes. Continue riding five miles a day, pacing yourself to stay within the 26- to 30-minute period. After a week, take your pulse again. You will probably find it lower than a week earlier because your body adjusted to the work load and your heart no longer needs to work as hard as it once did to satisfy muscle demands. You are conditioning yourself when the training effect takes over.

Younger men can build up the level of exercise activity more quickly. Women, while ordinarily less susceptible to cardiovascular disease, cannot match the work output of men if both are equally conditioned. Humans reach the peak of their physical capacity at around 17 to 18 years of age—the main reason Olympic Gold Medal winners in swimming are so young. If you are evaluating your own fitness and conditioning program and wonder about how fast you can progress, ask yourself:

• Did you spend a week at one activity level, and was it comfortable?

• Were you free from any unusual physical symptoms indicating you were working too hard?

• Did your pulse and breathing rates return to normal within ten minutes following the cessation of exercise?

If you answered all three questions affirmatively, then you can consider upping the workload to a higher level of activity—more miles on a bicycle or the same number of miles in fewer minutes. The temptation in building fitness is to progress from one level to the next too rapidly. Take your time! Be patient and consolidate your fitness at each level before moving on to the next. At some point, depending on your age, any preexisting conditions, weight, and consistency, you will reach a plateau—the highest level you can attain. Every person reaches a plateau eventually. You can tell when you reach yours by monitoring your heart beat and knowing your maximum capacity. When your pulse rate consistently reaches 70 to 85 percent of your maximum, and continued training does not reduce the rate, you are at or close to your plateau; but you will find many miles of pleasurable bicycling and improved physical fitness before reaching it. And when you do, you will be well-conditioned and fit to really enjoy cycling without fatigue and stress by maintaining your fitness plateau through continuing regular exercise.

## WEIGHT REDUCTION THROUGH CYCLING

With obesity approaching epidemic proportions in the United States, a bicycling exercise program plus diet control adds one more benefit. Bicycling can keep you slim, trim, and fit while you enjoy its other pleasures. If you're not already slim, trim, and fit, bicycling will help you reach your weight reduction goals.

At least one out of every five adults is overweight—that is, from

10 to 20 percent over the desirable weights noted in Table E. Most physicians and nutritionists concerned with weight control (along with most overweight persons) agree that those ugly, unhealthy pounds result from overeating. Foods when measured in Calories represent fuel the body turns into heat or converts to energy. The number of Calories a body needs to stay even varies according to body weight, sex, age, and activity level. During early adulthood, daily intakes of 3,200 and 2,300 Calories represent averages for men and women respectively. Table F defines other Calorie allowances for men and women at different body weights and three ages.

Like most averages, Calorie intakes and desirable body weights fit few persons exactly; but refer to them as a guide or a point of departure. If you deviate from the desirable body weight for your height, prefer the low side of the average rather than the high side. As for Calorie intakes, you can tell whether you are eating too much by weighing yourself every morning before breakfast. Daily swings in weight reflect different amounts of water retained in body tissues from day to day. But a daily chart of weights over a period of weeks will tell you the full story of Calorie intake. Small changes in Calorie intakes can affect body weight over time. For example, if every day you drank one bottle of a soft drink (about 105 Calories) over the total food intake necessary to maintain an even weight, you would gain about eleven pounds in one year.

Exercise, works the same way. You need not bicycle several hours a day to lose weight. A modest exercise schedule that shucks off 200 Calories each day will reduce your weight by about twenty-one pounds within a year — even if you don't diet.

While this chapter is not really aimed at developing a full program for dieting and weight control, look at the numbers in Table H. This table shows the relationship between bicycling and weight reduction. If you want to lose just one pound of body weight by hopping on your bicycle and riding at a moderate speed of 9 to 12 mph, you would have to pedal nearly forty-two hours. This is why so many weight watchers lose enthusiasm for exercising away extra pounds. But if you reduced food intake by an average of 200 calories per day, and rode your bicycle at moderate speeds for one hour each day, you would lose one pound in about 5½ days.

One pound of body weight equals 3,500 Calories. While bicycling

## TABLE E: Desirable Weights for Heights

| Height in Inches | Weight in Pounds | |
|---|---|---|
| | Men | Women |
| 58 | | 112 ± 11 |
| 60 | 125 ± 13 | 116 ± 12 |
| 62 | 130 ± 13 | 121 ± 12 |
| 64 | 135 ± 14 | 128 ± 13 |
| 66 | 142 ± 14 | 135 ± 14 |
| 68 | 150 ± 15 | 142 ± 14 |
| 70 | 158 ± 16 | 150 ± 15 |
| 72 | 167 ± 17 | 158 ± 16 |
| 74 | 178 ± 18 | |

## TABLE F: Calorie Allowances for Individuals

| Desirable Weight | Calorie Allowance | | |
|---|---|---|---|
| | Men | | |
| Pounds | 25 years | 45 years | 65 years |
| 110 | 2,500 | 2,350 | 1,950 |
| 121 | 2,700 | 2,550 | 2,150 |
| 132 | 2,850 | 2,700 | 2,250 |
| 143 | 3,000 | 2,800 | 2,350 |
| 154 | 3,200 | 3,000 | 2,550 |
| 165 | 3,400 | 3,200 | 2,700 |
| 176 | 3,550 | 3,350 | 2,800 |
| 187 | 3,700 | 3,500 | 2,900 |
| | Women | | |
| 88 | 1,750 | 1,650 | 1,400 |
| 99 | 1,900 | 1,800 | 1,500 |
| 110 | 2,050 | 1,950 | 1,600 |
| 121 | 2,200 | 2,050 | 1,750 |
| 128 | 2,300 | 2,200 | 1,800 |
| 132 | 2,350 | 2,200 | 1,850 |
| 143 | 2,500 | 2,350 | 2,000 |
| 154 | 2,600 | 2,450 | 2,050 |
| 165 | 2,750 | 2,600 | 2,150 |

at a slow 5 to 7 mph, a man weighing about 150 pounds burns up only about 2½ to 3½ extra Calories per minute (Table G). A woman weighing about 125 pounds burns less, about 2 to 3 calories per minute, for two reasons. First, more energy is consumed by the heavier man because he is bigger. Second, women use about 8 to 10 percent less energy because their systems work more efficiently. Table G shows net Calories per minute; that is, the calories consumed are due to the bicycling and are in addition to the Calories used to maintain normal body functions at rest.

As you would expect, the number of Calories burned goes up as bicycling speed increases. Further, since Calories used are net, they increase at a faster rate than speed increases. Table G shows that, as speed increases from 5.5 to 13.1 mph, or 138 percent, Calories used increase from 2.5 to 11.6 per minute, or 364 percent. Thus, if you intend to derive full benefit from bicycling to lose weight, pedal faster within the same time frame, and cover greater distances. The figures in Table G represent bicycling along relatively level roads. If you ride on roads with hills that have up to a 5 percent incline and similar decline, the Caloric consumption figures increase by 20 to 50 percent. Add another 6 percent for each ten pounds of body weight over the 150- and 125-pound averages for men and

## TABLE G: Caloric Expenditure During Cycling*

*In Calories/Minute*

|  | Men (150 lbs.)** | Women (125 lbs.)** |
|---|---|---|
| 5.5 mph | 2.5 | 2.1 |
| 9.4 mph | 7.2 | 6.0 |
| 13.1 mph | 11.6 | 9.5 |

Caloric expenditures for bicycling represent net values—over and above basal metabolism caloric expenditures for body at rest.

* On level roads. Add 20 to 50 percent for grades up to 5 percent (5 feet rise for 100 feet horizontal distance).
** Increase caloric rates about 6 percent for each 10 pounds of body weight above noted figures.
Large tires—add 1 Calorie/minute to above rates.
Sources: *Food: The Yearbook of Agriculture*, 1959, USDA.
  "Human Energy Expenditure," R. Passmore and J.V.G.A. Durnin, *Physiological Review*, 35:801, 1955.
  *Overweight*, Jean Mayer, Prentice-Hall, Englewood Cliffs, N.J., 1968.

women respectively. If you should be riding a bicycle with heavy tread balloon tires, add one Calorie per minute to each of the figures to account for the added rolling resistance.

Changing gears affects Caloric consumption less than you might expect. Important variables are distance and speed. Within the same time spans, the amount of work accomplished in traversing a set distance of level road or of climbing a specific hill relates only loosely to which gear you may be using. If you shift to a high gear, you will pedal at a slower cadence, to be sure, but the force on each pedal revolution will be greater than if you use a lower gear. A very fast cadence in a low gear will use more energy, but not as much more as you might expect. The actual differences have not been tested rigorously. However, unless you pedal with an excessively fast cadence or a very slow cadence, the average numbers shown in Table G will remain representative.

To help dedicated dieters mentally picture how many minutes they will need to pedal to work off certain foods, Table I shows exercise equivalents. A cola beverage in a 12-oz. can contains about 145 Calories. If you pedal along at a slow 5 to 7 mph, you must travel forty-eight minutes to spend the 145 Calories in the carbonated pop. But if you pedal along at a 15 to 18 mph clip, you can be back to zero weight after only twelve minutes of pedaling. You can figure all of the other foods similarly—and watch out for that slice of pecan pie!

Two other factors affect how many pounds you can lose while bicycling. First, when you engage in any kind of rigorous exercise, your body's basal metabolism level increases both during and after exercise periods. A sedentary person "lives cheap" in terms of food calories burned just to maintain an even body temperature and to move around from bed to table to desk and other low-key but normal activities. When this person embarks on a regular exercise program, his basal metabolism rate may increase as much as 10 percent. Maintenance of normal body functions throughout the twenty-four-hour day uses the bulk of the 3,250 calories burned by the average man in his twenties. So by increasing the basal metabolic rate (bmr), exercise burns up additional calories.

Offsetting the increase in bmr, however, is the training effect noted earlier. As you get better at bicycling, your muscles also become efficient. After riding along a road for an hour each day for thirty days, you won't burn up as many Calories on the thirtieth day as you did on the first day. This rise in efficiency would affect the figures in Tables G and H slightly. However, since these figures already average out a number of variables, and the increase in bmr uses up more calories between exercise sessions, they remain a useful guide.

Combining bicycling (or other) exercise with lower Caloric intakes makes for weight loss within a reasonable time period. And bicycling is an exercise you can enjoy and stick with without becoming bored.

### Table H: Bicycling Days to Lose 5 to 20 Pounds in Combination with Less Food°

| Bicycling (Minutes/Day) | Less Food (Calories/Day) | Number of Days | | | |
|---|---|---|---|---|---|
| | | To Lose 5 lbs. | To Lose 10 lbs. | To Lose 15 lbs. | To Lose 20 lbs. |
| 30 | 200 | 41 | 83 | 124 | 165 |
| 30 | 400 | 28 | 56 | 84 | 112 |
| 30 | 600 | 21 | 42 | 63 | 84 |
| 30 | 800 | 17 | 34 | 51 | 68 |
| 30 | 1,000 | 14 | 29 | 43 | 57 |
| 45 | 200 | 33 | 65 | 88 | 130 |
| 45 | 400 | 24 | 47 | 71 | 94 |
| 45 | 600 | 19 | 37 | 56 | 74 |
| 45 | 800 | 15 | 31 | 46 | 62 |
| 45 | 1,000 | 13 | 27 | 40 | 54 |
| 60 | 200 | 27 | 54 | 81 | 108 |
| 60 | 400 | 21 | 41 | 62 | 82 |
| 60 | 600 | 17 | 33 | 50 | 66 |
| 60 | 800 | 14 | 28 | 42 | 56 |
| 60 | 1,000 | 12 | 24 | 36 | 48 |

°Calculated at 7½ Calories/minute for about 10 mph with slight grades up and down.
3,500 Calories equal one pound of body weight.

## TABLE I: Bicycling Equivalent of Calories in Common Foods

| Food | Calories | *Number of Minutes to Equal Food Calories* *Bicycling Activity Level* 5 to 7 mph | 9 to 12 mph | 15 to 18 mph |
|---|---|---|---|---|
| *Beverages* | | | | |
| Cola, 12-oz. | 145 | 48 | 21 | 12 |
| Fruit flavored, 12-oz. | 170 | 57 | 24 | 14 |
| Ginger ale, 12-oz. | 115 | 38 | 16 | 10 |
| Beer, 12-oz. | 150 | 50 | 21 | 13 |
| Wines, table, 3-oz. | 75 | 25 | 11 | 6 |
| Wines, dessert, 3-oz. | 125 | 42 | 18 | 10 |
| Whiskey, 80 proof, 1½ oz. | 95 | 32 | 14 | 8 |
| Whiskey, 100 proof, 1½ oz. | 125 | 42 | 18 | 10 |
| *Cereals* | | | | |
| Bread, 1/16-lb. slice | 75 | 25 | 11 | 6 |
| Muffin, 2¾-in. dia. | 140 | 47 | 20 | 12 |
| Bun, Hamburger | 120 | 40 | 17 | 10 |
| Sweet roll | 135 | 45 | 19 | 11 |
| Saltine cracker, two, 2-in. sq. | 35 | 12 | 5 | 3 |
| Doughnut | 125 | 42 | 18 | 10 |
| Pancake, 4-in. | 60 | 20 | 9 | 5 |
| Waffle | 210 | 70 | 30 | 18 |
| Bran flakes, 1 cup | 105 | 35 | 15 | 9 |
| Corn flakes, 1 cup | 95 | 32 | 14 | 8 |
| Farina, cooked, 1 cup | 105 | 35 | 15 | 9 |
| Rice, puffed, 1 cup | 60 | 20 | 9 | 5 |
| Macaroni, plain | 115 | 38 | 16 | 10 |
| Spaghetti, plain | 115 | 38 | 16 | 10 |
| *Dairy Group* | | | | |
| Milk, whole, 1 cup | 160 | 53 | 23 | 13 |
| Milk, skim, 1 cup | 90 | 30 | 13 | 7 |
| Sour cream, 1 cup | 505 | 168 | 72 | 42 |
| Yoghurt, 1 cup | 120 | 40 | 17 | 10 |
| Malted milk, 1 cup | 280 | 93 | 40 | 23 |
| Ice cream, ½ cup | 145 | 48 | 21 | 12 |
| Cheese, cheddar, 1 oz. | 115 | 38 | 16 | 10 |
| Cheese, cottage, 2 tbsp. | 30 | 10 | 4 | 2 |
| *Desserts* | | | | |
| Cake, 2-in. section, 10-in. cake with icing | 345 | 115 | 49 | 29 |
| Gingerbread, 2-in. sq. | 170 | 57 | 24 | 14 |

TABLE I: Continued

| Food | Calories | Number of Minutes to Equal Food Calories | | |
|---|---|---|---|---|
| | | *Bicycling Activity Level* | | |
| | | 5 to 7 mph | 9 to 12 mph | 15 to 18 mph |

*Desserts*

| | | | | |
|---|---|---|---|---|
| Yellow cake, 2-in. section, 18-in. round cake without icing | 205 | 68 | 29 | 17 |
| Caramels, 3 med. | 115 | 38 | 16 | 10 |
| Chocolate mints, 2 small | 90 | 30 | 13 | 7 |
| Hard candy, 1 oz. | 110 | 37 | 16 | 8 |
| Chocolate bar, 1 oz. | 150 | 50 | 21 | 13 |
| Sugar, 1 tsp. | 15 | 5 | 2 | 1 |
| Cookies, 3-in. | 120 | 40 | 17 | 10 |
| Apple pie, ⅛ of 9-in. pie | 300 | 100 | 43 | 25 |
| Custard pie, ⅛ of 9-in. pie | 250 | 83 | 36 | 21 |
| Pecan pie ⅛ of 9-in. pie | 430 | 143 | 61 | 37 |

*Fats and Oils*

| | | | | |
|---|---|---|---|---|
| Butter or margarine, 1 pat | 50 | 17 | 7 | 4 |
| Salad dressing, blue cheese, 1 tbs. | 75 | 25 | 11 | 6 |
| Salad dressing, mayonnaise, 1 tbs. | 100 | 33 | 13 | 8 |
| Salad dressing, low calorie, 1 tbs. | 15 | 5 | 2 | 1 |

*Meat and Protein Group*

| | | | | |
|---|---|---|---|---|
| Beef & veg. stew, 1 cup | 185 | 62 | 25 | 15 |
| Beef potpie, 4½-in., 8-oz. pie | 560 | 187 | 80 | 47 |
| Chili, with beans | 170 | 57 | 24 | 14 |
| Hamburger, broiled, 3-oz. | 245 | 82 | 35 | 20 |
| Meat loaf, 3-oz. | 170 | 57 | 24 | 14 |
| Roast beef, 3-oz. | 375 | 125 | 54 | 31 |
| Steak, broiled, lean only, 3-oz. | 175 | 58 | 24 | 15 |
| Bacon, 2 thin slices | 60 | 20 | 8 | 5 |
| Ham, cured & cooked, lean, 3-oz. | 160 | 53 | 23 | 13 |
| Pork sausage, cooked, 2-oz. | 270 | 90 | 38 | 22 |
| Frankfurter, 1 | 155 | 52 | 22 | 13 |

## TABLE I: Continued

| Food | Calories | Number of Minutes to Equal Food Calories Bicycling Activity Level | | |
|---|---|---|---|---|
| | | 5 to 7 mph | 9 to 12 mph | 15 to 18 mph |
| *Meat and Protein Group* | | | | |
| Chicken, fried, ½ breast | 155 | 52 | 22 | 13 |
| Fish sticks, breaded, 5 ave. | 200 | 67 | 28 | 17 |
| Eggs, fried, 1 large | 100 | 33 | 14 | 8 |
| Baked beans, ½ cup | 155 | 52 | 22 | 13 |
| *Snacks* | | | | |
| Popcorn, popped in oil, 1 cup | 40 | 13 | 6 | 3 |
| Potato chips, 10 med. | 115 | 38 | 16 | 10 |
| Pizza, plain cheese, 5½-in. section, 14-in. pie | 185 | 62 | 26 | 15 |
| *Vegetables* | | | | |
| Carrots, 5½ x 1-in. | 20 | 7 | 3 | 1 |
| Celery, 2 8-in. stalks | 10 | 3 | 1 | 1 |
| Lettuce, 2 large leaves | 10 | 3 | 1 | 1 |
| Tomato, 1 med. | 35 | 12 | 5 | 3 |

# 8.

# Safety
# for Bicyclists

Along with more bicycles and greater mileage per bike is the growing
spectre of more injuries and deaths. Statistics can be frightening—1,000
killed in the United States during 1979 as a result of collisions between
bicycles and motor vehicles. You can bet that the unprotected cyclist
comes off second best in any kind of collision with a heavier—and
usually faster—car or truck. In addition, more than a hundred deaths
could be attributed to bicycle accidents not involving cars or trucks.
Estimates of accidents involving lesser injuries are not precise (only
those requiring a doctor's attention are reported) but exceed 1 million
in number. In one recent year, 330,000 victims of bicycle accidents
were injured seriously enough to require hospital emergency-room
treatment, and 710,000 required treatment in a physician's office.
Those two numbers alone total 1,040,000 cases. Of the injuries treated
in a hospital emergency room, about 40 percent involved lacerations,
with 20 to 25 percent of those above the neck. Contusions and/or
abrasions ranked second to lacerations. Fractures, usually to one of the
upper extremities, accounted for 14 percent of emergency room treat-
ments. Slightly more than 2 percent of emergency room injuries were
brain concussions.

Age was a definite factor in motor vehicle-bicycle collision deaths in
1979. Of the 1,000 reported, 400 deaths were youngsters age 14 or
younger, with another 360 in the age bracket from 15 through 24.

Those 1,000 deaths reported in 1979 are ominous, but it is amazing
that there weren't more, considering the enormous growth in bicycle
usage. There were an estimated 90 million bicycles around the country
in 1979; in 1941 the bicycle population was less than a third as large,
but there were 910 motor vehicle-bicycle deaths in that year. The

death toll for bicyclists involved in collisions with motor vehicles reached a low of 380 in 1954. All of these statistics are from the National Safety Council's records. Bicycle-related deaths not involving motor vehicles are not tabulated because no regular reporting system exists for collecting the data.

## HOW DO ACCIDENTS HAPPEN?

Bicycle accidents can be clearly divided into two types—collisions and falls. Collisions occur when a motorist strikes a bicycle that thrusts suddenly into a street from a sidewalk, driveway, or alley. Or, a driver may overrun a bicycle he didn't see at night because the bicycle wasn't lighted. A bicyclist may also collide with a pedestrian, tree, or other fixed object.

Falls result from a variety of causes—lack of skill in riding, carrying packages or another person that interferes with balance or steering, riding off curbs or steps, skidding or slipping on slick or loose surfaces, or catching wheels in a street-car track, drain slots, pavement crack, or expansion joint. Falls may result when a gear suddenly locks or a chain tangles in a gear cluster. Doing stunts such as rearing up on the back wheel to pull a "wheelie" also causes falls.

The differences between collisions and falls are important because falls are less likely to prove fatal; collisions cause most of the accidental deaths. Lack of riding skill and immature judgment lead to the greater incidence of accidents among children age 14 and under. Yet cyclists as young as 13 and 14 have pedaled across the country as Cyclemates (see Chapter Twelve) with only one minor accident attributable to riding. No car was involved. One other Cyclemate fainted while riding, for no apparent reason, and fell. I skinned a knee when my bike skidded as I rode through a banner for photographers at the start of Cyclemates II. Safe bicycle riding is possible even with youngsters if the cyclist is trained and remains alert.

Of the 850 bicycle collision fatalities, 450 occurred in an urban environment. According to a study of bicycle use and accidents in Raleigh, North Carolina, a school-age child rides a bicycle about 250 miles during the 6-month summer period, or about 313 miles over the year. Of 2,397 students studied in detail, all but 11 ranged in age from 5 through 14. Boys rode about double the miles of the girls. For this group the accident rate was 1.58 accidents per 1,000 miles, including those accidents for which parents provided first aid. Ordinarily, these minor mishaps are not reported. If only moderate or severe accidents (those reported by hospitals or physicians) are averaged, the rate during the test was .133 per 1,000 miles. During the three Cyclemates' trips covering nearly 12,000 bicycle miles, the accident rate was .167 per 1,000 miles.

A recent study of bicycle accidents by the California State Patrol found two emerging trends—a startling increase in fatalities (32 percent over a two-year span) and a change in the age groups affected. Accidents to young adults (age 15 to 34) increased from 25 percent to 41 percent of the reported accidents during the last twelve years.

The California Highway Patrol's analysis revealed that when accidents happen, the bike rider is often at fault. Riding on the wrong side of the road, making improper turns, running stop signs, and infiltrating the motor vehicle driver's right of way were cited as the four most common causes of bicycle accidents. The Commissioner stated, "Dramatic improvement is possible if bicycle riders keep alert at all times, exercise common sense, and follow the rules of the road."

## RIDING IN CITY TRAFFIC

Bicyclists have no more right than automobile drivers to ride their vehicles on public streets without some training and practice. Every state requires some kind of training before drivers are awarded a license to drive. Not so with cyclists. Lack of training, lack of skill in riding, and dumb mistakes cause most accidents. If you plan to ride in city or town while sharing roads or streets with automobiles, read and heed the following:

• Ride with the traffic and to the far right of the road or street. Both bicycles and automobiles have the same rights to space on public thoroughfares except on those limited-access highways where only motor vehicles are permitted. But bicyclists should recognize their vulnerability compared to drivers enclosed in steel boxes. Riding in the same direction aids car drivers to accommodate cyclists—and reduces relative impact if a collision should occur. Riding along the far right side of the street may be easy between intersections, but what about turns? When you approach an intersection, you can proceed straight ahead, turn right, or turn left. There's a safe procedure for each.

When turning to the right, the cyclist should make a tight turn—no swinging out to the left to make a wide, sweeping turn to the right. To make a tight turn, slow down, because you can't turn tightly while pedaling along at average speed. Slowing down on right turns also diminishes the hazards of gravel, wet slippery leaves or storm sewer grates often found near curbs or a pavement edge at corners.

If a car is alongside as you approach an intersection, determine as clearly as possible whether the driver plans to turn right. Recently manufactured cars include turn signals visible from the side. They provide one clue. Or, you might listen for a clicking turn signal. A rider following can see a turn signal from the rear and shout ahead "Car turning!" Or, look at the driver and signal your intention of turning to make sure he sees you.

Going straight across the intersection means looking to left and right to assure a clear roadway. If a car is alongside or close behind, you'll want to make sure he sees you and will not turn right into a line of bicyclists.

Turning left can be more of a problem. First, you will want to move into the left lane, just as you would if driving a car. Junior cyclists improve their riding safety and performance remarkably soon after passing a driver's test and earning a driver's license. When turning, make a sweeping turn to the left only when the lane is clear of oncoming traffic into the left lane of the intersecting street. When traffic permits, cut across to the far right side again.

At a busy intersection, principally at a traffic signal light which offers few breaks in the traffic, a better way to turn left is by making a "270." Instead of waiting for a break, go straight ahead. On the far side, swing around through the parking lot of a gas station or other access and turn right 270 degrees until you can proceed straight through the intersection in the direction you wish to go. With this procedure, you always remain in the far right lane and do not cross busy traffic lanes. This maneuver may take longer—but it's safer.

Hand signals may be controversial for some cyclists. The Cyclemates use both hand and audible signals. We want automobile drivers to be aware of our intentions. And, just as important, we want each rider in line to be aware of the leader's plans. If a rider stops, the one behind might run into him. So, we use hand signals and back them up with shouts—"Stopping!" or "Turning right!" Instead of the usual three hand signals, we use four—

Arm upraised for a right turn.

Arm directly out to the left for a left turn.

Hand and arm straight down for stopping.

Hand and arm down but moving slowly up and down to indicate slowing.

The first three of these signals are pretty standard. Some cyclists prefer not to use hand signals because they must remove one hand from the handlebars. If a cyclist cannot maintain control of a bicycle with only one hand, he shouldn't be riding on city streets. A cyclist should practice in a parking lot, bike path, or deserted street until he attains enough skill to control his bike with only one hand (see skill tests following).

• Stop at stop signs and signals. Police often complain that cyclists do not stop where signs are posted and, thereby, cause accidents. As any cyclist knows, stopping poses problems. One must either touch a foot to the ground or wiggle the front wheel to maintain balance. When riding with toe-clips on the pedals (a must for the serious cyclist), removing one foot from the pedals can be a nuisance. So, many cyclists slow down at stop signs, but do not stop. Observations during a study of bicycle usage in Davis, California, noted that bicyclists stop or merely slow down depending on traffic. Before a rider reached an intersection, he would look up and down the street. When his head sweep showed traffic present, he would stop to the point of placing his foot on the ground. But, if the intersection was clear, most riders continued across, disregarding the sign.

In another study at Davis, researchers found that car drivers and bicyclists chose different routes when traveling between various areas and the University of California campus. Bicyclists chose routes with an average of 4.9 stop signs and 1.8 stop lights; car drivers traveling between the same points chose routes with an average of 2.3 stop signs and 4.2 stop lights. After interviewing a number of student drivers and bicyclists, the researchers found that bicyclists seldom came to a complete stop at stop signs. They simply slowed down and continued through, traffic permitting. But they stopped completely at red lights. Car drivers, being subject to greater enforcement pressure, stopped completely at stop signs; but there was a 50-50 chance that they would go through a signal on a green light.

• Use streets which carry less traffic and which permit parking along the side. Arterials where no cars are parked almost always permit cars to drive at greater speeds than on side streets. Cars generally yield enough space between traffic lanes and parked cars to permit bicyclists to ride with relative safety. When cars are parked, however, bicyclists encounter another serious hazard—car doors opening without warning. If a door opens unexpectedly, the cyclist may swerve left into the traffic lane and collide with a car, if one is moving in that lane. Or the cyclist may collide with the open door. People in parked cars look for and can see cars approaching; they are much less likely to notice an approaching cyclist. Therefore, the cyclist must take the initiative and look for people sitting in cars. When you see a person in a car, slow down, move out slightly, or yell to let the person know you're there. If your bike is equipped with a good horn, sound it. Usually, you can tell if the person sees you, from head action or his eyes. If the car occupant shows no sign of observing you, approach slowly enough to stop quickly if the door should open suddenly.

• Avoid falls, because a car or another cyclist can run into a sprawled bike and rider and cause serious injury. Cyclists fall when they hit something, lose traction and slip, or catch a wheel in a road crack or hole. Every cyclist knows about avoiding storm sewer grates; they are deadly! Since grates are frequently found at corners, you have to watch the street at the same time as you keep an eye out for traffic. You can also catch a tire in a wide pavement crack, between a curb and pavement, or in a hole left where a chunk of pavement has settled. You must keep at least one eye open for such surface traps to avoid being thrown off—and mangling a bike wheel. Oil spots, wet paper or leaves, and loose sand or gravel can cause a narrow high-pressure tire to lose traction. Avoid slipping on these kinds of spots by not turning. Every time you turn, the tire generates a sidewise force; and, if the surface is slick, the sidewise force may exceed traction and the tire skids. By going ahead straight over slick spots, no side forces develop and there's little opportunity for the tire to skid.

Falls also occur when cyclists ride in groups, as on the Cyclemates' trips. Make sure the rider in front and in back knows what the group is doing *before* they do it. Riding too close can lead to collisions between riders. When riding in a group, know the skill level of the rider ahead. Leave at least one bike length between bikes. If you're traveling faster than 15 to 20 mph, leave two or more bike-length spaces between you and the rider ahead.

Pavement drop-offs sometimes lead to falls because of their suddenness. Rather than trying to climb back on the pavement, continue ahead off the slab until you see a good opportunity for slanting back onto the paved surface. Junk on the road can cause spills too—tree branches, bottles, sticks, cans, and parts that have fallen off cars. The small, light tires and rims on touring bikes won't ride over such junk without damage.

Railroad or street-car tracks are still another hazard. Sometimes wide joints between wood planks on either side of the tracks invite disaster. All of these openings threaten the cyclist, particularly when wet or icy. If possible, cross tracks at a 90-degree angle; if traffic won't permit a 90-degree crossing, dismount and walk across.

Bridges and overpasses present other problems, namely expansion joints with narrow cracks just the right size to trap a narrow bike tire. If traffic is clear, you can cut off at a 45-degree angle and avoid the slots. If car traffic prevents the angling technique, don't take chances—dismount and walk your bike across the joints. Bridges may also have steel manhole covers that can be dangerously slick when wet. Some bridges have narrow sidewalks for bicycle riders. When you share a walkway, remember that the pedestrians have the right of way. A narrow walkway along Lake Washington's floating bridge is posted, requiring bicyclists to dismount and walk around the draw-bridge area because of the sharp curves and of steel plates in the surface. Look, too, for mud, sand, and slippery mold on some bridges.

Obvious safety hints include: Ride with no more than one person on a bicycle, except for tandems. The rule is—a seat designed for each person on a bicycle. Yield right-of-way to pedestrians. Use only your own power—avoid hitching onto trucks or cars. When entering a street from a driveway, alley, or between parked cars, make sure the way is clear by slowing or stopping to look in all directions for children, cars, or other cyclists.

Learn the specific traffic code for cyclists in your community. Some towns and cities permit bicycle riding on sidewalks everywhere. Others permit sidewalk riding in residential areas but not in shopping or business sections. Local police departments publish rules of the road for cyclists; get a copy and memorize its provisions.

Wherever bicycle paths or trails are maintained, cyclists should use them, even if it means traveling extra distance. More and more cities and state highway departments are recognizing the need for physically separating bicyclists from automobile traffic. Bikeways and bike paths or trails are the answer; but if cyclists do not use the bikeways available, new ones will not be built. It's a case of "use 'em or lose 'em."

## COUNTRY AND SUBURBAN RIDING

Riding out of city traffic calls for different skills for safety. Cyclists should ride single file and to the far right—off the edge of primary traffic lanes if possible. When a shoulder is paved, ride there. If a shoulder is only gravel, remember that touring bicycle tires do not handle easily on unpaved surfaces, so ride on the edge of the pavement, using your best riding skill to remain close to the pavement edge without falling off. Riders in line should remain in line and not swing out into the traffic lane except to change position—and then only when traffic permits. Where shoulders are narrow and space to the right of the paved area restricted, keep a close watch on cars, and give ground readily if two cars pass near your position. Cars do not have a legal right of way over bicyclists on normal highways, and most motorists recognize their responsibility to share space; but you can't afford to take a chance on getting that rundown feeling by asserting your rights. It's better to give ground and continue on safely than to stand pat and be bumped.

Downhill coasting can be fun when handled safely. Here are tips from Cyclemates' experiences:

• Leave plenty of distance between yourself and the cyclist ahead. Before heading down a long slope, check your brakes to make sure they are working. Along the way, control speed with light braking to avoid a sudden stop at the bottom. You can go fast downhill, but anticipate changes at the bottom. Is there a sharp curve at the end of the hill? A bridge? Stop sign or signal? Gravel or slick pavement?

• Rushing down a hill directly behind another rider blocks your view; so stagger the line ever so slightly to keep a view line ahead. You want to see far ahead because you're going fast.

• When coasting fast downhill, keep at least a couple of fingers on the brakes to reduce reaction time.

• Wear sunglasses or clear glasses to help keep bugs and dust out of your eyes when coasting.

• When rounding curves while coasting downhill, remember to keep the inside pedal up. Catching a pedal while leaning around a curve can lead to a nasty spill.

• Ride scared when rolling downhill at 40 mph or faster. Be alert for anything that could throw you out of control, such as dogs or junk on the road. Think about skinning your nose or knees on the road surface if you spill.

• Don't take your eyes off the road. Instead of turning your head to look for traffic, listen for cars coming from behind. If riders at the end of a string hear a car, they can yell ahead (just say, "Car!," not a whole sentence). Use every opportunity to keep other riders informed of hazards from behind or ahead by shouting in both directions.

## COPING WITH DISTRACTIONS

Cyclists must continually be aware of cars backing out of driveways, and of children, dogs, and other distractions—in addition to auto traffic. A kid steps off the curb ahead of you—what is he going to do? Run off or stand in your way? If you have to swerve to avoid him, you could fall or collide with a passing car. With children around, slow down and be prepared for whatever action pops into their heads.

Horns or bells can be useful in warning off children, letting car drivers know you're around, and communicating with other riders in a group. (See Chapter Four.)

While dogs seldom bite, they can be a real hazard. They vary from the tired, indifferent mutts that couldn't care less about sixteen kids bicycling past to vicious, mean animals without a whit of kindness for unfamiliar humans—particularly those on two-wheeled vehicles. In between there are the casually interested, the barkers, chasers, and watchers with a yen to pursue. Bicycles and their pedaling action excite most dogs and start the canine equivalent of adrenalin coursing through their arteries.

Since bicyclists have been confronting dogs for years, the consensus suggests that your action be appropriate to the type of dog you encounter. To avoid one that comes dashing out from a yard, you may swerve into a traffic lane. Or you may actually hit a dog, lose control, and tumble. Sometimes a friendly, tail-wagging mutt can wander into your path and cause a tumble while welcoming you and your friends to the neighborhood.

Unfriendly dogs can be controlled by a variety of means. Ignore the half-hearted yappers, short-legged runners, and the barkers affirming territorial rights. If that doesn't work, yell at them with a startling blast —like "Hey!" shouted with authority in a sharp, loud tone. Or, "Get outahere!" What you yell means less than the harsh, sharp tone you use. Often the dogs will be startled and stop running. Then, speed up and you're away. Or you can slow down briefly, yell, and speed up again. On a level or going downhill, a good cyclist can sprint away from most dogs. Some alternative action may be needed if you're headed up a hill.

For determined chasers and vicious dogs, you may need to use one of the aerosol cans of liquid pepper or a home-made equivalent. A plastic squeeze bottle filled with household ammonia or detergent and water deters any dog if your aim is good and the can or bottle is within easy reach in your handlebar bag. Some of the commercial canned products, such as "Halt," include clips for keeping them handy.

A whip, stick, even a tire pump can be pressed into service to beat off a determined attacker. A well-aimed kick may turn back a close chaser. Just be careful not to run into something or lose control of your bike while fighting off a dog. Generally, your best protection from a dog nuisance is the sharp, authoritative yell and a controlled indifference as you ride on.

When carrying gear in a handlebar or pannier bag, make sure it is secure. When something falls off, a rider behind may swerve to avoid it and could fall. Also, if you notice something falling out of a handlebar bag, your attention is immediately diverted. When this happens while coasting downhill at 40 mph, you can lose control, possibly fall yourself, and block the way for a rider behind you.

PROTECTION. Bright clothing helps others to see you in the daytime. "See and be seen" should be the motto of safety-conscious cyclists.

Helmets are sometimes prescribed for cyclists for the same reason motorcyclists are required to wear headgear—protection of the cranium from direct, sudden contact with the pavement. Until youngsters acquire varied riding skills, a helmet could prevent serious injury. Children fall frequently—largely because they are just learning to ride and are careless. Kids can tolerate scrapes and scratches, but not head injuries—concussion, for example. Therefore, protective headgear of some kind—a football helmet, plastic cushioned cycle helmet, or even a thick, woolly watch cap helps prevent direct head-pavement contact.

## BICYCLING SAFETY AT NIGHT

Most bicycle accidents occur during daylight hours, mainly because most cyclists ride only during daylight hours. A study in Nassau

County, New York, revealed that 83 percent of bicycle accidents occurred during the day. But the rate of accidents was much higher for those who ride at night. Numerous suggestions for improving the visibility of cyclists at night are being considered by various city, state, and Federal government agencies.

Most common is the requirement that a headlight be visible from 500 feet away and that a red reflector or taillight be visible from 200 to 300 feet to the rear. Other suggestions call for luminous striping around the tires, reflectorized spokes, and stripes of reflective tape on the cyclist's outer garment. Luminous vests are available and make a lot of sense if you commute before sunup or after sundown. Many of the new bicycles include reflector panels on the front and rear vertical sections of the pedals to meet some state requirements. A two-way flashlight strapped to the left leg draws attention because of its motion. Although the two-way flashlight may also be strapped to the left arm, it moves less there than on the leg. One proposal calls for an outline of a bicycle stippled in luminous paint to the back surface of a jacket or vest.

## RIDING SKILLS

Balance and control are skills to be learned through practice. You can test your bicycle driving skills against the following standards adapted from "Skill Tests for Pedal Pushers," as published by the National Safety Council:

TEST NO. 1. A BALANCE TEST DURING SLOW RIDING IN A STRAIGHT LANE The course is a straight lane 3 feet wide and 60 feet long. Wide chalk marks on a level section of a school parking lot will do nicely. The rider taking this test starts from a standstill with the front wheel at one end of the lane. Very slowly he rides through the lane in not less than 30 seconds. Neither front nor rear tire should touch the outer edges of the 3-foot lane. Skill standards: (1) Neither foot touches the ground. (2) Time. Since a quick pass through the lane is easier than riding slowly, no less than 30 seconds is permitted, to test for delicate balance. (3) Wheels are kept within the borders of the 3-foot lane.

TEST NO. 2. DEMONSTRATION OF SKILLS IN PEDALING AND BRAKING. The arena for this test can be any paved level surface 25 x 100 feet. The rider mounts and rides 100 feet at average riding speed, brakes to a stop, dismounts, and parks his bicycle. Skill standards: (1) Balls of feet are on pedals while riding. (2) When braking with a bike equipped with coaster brakes, pedal cranks are approximately parallel to the ground

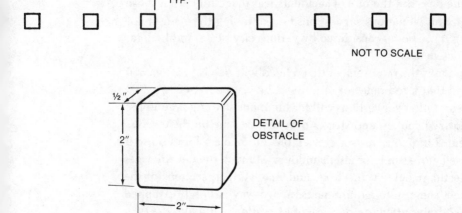

Fig. 48—Obstacle course for Skill Test No. 4. Obstacle blocks may be cut from wood or rubber to size shown in detail. When painted a bright orange or other light color, they can be easily seen aligned on a school parking lot or other relatively level riding area.

Fig. 49—Obstacle course for Skill Test No. 5. Twenty of the same-size obstacles detailed in Fig. 48 are aligned with only 5 inches between pairs.

and back pressure is exerted on rear pedal. For bikes equipped with caliper brakes, braking is equalized on both wheels or slightly more braking force on rear wheel. (3) Neither wheel is skidded during braking. (4) Bicycle is stopped approximately 10 feet from the point of brake application. (5) Rider dismounts and parks the bicycle properly.

TEST NO. 3. ABILITY TO RIDE ON A STRAIGHT LINE. The course for this test is a straight line 100 feet long and only 4 inches wide. From a riding start at slow or average speed, the rider must ride along the full length of the line while keeping both tires within the 4-inch width. No time is specified, as the rider must maintain enough speed to permit small changes in direction to correct balance. Skill standards: (1) Both tires are kept within the 4-inch line over the full distance.

TEST No. 4. ABILITY TO OPERATE BICYCLE IN CLOSE QUARTERS, TO REVEAL JUDGMENT AND ACCURACY IN RIDING PAST OBSTACLES. The course is laid out in a straight line with obstacles 5 feet apart as diagrammed in Fig. 48. The rider starts from a position far enough from the first obstacle to gain full control before starting through the course. The rider passes to the right of the first obstacle, weaves through the open space, and passes to the left of the second obstacle and on through all spaces alternating from side to side. At the end the rider circles and repeats the course on the way back. Skill standards: (1) Neither foot touches the ground. (2) Each obstacle is passed without a tire touching it. (3) Rider weaves from side to side, passing alternatively to the right and left of obstacles.

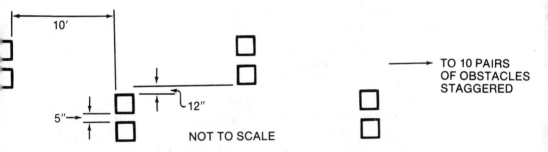

Fig. 50—Obstacle course for Skill Test No. 6. Staggered pairs of obstacle blocks are aligned only 5 inches apart.

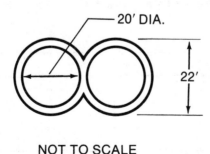

NOT TO SCALE

Fig. 51—Figure-8 obstacle course for Skill Test No. 7. Two 20-foot inside diameter circles overlap as shown for steering and balancing test. Riding strip between circles measures 12 inches.

Test No. 5. Ability to gauge the limited space between obstacles on a straight line. Obstacles can be the same size as those detailed in Fig. 48. However, twenty of the obstacles are aligned as shown in Fig. 49 to define the course. From a riding start, the cyclist rides slowly between each pair of obstacles without either tire touching. When the rider has passed through all ten pairs of obstacles, he circles and returns through the ten pairs again. Skill standards: (1) Neither foot touches the ground. (2) Each pair of obstacles is passed without touching them with either tire.

Test No. 6. Ability to gauge the limited space between pairs of obstacles spaced on a zig-zag line. The course for the double zig-zag obstacle test is detailed in Fig. 50. Obstacles are the same as those used in Tests 4 and 5. The pairs of obstacles are staggered off center by 12 inches. From a riding start, the cyclist rides at a slow speed between the pairs of obstacles without either tire touching an obstacle. After passing through the pairs of obstacles, the rider circles and repeats the performance in the opposite direction. Skill standards: (1) Neither foot touches the ground. (2) Each pair of obstacles is passed through without the tire touching either one. (3) Rider passes between every pair of obstacles.

Test No. 7. Ability to steer and balance while turning on a prescribed figure-8 course. The figure-8 course is laid out with 20-foot circles on the inside with lanes 12 inches wide, as detailed in Fig. 51. From a riding start and with both hands on the handlebars, the cyclist steers the bicycle through the figure-8 course. Skill standards:

Fig. 52—Course diagram for Skill Test No. 10. Course outline may be marked off in chalk on level pavement.

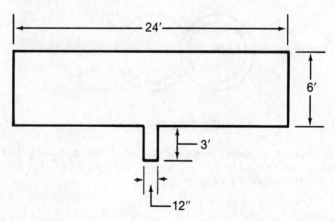

(1) Neither foot touches the ground. (2) Both hands are kept on the handlebars. (3) One full figure-8 is completed without touching any border of the course with either tire.

TEST NO. 8. ABILITY TO STEER THE BICYCLE SLOWLY AROUND THE SAME FIGURE-8 COURSE AS IN NO. 7 BUT WITH EMPHASIS ON MAINTAINING CLOSE BALANCE CONTROL AT SLOW SPEED. The rider starts from a standstill at any point in the figure-8 and slowly rides in the lane through the full figure-8 course in not less than 45 seconds without touching either wheel to the border of the course. Skill standards: (1) Neither foot touches the ground after starting from a standstill. (2) The full figure-8 is completed in not less than 45 seconds. (3) Neither tire touches any border line. (4) Brake is not used excessively.

TEST NO. 9. ABILITY TO MAINTAIN BALANCE AND CONTROL WHILE TURNING AROUND EASILY AND SMOOTHLY WITHIN A LIMITED AREA. The course for this test is a 12-foot-wide straight lane marked off on level pavement. From a riding start the cyclist passes along the left side of the 12-foot lane, turns clockwise and proceeds in the opposite direction without leaving the lane. Repeat the test by riding along the right side of the lane and turning counterclockwise. In each direction, the cyclist signals the correct left or right turn. Skill standards: (1) Neither foot touches the ground. (2) Proper signals are given for turns. (3) Border of the 12-foot lane is not touched by either tire during either maneuver.

TEST NO. 10. ABILITY TO TURN AND STOP WITHIN A LIMITED AREA TO SIMULATE AN EMERGENCY TURN AND STOP. The course for this test is laid out as detailed in Fig. 52. From a riding start at average speed, the cyclist enters the small, 12-inch-wide lane, turns to the right without either wheel cutting the corner of the lane, and comes to a full stop within the 6-foot lane. The rider then repeats the test with a left turn and stop. Skill standards: (1) Neither foot touches the ground until after the bicycle has stopped.

Scoring for each of the ten tests can be on a point scale as follows: 20 points, excellent; 15 points, good or acceptable; 10 points, average; 5 points, fair; 0 points, poor. Skill standards for each test represent guidelines for judging rider performance, with considerable latitude for scoring points on a subjective rating of smoothness and ease. A rider should pass each test with at least 10 points, or practice until he can perform with average skill. A rider who cannot pass each of the ten tests with at least average performance should not be permitted to ride on the streets.

# 9.

# Protecting and Transporting Your Bicycle

If your bicycle is stolen, your chances of getting it back are about one in fifty—or less. Although the rate of thievery now appears to be lessening, bikes are still being stolen for two basic reasons: (1) There are more bicycles to steal. (2) The demand for modern, lightweight, 5-, 10-, and 15-speed bicycles continues to be high. Although supplies are catching up with demand, bicycles are easily salable; so a quick turnover profit from stealing bicycles is still an inducement to the criminal.

In only one year in Seattle, Washington, more than 3,000 bikes were stolen, many from the University of Washington campus. These bicycles represent a dollar value of at least $200,000. With tongue-in-cheek, but with a bite nevertheless, campus and city police recognize, wryly, these four rules governing bicycle theft:

● The bicycle owner who can least afford the loss appears to be the first to be victimized.

● Effective planning for prevention of theft loss occurs after a bike is stolen.

● Like many auto drivers, bicyclists inherently believe "it won't happen to me."

● By ignoring the whole problem, cyclists figure the problem will simply go away.

Good bicycles cost too much for an owner to ignore the possibility of theft. So, what can you do to protect your bike? Recognize first that there are two kinds of bike thieves.

First, there is the casual thief, the joyrider, the youngster who sees a bike and decides to go for a ride. Sometimes, young boys will ride off on an unprotected bicycle for a joyride, possibly abandoning the bike in a convenient brush pile; sometimes he will dump the stolen bike in a lake or river to avoid being caught. Or, on a university campus, a student may see an unlocked bike and ride it to class on the other side of the campus with no intention of stealing it for good. These are the casual thieves. They usually take a bike on impulse with little thought of selling it. Casual thieves pose little hazard for the bike owner with even a modicum of bike sense. Almost any kind of chain, cable, and lock will stop the casual thief.

Second, there is the "for real" thief. Organized thieves steal bicycles in wholesale quantities, wheel them into a truck, and haul them away for sale in the next state or major city. Aside from shackling yourself to your bike or never letting it out of your sight, nothing provides absolute safety from organized thieves. But you can make stealing your bike so difficult that the professional thief will pick an easier mark and leave your bike untouched. Bike thieves' *modus operandi* runs something like this.

Thieves work in pairs, sometimes with a third driving the truck. One thief functions as a lookout. The other, usually wearing a long coat, carries a pair of compound-action bolt cutters strung from the ends of a rope around his neck. The bolt-cutters hang down below the waist with enough rope to permit opening the long handles to their full stroke.

When the thieves spot a likely bicycle, the lookout watches for casual passersby 'When no one is around, the thief with the bolt-cutters moves in. He leans forward over the target bicycle. The bolt-cutters are in position to snap through all but the heaviest chain. Snip! The bike is free. The thief hops on the bike and immediately rides it off to a prearranged meeting with the truck. A well-organized gang may include a rider to pedal stolen bikes to the truck, leaving the thief with the bolt-cutter and the lookout to capture more bikes in less time.

You can learn about security from the activities of both the casual thief and the professional. To protect your bicycle, select from these precautions and security measures, depending on your situation:

1. Never let your bicycle out of your sight. It only takes a minute for a thief to throw a leg over an unprotected bike and ride off. Richard Dowd, Merle Dowd's son, was well-indoctrinated in the never-let-a-bike-out-of-sight routine. One Saturday morning, he pedaled into

downtown Seattle—a 40-minute trip over the floating bridge across Lake Washington and up and down a few hills. The tickets to a rock concert he intended buying were being sold from a ticket booth on the third floor of a major department store—one with up and down escalators at both ends of the street-level floor.

But, alas, he had forgotten his lock and cable. He wasn't about to leave his 10-speed *Astra* on the busy downtown sidewalk while he shanked up to the third floor and stood in a ticket line that might extend far down the aisle. So he walked the bike through paired doors next to the revolving door, past the lingerie counter, up the escalator two floors, and stood in line with his bike alongside. He ignored the few surprised glances. No one stopped him going up or coming down —and he didn't lose his bike.

*Rule One.* Unless your bicycle is locked, don't let it out of sight in public.

2. Almost any kind of cable and lock will protect your bicycle from a joyrider or casual thief. Even one of the plastic-covered cables with a built-in three-disk combination lock is good enough as long as a bicycle is fastened to some fixed object. Thin cables and small chains frustrate only those potential thieves without bolt-cutters or pry-bars.

*Rule Two.* Use some type of restraining device to prevent the "honest people" from taking your bike for a casual ride. As long as your bicycle is seldom exposed to a professional thief, you may get by with a cable or light chain.

3. Heavy chain with links forged from alloyed steel at least ⅜ inch in diameter with deep case-hardened surfaces and a four-tumbler lock are needed for maximum protection. Why so heavy? Bolt-cutters will sever anything smaller with a quick snip. Reinhard Jaeger, supervisor of college police at Seattle's North Community College campus, has studied the operations of bicycle thieves and set up security measures that stopped bike thefts cold on campus. After a wave of thefts, Chief Jaeger examined many of the cables and chains students were using to secure their bikes. They were following published advice to "use a good chain with a good lock." When he asked hardware stores in the vicinity of the campus for a good lock and chain, clerks showed him a variety of cables, chains, and padlocks.

They told him that case-hardened links couldn't be cut and that combination locks were the best protection against picking. When store-owners who guaranteed chains and locks against cutting offered to let him test them, he took 24-inch bolt-cutters from his car and snipped every chain and lock shackle offered.

"I limited cutters to those with 24-inch handles. Anything bigger can't be concealed or easily used without attracting attention," Chief Jaeger reported. "None of the chains or locks being sold as 'theft-proof protection' would stop a professional. Case-hardening seemed to be the magic words. But case-hardening is a treatment where added carbon is introduced to surface steel only, and heat treated to produce a hard outer layer; it is intended mainly for wear protection. Once a bolt-cutter penetrates this very thin surface, the inside of a link is soft and easily cut."

Further tests by Chief Jaeger proved that anything less than ⅜-inch steel in chain links or lock shackles could be snipped with 24-inch bolt-cutters. Since chains and locks of that size were unavailable locally, he bought 4-foot lengths of chain with ⅜-inch hardened steel alloy links and attached them with a welded bolt to convenient railings around heavily traveled walkways on the campus. Students furnished their

Fig. 53—Bicycle secured with ⅜-in. steel chain and 4-tumbler lock. Note how the 4-foot chain is threaded through spokes of rear wheel, around main frame members, and post in shopping center.

own padlocks. The lock Chief Jaeger recommends is a 4-cyclinder key lock with heat-treated ⅜-inch alloy steel shackle (Fig. 53).

Special kits were assembled for sale through the student bookstore. Kits included a 4-foot section of the ⅜-inch chain covered with a tough plastic tubing to protect bike finishes, a padlock, and a plastic pouch with buckles for carrying the chain and lock on the bicycle handlebars. (The kits are not cheap, selling at cost for about $35.) The payoff? No more bikes stolen from the North Seattle Community College campus.

*Rule Three*. When bikes are exposed to professional thieves, nothing less than heavy chain and padlock will assure protection from all but the most determined thief. Costs may appear high, but the alternative could be loss of your bicycle.

Opportunity also plays a role in bicycle protection. Just as no house can be completely burglar-proof, neither can any bike protection system be absolutely safe. Tools other than 24-inch bolt-cutters, such as saws, cutting torches, and "space-age" implements, can break any portable protection if thieves are permitted to work unobserved for extended periods. But if a thief must employ obvious tools for more than a few minutes to penetrate your bike's protective shield, while people are walking nearby or in view of persons in nearby buildings, then he cannot work without fear of detection. Keeping bicycles out of isolated areas deprives a potential thief of his most important asset—unlimited working time.

*Rule Four*. Lock your bicycle to some fixed object near a sidewalk or path in full view of passersby or as many people in the area as possible. Avoid leaving your bicycle in some dark corner merely because it happens to be close to your destination. The more traffic nearby, the more assured is your protection.

How you lock your bike also makes a difference. A short cable or chain may provide only enough length to encircle a fixed object and an exposed portion of a front wheel. But with quick disconnect wing nuts or even a few turns with an adjustable wrench, the wheel could be freed from the frame and the most expensive parts of your bicycle removed. For best protection use a chain long enough to thread around a major part of the frame, the rear wheel, and a post or other fixed object (Fig. 53). One of the most expensive parts of a modern bicycle is the rear gear cluster and derailleur. Wheels may be quickly removed by cutting the gear chain and removing two nuts.

*Rule Five.* Lock your bike for maximum security by threading the chain through a rear wheel, around a frame tube, and around a fairly large tree, lamp post, steel railing, or bicycle stand structure.

If you expect any chance at all of recovering your bicycle should it be stolen, identify it and register it with local police or campus security forces. Courts have held that a bicycle must be positively identified before it can be returned. Further, a thief cannot be convicted unless the bicycle is positively identified as someone else's. Several means of identifying your specific bicycle are available:

• Serial number. Bicycles are numbered serially as they are manufactured. Often the serial number is stamped on a separate metal plate and the plate spot-welded, cemented, or riveted to the frame member at some inconspicuous location. If you keep a bill of sale with the number in a wallet or safe place at home and use the number to identify your bicycle from among many in a police bicycle impound, such proof of ownership will ordinarily be accepted. However, separate serial number plates can be removed—some more easily than others. If the thief removes the plate, you're sunk. For best identification, the serial number should be deep-stamped in the metal under the bottom bracket.

• Police registration. City police departments and college campus security forces have established programs for numbering and registering bicycles to aid in restoring recovered bicycles to their rightful owners. A bicycle to be registered is taken to a central location where a new number is metal-stamped on the frame, usually on the underside of the bottom bracket. The number is deep enough to prevent its being filed or ground off. Or, the number may be engraved with a motorized tool. The bike number and the registered owner are then added to an identification file. When a bike is recovered, police search the registration file for the number and owner. Bicycles that are returned to owners are usually identified through this system. Unfortunately, numbering and registration are spotty at best, and nonexistent in many locations. When stolen bicycles are transported out of a city or across state lines, they escape local registration lists. A state-wide system similar to the registration plan for automobiles, possibly with a license plate and a fee, would be necessary to effectively control the recovery of a large percentage of bicycles. States to date have resisted such a system because of the costs involved. But if your city or college maintains a registration system, by all means use it.

• Personal identification. To afford you a means of positively identifying your bicycle, engrave your driver's license number and/or your name under the bottom bracket with one of the new motorized engraving tools. These vibrating tip devices enable you to "write on metal" as easily as you write with a pen. Police departments sometimes make these available for identifying personal property as part of a community-wide program to forestall burglaries. Possibly your friendly bicycle shop owner will lend you one of his engravers. Your driver's license engraved deep into the metal affords positive identification if police should recover your bicycle, and could lead to its recovery if spotted for sale.

## TRANSPORTING YOUR BICYCLE

Bicycle trails, far-off vacations, and touring at a destination all call for some way to haul your bike along to the starting place. Bike racks for cars come in a variety of sizes and positions:

FRONT AND BACK RACKS. Racks that clamp onto the front or rear bumper offer an inexpensive and readily accessible means for transporting bicycles. Their one problem—potential damage to your bicycle. As you can see from Fig. 54, a bike strapped to a bumper rack hangs out in the breeze with no possible protection from any part of the car. One nudge from a car could easily bend a wheel, gear cluster, or pedals. Bumper carriers require a minimum of ½ inch between bumper and body. Many modern car designs do not leave enough space to accommodate the clamp ends. Therefore, another carrier may be required. Prices range from $15 to $30 depending on the model.

TRUNK BACK CARRIER. A rack that straps to the trunk offers nearly the same convenience as a bumper rack with less chance of damage to the bicycle from cars or trucks (Fig. 55). Racks will carry one or two bikes. One "Bike Caddy" (available by mail from Wheel Goods Corp.) straps onto a car in any of three positions to carry one or two bikes.

CAR-TOP CARRIER. Stowing bicycles for transport on the roof of your

Fig. 54—Bumper rack supports one or two bicycles. Elastic shock cord holds bicycle securely in place. Bumper-mounted bikes are subject to damage in case of even slight bumping from another car.

car (Fig. 56) offers several advantages. (1) Protection from traffic, as the bikes are out of the way and protected from other vehicles by your own car's bumpers. (2) Greater capacity. Most of the roof-top racks will carry at least four bikes. Some can be fitted with tie-downs for as many as six. But the roof-top carriers cost more—up to about $65 for racks that will stow four bikes. Two cross-bars are needed with their ends resting in the rain gutter or on rubber suction cups. Although the bikes appear cumbersome and ungainly when mounted upside down on a roof-top, this method offers the best combination, except for cost. You can make your own roof-top rack. Chuck Gnehm of the Mercer Island Cyclery designed his own rack to carry six bikes (Fig. 57).

Fig. 55—Trunk frame supports one or two bicycles out of harm's way. Trunk frame may also be used when bumper design provides too little access for attaching clamps.

Take-Apart. Hauling a bike on the back, front, side, trunk, or top of a car poses one further hazard—the possibility that it could be stolen. Chain and padlock help by complicating the theft. A better method may be to disassemble the front wheel from the bicycle frame and stow the bike in a trunk or rear seat (Fig. 58). Quick-disconnect hubs simplify the disassembly operation. One bike will fit into a remarkably small space, but two or more bikes can seldom be accommodated in less than a big station wagon even when disassembled.

Stowing your bicycle aboard an airplane when you fly to a resort or vacation destination no longer causes problems on major airlines. A box or plastic bag helps protect a bike in the baggage compartment

Fig. 56—When more than two bikes are to be transported by car, the car-top carrier provides space for as many as four, possibly six bikes. Carrier designs differ; most carry bikes with wheels in air. At least one carrier secures tires in channel tracks with bikes fastened to vertical posts.

Fig. 57—Charles Gnehm's home-made car-top carrier supports up to six bicycles. Main frame members are 2 x 6 planks covered with scrap carpet strips.

Fig. 58—After removing front wheel, bicycle stows easily in car trunk. Both wheels must usually be removed if two bikes are stowed in trunk or rear seat.

of your flight. Minor disassembly calls for loosening handlebars and removing pedals. You may wish to pack cardboard. or other stuffing around the rear cluster and derailleur.

Traveling by bus may not be so easy, as bus luggage compartments seldom contain enough space for an assembled bicycle. Rather than attempt to take your bike along on a bus, look for some kind of alternative transportation.

Amtrak passenger train service has drawn riders back to the rails. In contrast to the bus, baggage cars on trains offer ample space for bicycles. Fully assembled bikes can be transported on the same train as you travel, with little more than a baggage identification tag. But, if possible, supervise the loading to prevent other baggage from damaging wheels or gears. Partially disassembling the bicycle and packing it in a cardboard box for shipment will assure greater protection. Cyclemate bicycles were boxed in New York, Washington, and Halifax and shipped back to Mercer Island by train or truck.

# 10.

## Day Trips for Fun and Fitness

Bicycling off to the zoo and the beach or exploring the backroads and byways of your city, town, or countryside can be fun as well as good exercise. Bicycling affords greater mobility than walking and yet allows you time to savor the sights and sounds of the country or teeming city that you miss while driving or riding in a car. Then, too, you can cover more territory on a bicycle than by walking. But how do you plan trips, prepare for emergencies, and condition yourself physically to pedal the extra miles, sometimes in weather extremes?

As an individual cyclist or member of a group, decide first: What are your objectives? Sounds formal if all you're really thinking about is a leisurely jaunt through the park on a warm sunny day. Objectives need not be formidable or particularly challenging. But if you're interested in examining new, interesting sights and terrain while expanding your exercise or conditioning regimen, say so. That's your objective. Or maybe you'd like to plan trips for your family as Saturday outings to cement family relationships. You may want to concentrate on photographing seabirds while bicycling down an ocean beach. Or get out to meet new people and talk with those you see while on a leisurely junket. Maybe you plan a forty-mile trip because forty miles represents the next step up in your conditioning program. Your objective—to cover forty miles in four hours, or something similar. When you're after mileage, stopping to talk with strangers or to photograph interesting landmarks takes second place. But if you're exploring new territory, you will allow much more time for covering the mileage. Thus, stating, or at least considering, your objectives affects your planning.

Riding alone or in a group? Bicycling by yourself affords a great opportunity for contemplation and a chance to "get away." But riding in a group can be more fun—and more practical. In a group you can talk, compare observations on the terrain, play games, and encourage or pace each other when muscles rebel. In a group, every cyclist need not carry a complete repair kit, first-aid kit, and extra parts. You can split up the load. And, in case of an accident or a mechanical failure, others are along to call or ride for help.

Family groups are the simplest to organize and plan. For a day trip, all can participate in planning where to go and what to expect to see. Bicycling builds family togetherness two ways—by involving each member in the planning and by creating a situation where everyone does something together physically in an environment free from home distractions. Rather than use bicycles only for exercise, for errands, or to travel between school, tennis court, or playground and home, extend family bicycling to day trips. Later you may want to expand your bicycling horizons to weekend or longer vacation trips. On Saturdays a family can pack lunches in the morning and take off for the beach. Or explore a section of town being restored. Or—the list could be endless. But plan ahead and set up your objectives rather than have everybody mounting their bikes and heading out to parts unknown.

Ask the Visitor's Bureau or Chamber of Commerce in your community for information about places to see and visit on bike trips. A Visitor's Bureau lists museums, points of interest, industrial plants open for visitors, and scheduled activities. Also, ask for a detailed map of the area for planning trips.

A family I know owns a van-type station wagon that packs the family's four bikes. On a Saturday they may catch an early ferry for Bainbridge Island and pedal around the perimeter—a 45-mile trip; or they will ride off from their home on Mercer Island to explore the University of Washington campus. All-day trips keep every family member in condition for their regular summer bicycle camping trip to one or more of the San Juan Islands or into Canada.

Another family rides regularly on weekends for exercise and to keep in top physical condition for their summer vacation. They ship their bicycles by air or train to Mexico, Canada, or to a jumping-off spot near one of the national parks. From there they pedal off for a week's sightseeing. They have cycled through the Grand Canyon and Yellowstone-Teton National Parks and are planning a second trip along the western seacoast of Baja California.

School groups, possibly initiated by an interested teacher, afford an opportunity for junior high and high school students to bicycle regularly. The Cyclemates started from a small group (see Chapter Twelve). A bicycle club can be organized at school as easily as a French or drama club to sponsor short trips after school or on weekends.

Local bicycling clubs, such as the Cascade Club in Seattle, plan various trips and publish a schedule. Club members sign up for whatever trips interest them. Members handle their own planning for clothing, food, and emergency supplies and equipment. The American Youth Hostels operate a strong program, mainly in eastern states. See Appendix A for address. Local YMCA groups sponsor bicycle trips depending on the interest of youngsters and the inclination of an adult leader.

Two other national organizations encourage bicycle touring. The League of American Wheelmen (LAW) sponsors "century runs"—one-day trips covering 100 miles. Local chapters of the LAW organize day trips and overnight weekend jaunts for members. You can join one of the local chapters by contacting the League's national office. See Appendix for LAW's address. Any serious bicyclist should join the League of American Wheelmen to keep current with happenings of interest to cyclists.

The International Bicycle Touring Society sponsors one- and two-week "huff 'n puff" tours through such interesting and scenic areas as California redwood country, New England, the Lincoln Trail, the hills of Texas, and Europe's Austria, Brittany, and the Loire Valley. These tours depend on voluntary cooperation by members and cost less than commercial escorted tours. Annual membership dues are only a few dollars.

Bicycling magazines carry news of tours and bicycle clubs. *Bicycling, Cycling USA,* and *Cycle Touring* discuss grouping and trip ideas for bicyclists interested in joining with others for bike touring. See Appendix for addresses.

Keep an eye and ear open for news of bike tours sponsored by local park and recreation departments. One interesting series of day rides is sponsored by the National Capitol Parks Service in Washington,

D.C., for rides in and around the Capitol area. Madison, Wisconsin, Seattle, Washington, Denver, Colorado, and San Diego, California, are only a few of the communities actively supporting bicycling for fun and for commuting. Check your own parks department and local newspapers for leads to groups of cycling enthusiasts interested in day and weekend trips.

## PLANNING

Whatever your objective in bike tripping or touring, precise planning is a must. When you've worked at conditioning and can comfortably cycle from 20 to 60 miles in a day—where do you go? You can follow the lead of a group. Or you can plan your own family or small group trip yourself.

Start your planning with the aid of a large-scale map showing the area you're interested in traversing. City street maps available from gasoline service stations can be useful in plotting a trip street by street (small-scale maps of the whole state show too little detail for bicycle trip planning outside of cities). A medium-scale area or vicinity map will sometimes be printed on the reverse side of an oil company's city street map. While these can sometimes be useful, they may not show the byways and less-traveled roads and streets parallel to the main highways.

County maps drawn to large scale can often be purchased in sporting goods shops. These may be called "hunters' maps." Another source of large-scale maps that show every road and trail are sometimes available from real estate offices in a community; these maps help prospective house buyers find their way around an unfamiliar area. If your planned route extends beyond the limits of one community, acquire several large-scale maps and match them at the edges to plan continuous routes.

Some of the best sources of information on bicycle trips are the special paperback books published locally. In our area we have *Bicycling the Back Roads of Puget Sound.* Visit one or more of the bicycle shops in your area. If you do not see any of these local publications, ask the store owner for leads. Someone in nearly every major community publishes local trip guides.

When you have planned a trip on the map, check out the route by driving the whole distance first. You'll gain confidence for your first trips by noting such important points as shoulder widths, number and size of hills, traffic patterns, availability and spacing of restaurants, stores for buying lunch supplies, rest rooms, and points of interest to explore more thoroughly from your bike later. If you intend to lead a group of youngsters, plan to drive each route ahead as a precaution against surprises. If you are traveling with experienced cyclists who are competent to meet and overcome nearly any obstacle, you can skip the pre-trip drive, but if you are the least bit edgy about conditions along your intended route, hop in your car and check it out. You can drive a planned bike trip in a fraction of the time you will spend on a bicycle.

In your trip plans, consider driving part of the distance. For day trips or overnight weekend jaunts, transporting your bicycle by car, truck, or trailer opens up a much wider territory. If you live in the city, you could bicycle to the fringes and on to an interesting destination. But if you can load your bicycle onto a car rack (see Chapter Nine), you can skip the miles and time needed to reach a more interesting jumping-off spot. Also, you can plan on riding until later in the day, knowing that you can haul your bikes back home safely after sundown.

One way to enlarge your planning area is to draw a series of circles on a map with your home or group meeting place as the center. Figure the circles as travel time by car—one hour for the first, two hours, and three hours. Then, examine trip possibilities from a location starting at the edge of each circle. Much of the fun of day-tripping is in the planning. Look for interesting spots to visit and vary the type of terrain for increasing your biking experience.

Don't forget about eating! On a short day hike you can pack a sack lunch and stop at an interesting viewpoint to eat. Taking your food along avoids the necessity of detouring or scheduling time to find a restaurant. Some of the spots you'll be biking to support no food facilities. Or a snack stand may offer only hot dogs and soft drinks, as in a zoo or public beach area. On overnight or longer trips, as noted in Chapter Eleven, you may plan to camp and cook your own meals. Whatever your plans for eating, always carry an emergency supply of candy bars and water. You never know when an accident or bicycle breakdown will throw off your route timing. Even if you plan a lunch stop, you could be delayed; hence the need for a snack that you carry along.

Include clothing in your planning. Every season changes the needs for how much and what type of clothing you will be taking along. Weather permitting, riding shorts are most practical. If the weather is likely to be cold, wear warm wool shorts and wool knee socks; wool will keep you warm even in the rain. There's nothing as uncomfortable while biking as wet, tight-fitting blue jeans.

Follow the multi-layer plan proved most practical by hikers and search-and-rescue teams when the weather is cold. Instead of a single heavy jacket, wear a thermal undershirt and sweat pants over skiing "long johns." Or wear shorts over stretchy wool body suits or leotard-type leg, ankle, and foot coverings. One or more cardigan type sweaters worn over a light shirt can be unbuttoned when you're warm from cycling and buttoned up when you stop or when a chill wind is blowing. A windshirt, again borrowed from the skiers, worn on top of sweaters keeps chilly breezes from penetrating the loosely knitted or woven garments that trap air around the torso for warmth. Don't forget to wear some kind of warm cap or knitted hat that can be folded or pulled down to cover ears. And wool- or pile-lined mittens or gloves are an absolute necessity when riding in the cold. Feet also get cold, particularly if they are exposed to rain. Remember the advice of oldsters who say, "To keep your feet and legs warm, keep your head warm."

Rain poses special problems. No real answer exists for keeping dry while cycling in a steady rain. A rainproof jacket may shed the rain, but it will not permit your body to breathe. You can get as wet inside from body perspiration as you would from the rain in a tight jacket. A loose poncho with a hood will keep out most of the rain and the open bottom will prevent excessive sweat buildup. But, a poncho must be tailored to keep corners from catching in chain and spokes. A poncho also adds to wind resistance. Leggings to cover knees and legs exposed under a short poncho are some help. Bare knees will get wet in the rain, but the skin dries quicker than do wet jeans or slacks. One trick learned by the Cyclemates—tie plastic bags around the shoes and ankles to keep feet dry. A heavy rubber band keeps the plastic tight around the ankles. Legs can get wet and stay warm because they are moving, but wet feet can get mighty cold.

Hot weather clothing should be loose and light. T-shirts for the men and sleeveless blouses for women allow plenty of air circulation. Shorts or the popular jean cut-offs expose legs and thighs to the air for cooling. Some kind of a brimmed hat protects the head from the sun's heat during summer trips, although many prefer nothing on top Sunglasses protect eyes from the glare.

Clothing is a personal thing that varies according to age and trip length. Learn as you ride what works best for you. Just be prepared for changes in the weather. Stuff a windbreaker or an extra sweater in your pack even if the weather appears sunny at the start. Try different combinations of clothes as you ride, to get a feel for comfort on different trips. There's really no substitute for your own experience.

## EMERGENCY PLANNING

Two classes of emergencies can mar any bike trip, whether it's an hour long or covers two months: (1) Your bike can break down. (2) One of your group can sustain an injury. You need to be prepared for both.

For day trips you need carry only a minimum of tools and spare parts. Before you take off on any kind of trip more than a few miles from home, check your bicycle to make sure it is in top running condition (see Chapter Thirteen). If you've checked the hub cones to make sure they are tight without binding and are free from scratchy grit, you really don't need to carry cone-adjusting wrenches. On a day trip you would probably not want to remove a crank, the crank axle bearings, the rear cluster, or overhaul the springs in a brake. But you should be prepared for tire trouble and minor maintenance, such as replacing a broken brake or derailleur control cable.

On day trips bring along a 6-inch crescent wrench, tire wrenches, pliers, screwdriver, tire repair kit, and a pump. In your kit of spare parts include extra cables for the rear brake and rear derailleur. If your bike includes an internal rear-hub gear changer, don't attempt to carry tools for repairing it on a day trip. For longer tours, you will be better off with a 10-speed derailleur anyway.

Tire troubles cause most of the mechanical delays on trips. Although the lightweight tubular tires are easier to ride, heavier clincher tires will take more road punishment. For typical trips avoid the very light tubulars and select a tire with a heavier tread. In either case, carry an extra tube for clinchers and an extra tire and tube for tubulars. Some bicyclists own two sets of wheels—one set fitted with clincher tires and one set fitted with tubulars. Complete wheel-tire sets are necessary because tubulars will not fit on rims designed for clinchers—and vice versa. And make sure your tire pump will fit the valves on your tires. Practice patching a tube *before* you undertake a trip of any length longer than a few blocks close to home base (see Chapter Fourteen).

Consider security if your plans for a day trip call for leaving your bicycle unattended. At some spots on your trip, such as a fish hatchery or a waterfall, you might leave your bicycles and hike in some distance on foot. Any time your bicycles are likely to be out of view for more than a few minutes, take your chain and lock along—and *use* them. See Chapter Nine for recommended chains and locks to foil thieves. If your plans call for a picnic lunch where you can watch your bikes, leave the heavy chain and lock behind.

Carry a first-aid kit along for treating scratches and abrasions, stomach upset, or small injuries that might occur if a rider falls. For more than minor patch-ups, you'll want to call for help, so you need telephone numbers of every member of the group. Don't depend on asking the fallen rider as he may have hit his head and be knocked out. If you are escorting youngsters, your route planning might call for checking out telephone availability. When you drive a route ahead in preparation for a trip, note locations of telephones that are outside of stores, gas stations, or in small towns. Telephone locations are sometimes marked with road signs on highways, but seldom on the back roads where you will likely be traveling on day trips. If a rider is injured and cannot continue, call for help. If a telephone isn't nearby, flag down a motorist and ride to a telephone or haul the injured rider to a hospital. On organized tours a van or truck may accompany a group; this "sag wagon" can be helpful in emergencies and serve as a lift for riders who attempt to bicycle too many miles too soon. But you need not count on the sag wagon. Cyclemates were self-sufficient without one, and twice in three years an injured rider was carried to the nearest town by flagging down a car.

## CYCLING IN HOT WEATHER

Cycling in hot weather, which the Cyclemates encountered across the barren, intensely hot flatlands of South Dakota, and across the hot, humid plains of Iowa and Illinois, calls for extra attention to prevent heat cramps or heat stroke. You'll notice more sweating while riding under sunny skies—and that's good. Sweat is one mechanism the body uses to control internal heat balance.

You know how quickly you can work up a sweat working or exercising when air temperatures climb above 75 or 80 degrees. The more heat your body produces on a hot day, the more sweating occurs to keep your body temperature constant. While cycling at an average speed on a hot day, your body can sweat as much as three to five pints per hour, and higher than that during strenuous racing. Unless you replace this fluid loss, you may suffer muscle cramps or severe dehydration.

On hot days don't wait until you're thirsty to drink water. You know you're losing fluid constantly. If the air is dry and a wind is blowing, you may not even feel sweaty because the moisture evaporates immediately. Rather than stop for a big drink every thirty minutes to an hour, drink half to two-thirds of a cup of water every fifteen to twenty minutes—from the handy water bottle mounted on your frame. During rest stops, drink more water. For long jaunts in hot weather, you may need two bottles—or plan regular water bottle refill stops. Avoid sweet drinks, as they tend to make you thirstier. Chewing gum helps avoid thirst pangs.

Sweat pores exude salt along with moisture. You can get along without regular salt replacements more easily than doing without water, but why try? Instead, carry salt tablets and take one (600 mg) for every two pints of water or other fluid you drink. Don't overdo on salt; too much will actually reduce your tolerance to heat.

In addition to sodium chloride, small amounts of magnesium also disappear with sweat. To replace the magnesium, include grain cereals, green vegetables, and nuts in your diet. Salted nuts or peanut butter sandwiches will provide magnesium replacement without resorting to pills.

The human body is a remarkably adaptive mechanism. After riding under hot conditions for a few days, your body will adapt by giving off less salt and producing more sweat at lower blood flows. The blood vessels near the skin get even closer to increase the rate of heat transfer through the skin.

Recognize that if you do not maintain regular fluid and salt intake during hot weather cycling, you may be subject to dizziness, muscle cramps, and dulling fatigue.

## TRIP TIPS

When a group of more than five or six riders sets out on a day trip, decide at the outset how you will ride. You can ride single-file caravan style and stay relatively close together; all riders then follow the same course at roughly the same pace. An average rider can set the pace, and a strong, experienced rider may be assigned to bring up the rear. If anything should happen to one of the riders, the tail-ender can pedal ahead and stop the caravan. Sometimes the riders travel beyond shouting contact, but ordinarily each rider should cycle along within a few bike lengths of the rider ahead. Plan to leave gaps in the line-up, to allow cars to pass easily. In traffic only a few bicycles will be able to get through a green signal light unless you bunch up while waiting and all buzz through together. Therefore, the lead group should remain in eye or ear contact with following groups when traveling caravan style.

On short trips, an alternative to caravan style is a succession of destination stops. You can lay out an overall plan, then break it up into segments. Each rider, or small groups of several riders, then take off on their own with a plan to meet again at the first break stop. When all the riders check in at the first break stop, take off on the second segment—and so on for the rest of the trip. Series riding works best for experienced riders. When youngsters or riders new to day trips are along, the safest course is to ride caravan style.

Riding loaded bicycles calls for some getting used to. Most of the extra weight—lunches, extra clothing, tools, and spare parts, should be stowed in double pannier bags on a rack over the rear wheel. Make sure the weight is evenly divided between the two bags to maintain balance. A few items, such as candy bars, sunglasses, and the like can be carried in a small handlebar bag. Inexperienced riders carry their gear in a day-hike bag strapped to their back, but they soon learn that the constantly shifting load reduces efficiency and soon becomes an annoying nuisance. For best cycling you want your load as low as possible.

Extra weight seldom bothers a cyclist while traveling on the level or on gentle hills, but when climbing larger hills you'll want to shift into lower gears sooner to maintain cadence without straining leg muscles. Going down hills you'll find the extra weight serves to build up momentum and you'll need to brake sooner than when traveling light. With more weight to control, don't hesitate to begin using brakes while you're still under firm control.

Day-tripping should be more than just exercise. But unless you build up your muscles and condition your entire body, even a short trip can be tiring. When you begin pushing tired muscles to keep up with the group, much of the fun evaporates from day-tripping and the rest of the day becomes a real drag. The answer—build up your endurance through an organized conditioning program.

## CONDITIONING FOR TOURING

Only you can set a conditioning regime to get in shape for cross-country or weekend touring that suits you individually. Nearly every cyclist approaches touring with a different background and different "now" conditions. An under-30 man or woman used to regular exercise can expect to turn more miles at the beginning than an over-40 desk jockey who has done little more than walk to his car twice a day for the past five years. The benefits from a regular bicycling conditioning program are spelled out in detail in Chapter Seven. Conditioning for touring involves building your physical reserves and discipline for jaunts longer than those to the supermarket and back.

Regular riding remains the key to conditioning for touring. You learn by doing! Cyclemates easily did 80 to 100 miles in a day; but they were doing mileage every day, and in their training they built up to those distances. Plus, youngsters take on conditioning easier and faster than adults—even young adults. If you long to climb on a bike and ride fifty miles—or to take on a "century run," follow these tips:

• Depending on your age and how much exercise you have been getting, you may want to see a doctor before beginning a regular conditioning schedule. And if you're over 40, ask your doctor for an electrocardiograph test under stress. He'll check your heart's performance while you ride a bicycle or jog on a treadmill. Then follow his advice!

• Begin riding one or two miles a day for the first week. But ride every day if you are new to a bicycle. Your body will take time to adapt to a narrow saddle, continuing exertion, and a leaning-forward stance. (Don't attempt serious touring with a sit-up bike equipped with flat handlebars.) Don't miss a day if you can possibly avoid it. Ride in the rain when the weather turns sloppy. Get used to heat while riding your daily stints. Regular riding is important; more so than the number of miles you begin with.

• Add more miles to your daily jaunts by the week—not by the day. If you ride two or three miles per day the first week, jump to five or ten the second week—or possibly the third week. Don't try to up your mileage per week in big jumps at first. You'll find it easier to increase mileage from 10 to 15 than from 5 to 10—so take it easy until your entire system adapts to the extra work. Your legs don't do all the work; you must also condition your heart, arms, vascular system, lungs, diaphragm, and back muscles. All must toughen up together.

• Practice efficient riding techniques as you ride, as noted in Chapter Six. Remember ankling, cadence, and gear shifting. While you're riding, practice good form and you'll learn about cycling as you ride.

• Recognize your body's needs during conditioning. Plan to sleep regularly and long enough to rest thoroughly. You'll find yourself eating more to provide energy. During warm weather be sure to drink plenty of fluids to prevent dehydration (see page 148).

• Work harder each week to gain the benefits of the training effect from exercise. If you were riding two miles last week, try five next week. To gain endurance, keep pushing to increase the number of miles you ride. Discipline yourself to increase cadence until you are huffing and puffing during at least part of your daily riding. To ride farther next week, your exercise this week must be more intense and last longer—keep pushing in steps. How big those steps can and should be will depend on your starting condition, your age, weight, and the regularity of your biking. Read Chapter Seven again for an idea of how fast you can build mileage into your daily trips.

Getting ready for touring means riding miles and miles and miles. You'll know you're ready for a thirty-mile trip if you can pedal through twenty-five miles without undue fatigue. And twenty-five miles is a big step toward fifty—and on to a "century run."

# 11.
# Long-Distance Touring

Okay! You've been on day trips and extended trips with an overnight stop at the far end before touring back. Now what? Touring for a week, two weeks, or two months can be your next step up to the fun of bicycling. People who travel by car miss so much! Why not plan your next vacation around bicycling? Or combine bicycling with car tripping to extract the most from your precious vacation weeks. By packing your bicycle on your car or shipping it by air or train, you can quickly cover the uninteresting miles between your home base and any number of scenic or interesting locations. Then, at your destination, ride off on your bicycle to savor the sights and sounds in a leisurely way.

You'll need to consider new challenges when you lack proximity to your home base. And that's the purpose of this chapter—to help you prepare for the big step beyond day-tripping.

## GETTING IN SHAPE

Long-distance touring taxes muscles seldom used unless you're an ardent bicycle commuter or spend successive days or weekends pedaling for hours at a stretch. If you can comfortably negotiate day-trip mileages in the 40 to 60 range, you are well within hailing distance of the 80 to 90 miles common for extended bicycle trips. But decide on your objectives, as noted in Chapter Ten. Long-distance touring may concentrate on photography or on wine trails in California, Revolutionary War history in New England, Civil War battlefields in Pennsylvania, or the scenic splendor of our famous national parks. A day's pedaling may cover only 40 to 50 miles when you program many stops along the way.

Long-distance touring adds two dimensions to the section on conditioning in Chapter Ten: (1) Possibly more miles per day. (2) Continued mileage day after day. Unless you pedal those miles with more than average efficiency by ankling and maintaining a steady, comfortable cadence, long distances can become a tiring chore. Therefore, part of conditioning involves practicing and continuing to be aware of good form while riding under varied conditions—wind, hills (both up and down), and gear changing smoothly and at the right time. These aspects of effective cycling are discussed in Chapter Six. Before you take off on a long-distance tour, review those points. You can refine your cycling form while completing your detailed trip plans.

## PLANNING

How far can you pedal consistently in one day? An average of 40 to 50 miles per day may be right for a leisurely trip with limited distance objectives. On a Cyclemates tour when we were interested in distance because of the limited time available for crossing the breadth of the, United States, an average between 80 and 100 was more reasonable. Who's to say what is a good distance for planning? How many miles you travel will depend on the kind of trip you plan. You can cover more miles if you work hard and stay on your bike for many hours a day.

As one example, here's how we planned the Cyclemates tours from Mercer Island, Washington, to New York City, Washington, D.C., Halifax, Nova Scotia, and Williamsburg, Virginia. I wrote to each of the states along the routes. I received an official state map, but I also received special notes about those highways, including Interstates, where bicycling was not permitted. So, we had to plan our route on the less well-traveled highways. We always went up Stevens Pass over Washington's Cascade Mountains on U.S. Highway No. 2, even though it was nearly 1,000 feet higher in elevation than Snoqualmie Pass, the route of I-90. Stevens was a two-lane highway and Snoqualmie was four-lane. Climbing Stevens to the ski patrol hut where we slept the first night was 86 miles—much of it *up*.

I planned about 80 miles per day, which is not difficult under normal conditions. On Cyclemates I, our longest day was 136 miles. Cyclemates II topped that record with a run of 142.7 miles across the plains of South Dakota. The group in Cyclemates III really set a new record by pedaling 189.2 miles from 6 A.M. to 10:30 P.M. to arrive at Medicine Hat, Alberta. This record was broken on Cyclemates IV, when we rode 194.7 miles across eastern Kansas. Some days we rode 60 miles before lunch. But 80 miles per day was a fair average. We stayed flexible and didn't plan each day's trip ahead. Ordinarily we rode four, five, or six days—then stopped for a day. Sometimes we detoured from our planned route to see some place of interest. We were not trying to set a record or to merely cover the distance between Mercer Island and some distant point; a main reason for our going was to have fun and enjoy our trip along the way. Touring Banff in '72 was a great treat. On Cyclemates II we toured both Glacier and Yellowstone National Parks and took in the sights like other tourists.

In planning, I looked for towns at reasonable intervals. For the Cyclemates II trip to Washington, D.C., the most direct route would have taken us through lower Idaho, but distances stretched to 100 miles or more with no towns at all. So we went out of our way through Glacier National Park again—with a different group of kids. Since we didn't pack much food, we depended on towns or crossroads stores for food. The Glacier National Park detour gave the second bunch a scenic trip, and I enjoyed it as much the second time as the first.

Highway 2 crossed the top tier of states and was the obvious choice to New York. Originally we had decided to go through or around Chicago, but so many of the highways there are either toll roads or four-lane limited-access highways that we would have had to detour much too far south. Instead we went across upper Michigan.

We looked for campgrounds as well as towns when planning a route. We did not look for touristy state and national park sites, but stayed in many small city or county campgrounds. Also we often slept overnight in churches. Although we knew our route generally, if the local people suggested an alternative way to go, we might take that.

And we didn't feel limited to a specific overnight stop ahead, but played it by ear. (This led to a problem for us in Montana, on Cyclemates II, as related in Chapter Twelve.)

Look, too, at other factors when planning daily distances. Mountains need not be major obstacles. The Cyclemates pedaled to the top of Stevens Pass in one day. On flat, uninteresting country, you might consider lengthening the daily mileage to put the flats behind you and go on to more captivating terrain. Through a landscape as scenic as the Canadian Rockies, a 50-mile day leaves extra hours for sightseeing.

Weather obviously affects the practical distances for planning. A strong headwind can be a more difficult deterrent than climbing a mountain pass. Extreme heat may call for a plan to rest during the hottest part of the day and cut the daily stint to a more comfortable 50, 60, or 70 miles. But for a long-distance trek of several hundred to more than a thousand miles, figuring an eighty-mile day can be a fair average as long as you do not plan to cycle every day. Instead of turning a tour into a grind, plan off-days every four to six days for a change of pace, a chance to launder personal clothing, and to rest, see a movie, or take in local sights.

Eating along the way involves trade-offs between cost, time, and personal interests. If you plan to camp out in tents, then cooking your own meals may make sense. But carrying utensils and a stove, packing the ingredients for meals to be cooked in camp, and the time required to cook and clean up after each meal impinge on other objectives. Packing full cooking gear adds weight, although lightweight kits designed for mountain climbers and efficient stoves can control weight—at a price. Probably the biggest drawback to cooking meals is the time required. Cooking two meals, breakfast and dinner, while eating sandwiches for lunch can deduct as much as three or more hours from each day's available cycling time.

On Cyclemates' trips we ate breakfast in a restaurant, made up meals from a store for lunch, and picked up quick do-it-yourself meals at night—along with other alternatives noted in Chapter Twelve. Planning to eat all three meals in restaurants presents two drawbacks: (1) You must time your trip segments to put you near a restaurant three times a day for meals. (2) Costs of eating three prepared meals a day can escalate the cost of touring beyond the means of some youngsters and families.

Sleeping and personal care (showers and laundry) should also be planned in advance. Some touring cyclists plan daily segments between towns where motel accommodations are available. There's nothing like a hot shower and a clean change of clothing to refresh a tired, dusty body wearied from a day of cycling under a burning sun. But again, cost can be a determining factor.

Camping along the way offers a low-cost alternative. Individual back-pack tents weigh as little as four pounds, complete with poles. They can be set up or struck in a few minutes. Many campgrounds include showers or are located near a body of water suitable for swimming. If you plan to camp along the way, select a tent that is, first of all, lightweight. Treated nylon tents developed for mountaineers offer the best combination of light weight and rain resistance. Make sure the tent includes a zippered mosquito net and a sewn-in waterproof floor. You will not always be camping among trees, so pack your own take-apart poles. Single or double tents can be selected according to the make-up of the group.

Along with a tent you'll need sleeping bags and either an air mattress or a roll-up foam pad. Down-filled bags offer the greatest warmth with minimum weight. A ½-inch foam pad that rolls into a tight bundle affords good insulation from the ground and some padding for hip bones; or, to save weight, a ¾-length lightweight air mattress fits under shoulders and hips. After a day of pedaling, most cyclists experience little difficulty in sleeping at night. All of these necessities for camping can be packed in double pannier bags with plenty of room left for clothing and personal articles. See Table J for a checklist of camping essentials.

## TABLE J: Camping Equipment

| | |
|---|---|
| Nylon mountaineer tent | Mess kit |
| Sleeping bag, down or lightweight | Swiss Army knife |
| ¾ air mattress | Water container |
| Stove, propane | Matches in waterproof container |
| Propane fuel cylinders | Detergent |
| Cook kit (pans) | Scouring pads |
| Utensil set (knife, fork, spoon) | Dish towels (two) |
| Long-handle cook spoon | Nylon avalanche cord, 50' |
| Pancake turner | Flashlight, lightweight |

## SPARE PARTS AND TOOLS

In addition to the tire repair kit and a few tools you would expect to carry on day or weekend trips, consider extra parts. You may need springs and adjustment screws or extra cables for brakes. Certainly you should carry brake pads to keep caliper brakes in top operating condition. On a long tour your spare parts kit could also include spare spokes and extra cables for front and back derailleurs. You'll need a good tire pump for the group; preferably one you put your foot on while pumping, instead of the lightweight frame-mounted pumps. Carry complete spare bearings for front and back wheels, bottom bracket, and pedals. Headset bearings will seldom fail if they are properly lubricated before starting.

A complete tool kit should include those items listed in Table K. Some of the tools can do double or triple duty, such as the two sizes of adjustable jaw wrenches and the all-purpose pliers. If your bicycle includes screws with the cross-head Phillips slots, make sure your kit includes a Phillips screwdriver that fits.

### TABLE K: Bicycle Tools and Spare Parts

| | |
|---|---|
| | Pliers |
| Tire repair kit | Crescent wrench, 6″ |
| Chain rivet tool | Pair cone wrenches |
| Tire irons | Spare tire |
| Tire pump | Spare tube |
| Air pressure gauge | Brake shoes |
| Screwdriver (slot) | Front and rear brake cables |
| Screwdriver (Phillips) | Rear derailleur control cable |

## SAG WAGON

Organized tours, particularly those run by operators for profit, frequently include van-type truck or station-wagon support vehicles— the infamous "sag wagon." The role of the sag wagon can be twofold: (1) To carry much of the camping gear, tools, spare parts, and miscellany that add weight to the touring bicycle. (2) To afford an alternative means of transportation for riders who may not be able to maintain the normal pace of the group or who become ill en route.

Alternatively, groups such as the Cyclemates travel with everything they need packed in their panniers and handlebar bags. Part of tour planning involves one major decision—to travel with or without the sag wagon. When everything including camping gear must be packed on bicycles and hauled up and down hills and mountain passes, only essentials remain. Traveling on a bicycle without an auxiliary vehicle calls for an austere lifestyle on the trip. When a sag wagon is available to carry the heavy gear, you can take some of the comforts of home along. But, somehow, part of the challenge also disappears. You're a cycling group in name only.

Costs increase significantly when a sag wagon is included. There is the cost of driving the distances plus the expenses of the driver. Pedaling eighty miles a day affords a challenge to the touring cyclists; but driving eighty miles a day can bore even the most interested support person—so a driver must usually be paid.

If the Cyclemates can carry all the gear they need to travel coast to coast on their own bicycles, who needs a sag wagon? I recommend that you plan your trip without the psychological menace presented by the sag wagon. If you know that every time you tire of pedaling, you can pack your bike in the wagon and ride a few miles, most of the challenge and much of the fun disappears. You're really only a part-time cyclist.

### TABLE L: Personal Articles and Clothing

| | |
|---|---|
| First-aid kit | Rain jacket or poncho |
| Suntan cream | Sunglasses |
| Insect repellent | Sewing kit |
| Ditty bag with toilet articles | Towel |
| Complete change of clothing | Toilet paper |
| Sweater | |

## WEATHER

On any long-distance tour you're likely to encounter nearly every kind of weather from cold, drizzly rain to scorching heat. Because touring should be fun, most trips are planned for spring, summer, or early fall seasons in those parts of the country subject to winters and summers with extremes of temperatures. Even so, you may encounter cold 'while cycling in the high altitudes common to mountains; and many stretches of the country bake under summer sun during the middle of the day.

Part of your planning calls for packing clothing to suit the extremes of the weather you will likely encounter. Extra cardigan sweaters for cold; lightweight, airy shorts, T-shirts, and blouses for hot weather, and some protection from the rain should be included in your packs. A light rain jacket or short poncho can keep you pedaling during most spring to fall rains. For more information on clothing, see Chapter Twelve.

If you stay inside on rainy days, you're likely to find your planned timetable goes awry much too often. Further, rains can come and go in any one day. Snow can be another problem, though; snow makes pedaling hazardous as well as uncomfortable. So there's a limit on the different kinds of weather you can prepare for.

## GROUP SIZE AND MAKE-UP

One natural group is the family. Biking holidays where the whole family takes to the hills and back roads are becoming the "in" thing. These trips test the mettle of every family member and provide a change of pace from the driving or airline trips to a resort destination. While leadership and compatibility occur naturally in family groups, these factors can make or break a bicycle tour for other groups.

A strong, responsible adult leader can conduct a tour for youngsters. The Cyclemates proved that as many as sixteen junior high school boys and girls under the leadership of one adult could successfully cycle thousands of miles without a sag wagon—and have fun meeting the challenges that inevitably pop up along the way.

Adult groups that gather for specific "huff 'n puff" tours organized through the International Bicycle Touring Society will usually be made up of experienced cycle tourists. Like devotees of any other pursuit, cyclists tend to be flexible thinkers and generally compatible because they are "something special" and know it. Touring cyclists have already met and conquered a wide variety of challenges and tend to make good cycling companions. Tours sponsored by local chapters of the League of American Wheelmen also attract compatible cyclists. There you can sample the groups on short trips before committing yourself to an extensive week- or month-long tour. Plan to join the bigger groups in either the IBTS or LAW in company with one or two close friends. Then you can relate to the group at two levels—closely and at whatever distance works out best.

Cycling shops can take the lead in arranging for local tours as one method of building a clientele. The Mercer Island Cyclery, for example, organizes weekend day trips around the Puget Sound area. Once you get the yen to tour, you can usually find one or more companions to share your interests. Many newspaper and magazine stories tell how one person or four or more cyclists have left on a tour and found riding companions along the way. If you begin cycle touring alone, you will probably not be lonely for long.

# 12.
# Cyclemates
# Tour Cross-Country

Fifteen boys and girls cycled across the United States with me during the summers of 1970 and 1971, and sixteen accompanied me across the continent in 1972 and 1976. The boys and girls were from my classes at North Mercer Junior High School on Mercer Island, Washington. The map in Fig. 59 shows the four routes we took. Cyclemates I (Fig. 60) pedaled 3,597 miles to the west access ramp of New York City's George Washington Bridge in sixty days. Cyclemates II (Fig. 61) trekked across the middle part of the United States, 3,691 miles to the Washington Monument in Washington, D.C. President Nixon received all of us at the White House on August 10, and expressed his appreciation for a group of turned-on youngsters willing to accept and carry through such a challenge. In 1972 Cyclemates III (Fig. 62) spent nine weeks and three days climbing up and coasting down the mountains of western Canada, traversing the endless plains of middle Canada, and ogling the unusual sights and scenery as we circled the Gaspé Peninsula of eastern Canada to end up in Halifax, Nova Scotia, 4,535.6 miles from home. On Cyclemates IV in 1976 we were joined for the first time by an adult, Mary Gnehm, the mother of two boys who had gone on previous trips. We cycled 3,986 miles to historical Williamsburg, through the Rexburg floods in Idaho, over Independence Pass in Colorado (12,095 feet high), then across the plains and the Appalachian Mountains on a route close to the Bikecentennial one. All four trips began from the parking lot of North Mercer Junior High. All riders who started each trip finished the full distance.

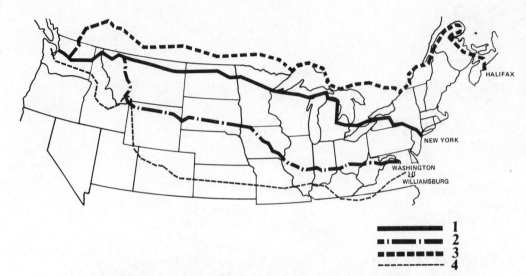

1
2
3
4

Fig. 59—Cyclemates' four cross-country tours began at the parking lot of North Mercer Junior High School, Mercer Island, Washington. Cyclemates I ended at the west end of the George Washington Bridge into New York City. Cyclemates II ended at the Washington Monument. Cyclemates III ended in Halifax, Nova Scotia, after touring the Gaspé Peninsula. Cyclemates IV ended in Colonial Williamsburg, Virginia.

Fig. 60—Roster for Cyclemates I—(standing from left to right) Walt Mauldin, Carl Malmfeldt, Mike Evans, Dennis Early, Kathy Horrigan, Nancy Bolger, Anne Simpson, Gail Stevens; (kneeling) Dave Dunnington, David Heston, Brian Gribble, Andy Rice, Laura Dassow, Mary Strachota. Not shown: Lisa McMillan. Center—Frances Call.

Fig. 61—Roster for Cyclemates II—(left to right) Elaine Bracken, Hanne Petersen, George Goodstein, D.R. Mendel, John Stuckey, Peter Gnehm, Maiko Blow, John Mudge, Chris Simpson, Frances Call, President Nixon, Kevin Lamb, Mary Pagel, Sue Hall, Brent Larson, Nancy Bolger, Allison Johnston, Randy Parker. Nancy Bolger (third from right, white shirt) rode with Cyclemates I and was living in Washington, D.C., when Cyclemates II arrived.

We pedaled every inch of the distance. The hills included the "Going to the Sun Highway" over the Continental Divide in Glacier National Park, Powder River Pass 9,666 feet high in Wyoming's Big Horn Mountains, and the Rogers Pass Highway over the Continental Divide on the Trans-Canada Highway. Highest of all was Indepen-

Fig. 62—Roster for Cyclemates III—(left to right, standing) Drew Hendel, Chris Lewis, Richard Gnehm, Robb Flem, Kathy Rousso, Jo Ann Davenport, Margaret Tivnan, Paul Wilhelm, Nancy Moore, Frances Call; (kneeling, left to right) Laurie Sutter, Dan Zak, Gary Fromm, Patti Daly, Jean Marshall, Duane Eng, Nancy Engman.

Fig. 62a—Roster for Cyclemates IV—(left to right, kneeling) Karen Schaps, Linda England (behind), Kay Roberson, Hilary Morrow, Art Sidel, Andy Hamp, Mark Travis; (standing) Sandy Rodgers, Lucia Pirzio-Biroli, Jack Whiteford, Eric Muller, Kris Embrey, Mary Gnehm, Jeff Morgan, Frances Call, Peter Travis, Sandy Gehres, Steve Gill. We were cycling through a snowstorm atop Chinook Pass in Washington.

dence Pass, 12,095 feet up in the Colorado Rockies. Actually, although the highways over the Continental Divide in both the United States and Canada are higher, the hills we pedaled over around the Gaspé were more tiring and difficult. Hills and mountains are not all that hard to negotiate with an operational 10-speed bike. We geared down and, with a consistent cadence, churned right on up to the top. Pedaling up long grades can be physically taxing, of course, and we often stopped about every thirty minutes on a consistent climb, not only to rest but to snay pictures and take in the spectacular scenery.

We packed everything we needed for 3,000 to 4,000 miles-plus of bicycle riding on our own bikes (Fig. 63). Each cyclist carried his or

Fig. 63—Loaded Cyclemates' bicycles include double panniers, sleeping bag on rear carrier, water bottles on seat post, and large handlebar bag. Cyclemates carried everything they used on the trip except food.

her own tent and sleeping bag, personal clothing, sundries, and part of the group load. Four of the boys packed our spare parts (see Table M). Another packed a heavy-duty tire pump. The first year we started with light handpumps to cut weight, but they fizzled out. On the last two trips we carried the kind you can put your foot on and fill a tire with high pressure air in a hurry. Two of the girls carried note paper, envelopes, and stamps to write thank-you notes after we stayed in a church or some other place overnight.

One key objective of the trips was to teach self-reliance and resourcefulness. No, that's too formal; teaching implies a class setting with me lecturing. The Cyclemates learned from experience. And they learned well. For openers, each student had to earn at least half of the money he would need for the trip. We sponsored car washes on Saturday, bake sales, and other group activities to help raise the cash. Some of the kids earned all of the money they spent on the trip. During the early trips, we budgeted $3.50 per day for food plus personal amounts for laundry, entertainment, and lodging. This rate went up to $4.25 a day by 1976, and hit a high of $7.00 per day on the shorter 1980 Cyclemates' tour. But on all the rides we had to scrounge a lot. Also, the kids learned to cope with a variety of problems they never encountered at home. They became quite ingenious in stretching their cash. This is what kept their trip cost down to only $210 on the early trips. On top of that, we paid air fare one way plus the cost of shipping our bicycles back. Total cost—about $500 apiece. That was incredible, even in those days when a dollar went much farther.

What do youngsters gain from a trip like the Cyclemates' tours across continental America? First, they accept a real physical challenge —and find themselves equal to it. They see the United States or Canada in detail such as few teen-agers—or adults—ever have. Some of their friends at school thought the Cyclemates were looney—right out of their tree. But I've seen quiet kids grow like you wouldn't believe. They learn about money—earning their ante beforehand and spending each day's cash only after choosing from numerous alternatives. They learn responsibilities to a group. And they learn early how much they can accomplish—if they try. My challenge was to get them to try, to inject them into situations that required innovative answers or a stick-to-it-iveness they couldn't learn from their routine at school. Bicycling coast-to-coast offers kids the chance of a lifetime to do something few youngsters or few adults ever tackle.

As a learning experience, there's little to equal the variety of happenings on a long bicycle trip. If you can't manage a full summer, make it a month's tour. Keep the itinerary relatively local. Or strike out for two weeks. Cutting a tour down to a week reduces the overall impact. A week's tour can be fun and a learning experience, but it can't match a cross-country trip.

Peyton Whitely, an assistant city editor for *The Seattle Times*, rode with Cyclemates III from Mercer Island to Wenatchee, up and over the Cascade Mountains and deep into the heartland of Washington's apple country. After riding for two days with us, he wrote:

> The members of Cyclemates III are an admirable bunch of kids. The girls are too young to be called women and the boys aren't old enough to shave, but they are setting out on an adventure as difficult as almost any imaginable.
>
> The idea of pedaling a bicycle to Halifax, Nova Scotia, from Mercer Island seems a little like earlier times when young men and women went in search of their fortunes. Today, it seems, many young people are more willing to use someone else's gasoline and hitchhike. The Cyclemates depend on nothing but their own strength, determination, and preparation.

## HOW DID IT ALL START?

Just before school dismissed for the summer vacation in 1969, I suggested to my students that they tackle something physically challenging during the summer. We considered mountain climbing, hiking, and bike riding, among others. They liked the idea of bicycling, so I suggested, "How many would like to ride around the Olympic Peninsula?" Olympic National Park occupies most of the peninsula which forms the northernmost tip of the west coast of the United States. By highway and ferry across Puget Sound, the trip totals about 250 miles.

That was the beginning. Out of thirty kids in the class, twenty-five were all hot to go. I figured that was too many, so we drew slips out of a hat—seven boys and seven girls. After school was out in June, those fourteen rode with me around the Olympic Peninsula—a six-day trip.

We didn't just pick up and head off for the Pacific Coast. We figured we should train a bit to get in condition. Our first ride was around Mercer Island—about 15 miles. We were exhausted after the trip. We stopped and gorged on ice cream and wondered how we would ever manage a trip around the Olympic Peninsula. On our next ride we circumnavigated Lake Sammamish—about 23 miles. I can remember a parent saying, "I'll be home all afternoon if you have to call." Now, 23 miles is nothing; we've done that much before breakfast, but back then it was no small thing. After a few more trips around Mercer Island, we figured we were ready for the Olympic Peninsula.

I figured our itinerary for about 30 to 40 miles a day, to keep the pace leisurely. But the first day we pedaled 48 miles—and it was hard because we had all made up our minds that it would be hard. On the sixth night we stayed at a motel in Port Angeles. It was something to look forward to. When we finished, we thought we had conquered the world.

A couple of weeks later, I led a second group of sixteen boys and girls (including those who had missed out the first time) around the Olympic Peninsula. These two groups formed the nucleus for Cyclemates I. During the fall of 1969 we took trips almost every Sunday. We'd take the ferry to Vashon Island and pedal around the perimeter road—about 40 miles. Or Bainbridge Island—45 miles. A trip around Lake Washington totals 65 miles. We learned by doing. We had camped out using plastic tarps on the Olympic trip, but during the fall and winter, rain caused us to pack more gear—all on our bicycles.

Around Christmas we began thinking about a summer trip. When one of the kids piped up with, "How about coast-to-coast?" I thought it sounded impossible. That was just too far! But I dug out maps and began figuring. We knew by now we could make 80 miles a day over almost any terrain. At that rate we could do it! The more we looked and talked, the more plausible the whole adventure sounded. Shortly after Christmas we began serious planning. The details of how we planned for Cyclemates I are in Chapter Eleven. While flexible routing can be helpful, it also led to one embarrasing incident.

Before we left Mercer Island, we planned our route through Great Falls, Montana. Knowing our plans, Ross Hidy, pastor of Holy Trinity Lutheran Church on Mercer Island, arranged a surprise dinner for us with a friend in Great Falls. We didn't know anything about it, of course. But we kept in contact with parents by telephone about every three days, so he figured when we would be in the vicinity of Great Falls. As Reverend Hidy tells the story, his friends arranged a big Mexican dinner for us at their house. They knew we had stayed overnight in a town about 100 miles north the night before. Great Falls was an easy day's ride and the weather was ideal. Then, about 5 o'clock in the afternoon, Pastor Hidy received a long-distance call from his friend. "Where are the Cyclemates?" he asked. "We've had the state patrol looking for them, but they've disappeared!"

Although there was no particular reason for Reverend Hidy to be concerned about our safety, he was embarrassed that his friends had prepared a big feed and we weren't there. It wasn't until one of the girls called her parents that Reverend Hidy found we were camped at Wolf Creek, many miles south of Great Falls! The moral of the story is make certain that those who wish to accommodate you realize you have a flexible schedule.

## LOADING THE BICYCLES

Each of the Cyclemates was responsible for his or her own camping equipment and clothing. We carried tarps to keep off the rain and dew; they were light and easily set up when trees were available. Later, we decided on tents.

Each boy and girl carried a sleeping bag and individual tent (which provided privacy). (Fig. 64) The little individual backpacker tents included stakes and poles, so we didn't need trees for stringing up a

Fig. 64—Camping in a park outside of Ashland, Wisconsin, Cyclemates I pitch their individual mountain tents for the night. Bicycles receive regular maintenance by boys in mechanics' corps.

tent. In Canada we needed mosquito netting on the tents too—swarms of mosquitos everywhere. And at Revelstoke, Canada, it was cold and wet.

One night in northern Minnesota the skies unloaded—six inches of rain in one night. Of course we were soaked, sleeping bags and all. The next morning we biked into the nearby town and dried our clothes and sleeping bags in a laundromat. The worst thing was getting our sleeping bags wet. Some of the kids tried plastic rain flys over the tent, but soon discarded them—too wet and messy to fold up. We learned to pack all our gear in plastic bags.

Tent, sleeping bag, and a minimum of clothes, usually shorts and short-sleeved shirts were basic for everyone. On the Canada trip, we knew it was going to be cold, so we packed extra sweaters and jackets. A light rain jacket is all we ever took, because nothing will keep you dry while riding in the rain. Anything waterproof condenses perspiration inside, so you may as well be wet from the rain. Pedaling kept us plenty warm even while riding in the rain. Mainly we needed rain protection in camp.

### TABLE M: Spare Parts and Tools Carried on Cyclemate Tours

| *Spare Parts* | *Tools* |
|---|---|
| Spare tires (4) | Clincher tire repair kit |
| Spare tubes (4) | Screwdriver |
| Front & rear brake cables (1 of each type) | 6" crescent wrench |
| | Long-nose pliers with wire cutters |
| Front & rear derailleur cables (1 of each type) | Spoke wrench |
| | Allen wrenches (assorted sizes) |
| Derailleur | Cotterless crank tool |
| Crank cotter | Tire wrenches |
| Brake shoes (6) | Chain riveter |
| Bearings (range of sizes) | Cone wrenches (pair) |
| Pedals (various) | Freewheel remover (for all bikes |
| Rear cluster | in group) |
| Chains and links | Tire pressure gauge |
| Spokes (sizes for all bikes) | Pump (heavy duty) |
| Rear axle | Pedal wrench |
| Rim liners (2) | |
| Assorted nuts, bolts, screws, & spacers | |

Each Cyclemate took miscellaneous gear—usually a camera and stationery—that sort of thing. This personal gear along with a half-dozen candy bars for emergencies went into the light handlebar bag. And a water bottle was strapped to the frame.

Group equipment—spare parts, first-aid kit, tools, air pump, tire gauge—was divided among the kids, with the boys carrying the heavy gear (see Table M). All of the heavy, bulky gear was divided between the two panniers that ride over the rear wheel. The sleeping bag rode behind the saddle.

## FOOD ON THE ROAD

With just a few dollars a day for food, menu planning and food buying get basic in a hurry. Pedaling 60 to 130 or more miles a day burns up plenty of calories (see Chapter Seven). Eating was not a group affair except on special occasions. Each kid learned to be self-sufficient. On our last tour we figured our $7 allowance as an average of $2 per meal plus a dollar for pop and snacks—candy bars, milk-shakes, and an occasional burger. We usually spent more than $2 for breakfast and less than $2 for lunch.

Breakfast was our big meal—to get set for the day. We always ate in a restaurant. That's another reason for planning overnight stops near towns. Breakfast was eggs and bacon—sometimes on a stack of hotcakes. On many a morning a friendly restaurant owner would just keep piling on more hotcakes; they're filling and pack plenty of calories when flooded with maple syrup. Everybody paid for his own meals out of his daily food allowance. I didn't check—it's the spirit of wanting to learn to live on a budget.

Lunch was another big meal—mostly peanut butter and jelly sand-wiches with various trade-offs depending on the weather and the store. Kids love to shop in supermarkets! Two would usually split a quart of milk. When it was hot—and it was plenty hot some days, particularly crossing South Dakota on our way to Washington—we were thirsty. So we drank quantities of pop. But a can of cold pop costs 30¢ to 50¢. The kids soon learned that pop in big, returnable bottles costs much less than individual 12-oz. cans. So two might split a quart. Better still, they bought soft-drink powder and mixed it with water for their drink bottles. Even warm, that was better than a continuation of nothing but plain water.

Another lunch favorite was cheese and tomato sandwiches. It's hard to buy small quantities of cheese, so I would find someone to split a package of eight slices with, and each of us would buy a tomato. We would sit against a building and use a grocery bag for a table. Frozen whole strawberries were another treat—along with the usual peanut butter and jam sandwiches. When you open a container of frozen strawberries, they are solid and immediately collect frost on the outside. By the time you have spread the sandwiches, a few of the berries were thawed enough to eat—*delicious!* And the moisture in them helped quench our thirst.

We really didn't worry too much about balanced nutrition. Eggs and bacon in the morning plus peanut butter at noon provided plenty of protein. Bread and the jam, plus candy bars, kept energy levels up. And we drank quantities of milk and often splurged on ice cream and milkshakes. Since each kid was responsible for managing his or her own food money, two or more would buy certain items, sharing the cost. One boy might say, "How many for peanut butter and jelly?" Say nine hands went up. That boy would then duck into the store and come out with two loaves of bread, having actually counted the slices to make sure there were at least 18 or 36 slices, depending on demand. He would buy a big jar of peanut butter and the biggest, cheapest jar of jelly or jam he could find. Although I sometimes objected to the quality, I didn't say so, because that was his decision. Too many complaints from the others and he would know enough to buy a better quality next time. When he divided up the bread, peanut butter, and jelly, he also split the cost. Say it all came to $3.00; he would split it nine ways. It really is surprising how much food you can buy that way. If I decided I wanted a banana and a bag of peanuts, I would buy them separately. At times, someone would buy a can of vegetable soup and eat it cold—very refreshing and filling when you're hot and thirsty.

At some grocery stops, the manager tossed us a bag of candy bars— sort of like feeding animals. Sandwiches can be tiresome after several days, so if there was a restaurant across from the supermarket, one or more of the kids went in for a bowl of soup.

Dinner was our most variable meal. Often we would eat cereal and fruit. Milk on the cereal tastes particularly good when you're thirsty. We added canned or fresh fruit to the cereal, or ate fruit out of hand. Sometimes we had sandwiches again for dinner. If there was a restaurant available, some of us occasionally sampled their low-cost "blue plate special."

When we stopped in a church with a kitchen in the basement, a favorite treat was French toast. The kids loved to cook when they had an opportunity. If two of the girls decided to cook French toast for the group, they took orders and planned how many slices of bread they would need. Then, off to the store. One counted the slices in the loaves of bread to make sure they were getting the best buy; the other bought the eggs, milk, and syrup. They whomped up a tasty feed for very little cash. To top if off—fresh fruit.

Planning lunch and dinner was a favorite topic of chit-chat while we rode. Each of us soon got to know what the others liked. We would team up with different partners to turn mealtime into a real event. The kids learned to scrounge. At breakfast they might take a couple of packets of instant oatmeal with them into the restaurant and order a cup of hot water along with their eggs and bacon. Hot oatmeal with plenty of sugar plus possibly the jam that came with toast added more protein and energy food in the morning. They helped themselves to the little salt, pepper, sugar, mustard, and catsup packets, and stored them in their handlebar bags. At lunch a little mustard on cold cuts added a zingy taste. Some bought sardines for sandwiches. And—kippered herring! The boys sometimes ate several cans, particularly on hot days. The salt in the herring not only tasted good but replaced salt sweated out while pedaling. Occasionally we would luck out and get invited to a big meal by the friendly people we ran into. Believe me, some of them didn't know what they were getting into when they asked us to a spaghetti feed or a barbecue.

One hot day about lunchtime the kids saw some people outside in a yard and asked them if they might sit and rest under their trees. The people were very friendly. The man said to call him "Farmer Brown." Mrs. Brown brought out cold lemonade and cookies. We learned that the Browns' son, daughter-in-law, and seven grandchildren were visiting for the day. Presently, tables appeared outside, and the women started loading them with food. Since the Cyclemates believed the Browns were going to have a picnic, they got up and started to thank them and tell them goodbye. Farmer Brown exclaimed, "Oh, no! You can't go now! We have your lunch all ready!" And what a feast it was! So many good things to eat, and lots of it.

Once in Montana a woman passed us in a pickup truck—then stopped ahead until we caught up. She asked us the usual questions: Where were we headed, where had we come from, how many miles had we pedaled, and so on. It was shortly after lunch, and we talked for about ten minutes alongside the road. She invited us to see her ranch. We all piled into a stake truck, and she drove us over her 4,000-acre spread, —beautiful! We met some of the nicest people that way. They were entranced by the idea of fifteen junior-high kids taking off on a cross-continent journey, and wanted to talk and learn more about our experiences and plans.

Looking ahead during the day toward dinner and breakfast the next morning sometimes called for questioning or a long-distance call. In Idaho, Montana, and parts of Canada, stores and restaurants can be many miles apart. Before we camped I wanted to know how far we had to ride to find a restaurant open for breakfast. Also—was there a store near the campground? If not, then we would need to buy dinner supplies ahead. We consulted our map. We might find a town marked, but was there a store and/or restaurant? I gave this job of reporting on upcoming stops to one of the boys—our PR representative. I usually checked out his findings. After you've ridden 20 miles for breakfast only to find the restaurant closed and you ride another 20 miles before eating, you learn to ask the right kinds of questions! If there was to be a ride before breakfast the next morning, we bought an extra orange or extra doughnuts to eat when we first got up. And we always stocked a reserve of candy bars in our handlebar bags; when we ate those, we replaced them at the very first opportunity.

Staying in churches simplified many overnights, particularly when the weather was bad or threatening. I never called ahead. Can you imagine the reaction if I had called and said, "I'm an old-maid school-teacher from Seattle and I have fifteen kids with me. Can we stay in your church basement for the night?" Instead, we simply rode up to a church and asked in person. With all the kids visible, it was a soft sell. In the course of three summers, we stayed in about sixty churches and were turned down only three or four times. Maybe a basement was being remodeled and was a mess—or maybe there wasn't a basement. Only twice were we turned down with a flat "no."

We never had a complaint after staying in a church. One reason was that I detailed two of the more reliable kids to inspect the premises— pick up papers and make sure the kitchen was spotless if we had used it. Then, within three days, our letter-writing pair drafted thank-you notes and mailed them back to the church, expressing our appreciation.

One hot day near Frankenmuth, Michigan, a man stopped the bicycling brigade to get our "story," a common occurrence. He offered to buy each of us a coke. After hearing we planned to stop over in Frankenmuth, he drove on in search of Joseph Lier, called "Mr. Scoutmaster Joe" for his thirty-five years in scouting. When Joe heard about the Cyclemates, he adopted the group during our stay in his home town.

Nationally known for its Bavarian Festival each June, Frankenmuth receives well over a million tourists yearly, but even a mere sixteen visitors were important to Scoutmaster Joe. The Cyclemates had planned to camp outdoors that night, but Joe offered us the use of the beautiful new Scout building. We dined at the century-old Zehnder's Restaurant, famous for its all-you-can-eat chicken dinners. When manager Edwin Zehnder heard about the Cyclemates, he hosted all our dinners himself, declaring, "No kids leave here hungry!" And none did. Next morning at six o'clock four Scout mothers came to the Scout building and prepared breakfast for the early risers.

Riding for hours may sound boring. We didn't find it so. Most of the kids yakked it up much of the time—pointing out the sights, planning their next meal, or looking ahead to an overnight stop. On the road, one girl's job was to plan which girl would lead and when to change. One of the boys did the same for the tail. A girl always led because boys set too fast a pace—that is, unless we were heading into a strong wind. Then the boys would take turns leading to break the wind. The others found it easier going by following closely.

We used hand signals to communicate while riding. I rode at any spot in line, and I always knew who was bringing up the tail. When the boys changed position, they let me know. When someone had a flat tire, he would let me know by shouting and we waited. Otherwise, if I looked back and saw the tail was not there, I knew someone had a problem. I slowed the pace until whoever had dropped behind had caught up. If we had been riding steadily for more than an hour and a good rest spot appeared nearby, we'd wait and regroup before pushing on.

The kids conscientiously observed the country they rode through. Even on the seemingly endless plains of Canada (Fig. 65) small differences in the landscape appeared often enough to warrant conversation. And of course there was always talk about lunch—or dinner and the weather. Cyclemates I played games much of the time—the alphabet game, matching pairs, and others. They had expected the time to pass, slowly and were prepared. Later groups found they didn't have to worry about boredom, so they relaxed and enjoyed the sights.

Historic points of interest marked by monuments and signs afforded another diversion. We stopped and read the full text of those big cast plaques that appear frequently along western highways. Most people zip by in their car with barely a chance to read the title. When people ask, "What is there to see?" I remind them of how much more interesting it is to walk around a historic part of town than driving through. We all see so little from the car window as we zip past at 70 mph. But,

Fig. 65—Riding single file, Cyclemates III cross seemingly endless plains of middle Canada on their way to a record 189.3 miles in one day.

at 15 to 18 mph we discussed the geology, the ever-changing scenery, animals, vegetation, and farming activities. Through the cities we were so busy paying attention to signs and traffic, we didn't have a chance to get bored (Fig. 66).

Rest days also provided a change of pace from riding. Usually, we rode five days and rested one. But we might rest after four or continue on for six days. It's not much fun laying over a day in a camp by the side of the road. We preferred to break at a small town where we could swim, wash laundry, and take in a movie. Townspeople were most friendly and accommodating. We spent much of the time talking with people in town, posing for the local newspaper photographer, or enjoying an enormous picnic a group might hastily organize for us.

On the road we broke for a rest after thirty minutes to an hour and a half, depending on the terrain. After thirty minutes of churning away at five mph in low gear up a long mountain grade, a rest relieves muscles and lungs. After one to two hours riding on fairly level terrain, you get a little saddle sore—so, it's rest stop again. A drinking fountain or a "pop stop" afforded an excuse to break for a few minutes. And at crossroads gasoline stations, restrooms got a heavy workout. In between filling stations and restaurant restrooms, the familiar bush or big tree— even rocks—afforded privacy for a relief stop.

WEATHER. On a cross-country trip riding an average of eighty miles per day, we Cyclemates couldn't pick only warm, comfortable days for riding. We encountered just about every kind of weather there was except heavy snow. One of the really difficult runs was the Cyclemates III climb to the summit of Stevens Pass. From Mercer Slough, elevation 30 feet, we pedaled eighty-six miles to the summit at Stevens Pass, elevation 4,061 feet. During the last seventeen miles we rode in a freezing-cold drizzle along with fog so dense we could barely see the opposite side of the two-lane highway. We could hear the cars coming up behind us before they could see us.

During most trips, Cyclemates wore shorts and didn't worry about the rain. Pedaling consistently kept us warm. But during the early stages of Cyclemates III, pedaling over Stevens Pass, through Revelstoke Park, and over Rogers Pass, it not only rained practically every day but temperatures hovered around 40 degrees. Wool knee socks helped keep lower legs warm even when wet. But our feet were another problem. Some of the kids slipped plastic bags over their tennis shoes with a rubber band around the ankle to keep socks and shoes as dry as possible. Unless we were climbing steadily, pedaling didn't keep our feet warm when a cold, drizzly rain soaked through shoes. By keeping our feet dry, we were more comfortable.

Hot, sunny weather posed different problems—heat exhaustion, sunstroke, or just plain hot, sweaty pedaling. Most of the kids wore something over their heads to keep off the direct sun. I usually wore a bandanna folded and tied over my hair. Some of the girls wore floppy short-brim hats, but they would blow off unless tied under the chin.

Operating the bicycles in rain or snow caused few problems except

Fig. 66—Cyclemates III pedal past the town clock in Halifax exactly on schedule, 3:00 P.M., August 9, 1972, ending their cross-country bicycle trip.

for safety. Brakes do not function as well on wet rims as on dry rims. Stopping in the rain with wet brakes is much like braking a car on ice or snow. You can't stop as quickly, so you allow greater distances for stopping. Holding the brakes on while coasting down slight grades will keep the rims dry in anticipation of heavier braking later at the bottom of a downgrade.

Riding in snow or on wet pavement calls for constant attention to avoid spills due to slips. Gravel or sand always poses hazards but is especially so when wet or icy. Before leaving on Cyclemates III across Canada, we practiced riding up and down hills in light snow. Climbing hills around the Lake Washington area in 3 to 4 inches of snow was not much different from riding on wet pavement. Coasting downhill called for greater care to prevent sidewise skids. Although small tires afford little road contact, they cut through light snow. During any riding on wet or snowy surfaces, be especially wary about sudden changes of direction, quick stops, or quick applications of pedal power. Slow and easy are the two watchwords for riding in snow.

## PERILS OF PEDALING

Only two accidents, neither of them serious, marred all three Cyclemates' trips. On Cyclemates I we were riding along on a pleasant morning in North Dakota when Mary passed out—fainted while riding. She just went plop—right to the ground, hitting her head and knocking herself out for a few seconds. I didn't want her to ride, obviously, so we flagged down a car. A couple from Michigan driving a van picked up the girl and me. We piled both of our bicycles in the back. It was forty miles to the nearest hospital. While we were gone, I instructed the kids to continue on to the next crossroads, about five miles ahead, and stay there until I could get back to them.

At the hospital Mary was checked out. She was shaken up a bit, but otherwise okay. We walked back to a motel from the hospital in Rugby, North Dakota. We had not stayed in a motel up to that point. The girl lay down for a nap while I prepared to get back to the others. While in the hospital we had met a rodeo cowboy who was being X-rayed to assess damages from a fall the previous day —July 4th. He offered me a ride along with my bicycle back to the crossroads to join the kids. We cycled on into Rugby, a three-hour trip. That night we all stayed in the motel—girls in one room, boys in another, with sleeping bags on the floor. Who got the beds? They drew straws.

Next day I declared a rest day, as I wanted a doctor to look at Mary again. But we couldn't afford a second night's stay in the motel. So at 7 A.M. I knocked on the door of the Catholic Church in town. The priest answered and I said, "Father, I have a problem."

"Come in, my dear," he answered. I could tell he was already mistaken about my problem. After explaining what had happened, he dragged out the keys to his car and handed them to me. "You're going to need to get her bike fixed. By all means settle in here."

After driving back to the motel, we rode to the church and planned a clean-up, laundry, and rest day. Mary's bike was unridable, with a bent front fork. Two of the boys and I loaded the bike into the priest's car and headed for Minot, North Dakota, in search of a bike shop. There was no replacement fork available, but we were able to unbend it enough to make it ridable. After a day's rest and a second okay from the doctor, Mary and the rest of us rode on. We were able to find a new fork in Minnesota, but it wouldn't fit. In the end, Mary rode the bent fork all the way to New York City.

Cyclemates II made it across the full distance from Mercer Island to Washington, D.C., without an accident.

On the Cyclemates III trip across Canada, one of the girls leaned over to brush glass bits from her tire—and stuck her hand in the spokes! Of course she tumbled down, quite bloody. Then the girl riding behind ran into her. So, with the two of them hurt, I flagged down a car and we rode to the hospital. I left my bike with the kids but hauled the other two with us in the car. The front wheel on the second bike was badly bent.

Again we were lucky. All the one girl needed was a clean-up and a bandage dressing. The second girl wasn't hurt, just shaken up a bit. I hitchhiked back to the group and we rode into town. That night we camped in a little town park on the outskirts and encountered the only disagreeable incident in all three trips.

We spent most of the evening eating, putting up tents, and working on the bikes. The rim was out of round by about 2 inches. The two boys who specialized in repairs removed the wheel, took off the tire, and removed all of the spokes. They first recurved the rim to run true, then relaced it. With our packet of tools we could fix a remarkable variety of troubles. We went to bed at dark. About 2 A.M. I was awakened by headlights and revving engines. Then several cars began racing around our tents, running over the tent pegs in one case. I was hoping they would go away, but they kept driving around and around, seemingly getting closer each time. Finally, I crawled out of my tent and stood in the track, ready to jump to the side. But they stopped—a bunch of drunken teen-agers. I asked them to get out and leave us alone—and they left. A couple of hours later, a Canadian Mounted Policeman showed up, and I gave him the license numbers I remembered. He called on his radio for identification and found that the wild bunch were frequent troublemakers.

City riding posed other perils. I always took the lead through towns because I was alert to such hazards as car doors opening, street drains, and traffic signals. Also, I knew where we were going to turn and the route ahead. If I hadn't done the leading, the lead girl would have been looking back for my signals and might have taken her eyes off possible hazards ahead.

We worked out a system for getting through big cities. Bypassing them could cost at least a full day of travel time, and in the East cities are close together. Our strategy was to get up at the crack of dawn— say 4:30 A.M. I had an alarm clock. Then I would wake the girl assigned wake-up duty, and she roused the others. We would pack up and hit the road before anyone else was up and bomb right on through the city. In Cincinnati I remember passing one of those trucks washing down the streets—it splashed us with water as we went by. But there was hardly a car in sight. By the time traffic began to build up, we were through the city and heading out the eastern fringe with light traffic. We zipped through Cincinnati in about an hour and a half—then stopped to eat breakfast. We went straight through Montreal on Cyclemates III the same way. In preparation for an early morning city run, we bought snacks the night before to hold us till breakfast. The kids didn't mind—but I missed my morning cup of coffee.

We crossed the bridge over the Straits of Mackinac the same way. Ordinarily, cyclists are not permitted to ride across the bridge— with some justification. Expansion joints with long thin tongues of steel interleaved separated roadway sections. The spaces between these steel fingers can easily catch a tire and tumble the rider head over elbow onto the pavement. So the bridge authority normally hauls bicyclists across in a truck. But we were determined to ride the whole distance. We puzzled over the problem for several days in advance.

At the west end of the bridge I talked to a policeman and asked where I could call the head honcho of the bridge authority. I called from a phone booth while we were in a post office picking up mail. When he came down, we chatted for a while.

"We want to ride the whole distance," I said.

"Fine, you can ride across—if you start at five thirty in the morning."

We camped early that night and started across the next morning at 5:30—before breakfast again. There were no cars, and we first stopped to lead our bikes across the gratings, then rode across at a 45-degree angle to avoid catching tires. If there had been cars, we couldn't have angled across the expansion joints.

## COMMUNICATIONS

Parents were concerned about us, of course, and the kids liked to call home occasionally. That family would then spread the word to the others. During Cyclemates III, a local radio station broadcast daily reports. Sometimes, as near noon as convenient, I would call the station with a status report. A surprising number of friends followed Cyclemates III daily through these reports. Cyclemates IV called Seattle radio station KVI twice a week and disc jockey Bob Hardwick filled in the details of our trip for interested listeners.

Mail stops were high points of the trip. We had marked mail stops on our general route. The pace quickened for quite a few miles before we reached these post offices. The kids would wait until one of the girls would call for mail at General Delivery. She would parcel out the letters and packages, and we'd all sit on the post office steps and read through every letter. Later, the kids would read them again and again. Packages from home included goodies that were usually shared and gone the same day.

On entering a new state or province, I contacted the state police to tell them who we were and to detail our planned route. I wanted parents to be able to contact us in case of an emergency. Sometimes a patrol car would stop and talk with us after receiving a radio report.

## TRAINING AND SELECTION

All four of the Cyclemates cross-country groups were tops, as the shorter tour groups have been, too. And everyone who started finished the full distance. That's pretty amazing to many people, but in selecting the ones who made up each group, I had experience to go on. All fall and winter we took trips. Kids would ask to go, and we would take day trips—sometimes staying over Saturday night. Occasionally I would deliberately schedule a long, grueling day to see how new riders handled themselves in camp when they were tired, hungry—possibly soaking wet from the rain. Some kids dropped out. They thought it would be fun, but it turned out not to be their cup of tea.

Most of the kids were in my classes at one time or another, so I could see how they behaved and how they worked. If they wouldn't work for me in class, I figured they wouldn't work for me on a trip. I shied away from the school leader or "big shot" type. I didn't want a strong leader among the group. That kind of boy or girl will take over, and the others would have little opportunity to develop their own leadership skills.

I didn't often select top scholars, either, although I didn't shy away from them. I looked for the kids who were determined, quiet perhaps, but kids who were constantly aware of what was going on around them. I selected kids who would gain from the trip and learn the most from their experience. During training trips I drove them hard to see how they reacted. I'm a real stickler on politeness, saying "thank you," and making a good impression on people. I can't tolerate brats. I corrected them when they made mistakes. It was all right to make a mistake, but I didn't want them doing it again. So I sized them up. How did they take correction? What was their attitude? Did they hold a grudge?

I looked for cliques too. After we came in from a trip, we'd sit around on the floor and evaluate a trip. "Susie, you delayed the group this morning because your saddle bags were not packed. You could have done that the night before." Or, "Mary, you always save a seat at a restaurant for Penny. You two ride together all the time. Shouldn't you mix with the others?" If they reacted negatively to such correction, I didn't think they would make good group companions over a two-month period. On the trip we were like brothers and sisters —sharing the same bathroom and sleeping in the same big basement at times. We couldn't tolerate too many quirks.

Finally, since they were my responsibility, I made the final selection. I'll admit I've been lucky. All of the groups took the rain, the cold, the heat, and the long days without griping. I'm sure they benefited and matured. ·More groups of this kind could help kids learn and develop by making mistakes while doing something challenging. Too many programs fail to allow the kids a chance to grow and develop on their own. They won't learn with highly structured, spoon-fed programs where all the decisions are made by adults. I've found that kids react marvelously to a challenge—they get too few these days in normal activities.

Cyclemates proved that kids have spunk. They can be stimulating companions if given half a chance. Parents have told me how much their youngsters grew and matured during their eight weeks on the road. They came back much more independent—and helpful. I know that over 150 kids from Mercer Island homes can look back all their lives on an experience few kids their age ever get a chance to live and enjoy. There's really no reason why more can't do the same.

Fig. 67—Jacket patches for Cyclemates II, III, and IV. Cyclemates I, who pioneered the route from Mercer Island to New York City, had no identifying patch.

# Part 2
## Maintenance and Repair of Bicycles

# 13.

## Keeping Your Bicycle in Tip-Top Working Order

Your bicycle with all of its gears and bearings plus the many moving and nonmoving adjustable parts remains basically a simple machine. It has two wheels which rotate on ball bearings. The rear hub may be limited to one speed or be fitted with either of two types of gear-changing mechanisms, as explained in detail in Chapter Three. The headset and handlebars allow you to move the front wheel to either side while riding, and the pedal mechanism turns your leg power into rotating power to drive the rear wheel. The bicycle really is that simple.

Unless you are interested in overhauling bicycles, information about lubrication, adjustments, and the simple repairs you might need to make on a trip should be enough. Basic information in this chapter will help you keep your bicycle in tip-top running order. Chapter Fourteen deals with the simple repairs most cyclists prefer to handle themselves—repairing a punctured tire, replacing a worn chain, replacing and adjusting brake pads, and fixing gear-changing and brake cables.

If your fingers turn to ten thumbs when trying to fix anything mechanical, you may not want to tackle anything more difficult than patching a leaky tire. On the other hand, if you understand about wrenches, bearings, adjusting sleeves and cables, most of the information you need can be found right on the bicycle. You can adjust components by analyzing each function and correcting the fault. Bicycle parts are really not that complex. As you follow the part-by-part information in this chapter, note the suggestions and adjustment criteria that will help you keep your bicycle in good condition. When some part is buggered or broken, you will need to visit a cyclery or order a replacement by mail. Practically, you may find that a trained mechanic with special tools to replace or overhaul a mechanism costs less in time and money than doing the job yourself with makeshift equipment.

A few years ago when 10-speed bicycles became popular, few experienced bicycle mechanics staffed cyclery shops. Now, nearly every bicycle shop is equipped with special tools and the know-how to fix major problems or to overhaul major components of your bicycle. As an individual, you need not feel compelled to become so knowledgeable that you could fix any conceivable fault that might afflict your individual bicycle. You should, however, become familiar with routine maintenance, lubrication, and those adjustments that keep your bicycle functioning smoothly and easily.

You can follow a two-step procedure in maintenance. First, check each element of your bicycle for top operating condition. Second,

Fig. 68—Bicycle parts and components.

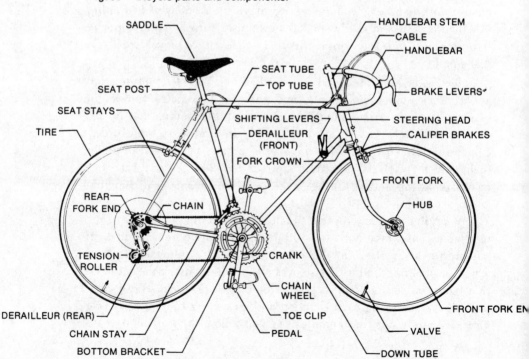

depending on what you find during this check, adjust or correct any malfunctions. Before a pilot takes off in his small airplane, he makes a pre-flight check to assure that controls are operating and the engine is functioning as it should. You can do the same with a pre-ride check.

## TIRES

Bicycle tires are vulnerable to glass, nails, and wear. Before you start on a tour or even a jaunt around the block after a spell of not riding, check tire pressure first. Table N notes optimum tire pressure according to tire size and the rider's weight. Tires should be inflated hard to get maximum mileage, easier riding, and lighter steering. Soft tires are dangerous. For long life, keep gasoline and oil off tires, as these fluids cause tire rubber to soften and to deteriorate chemically.

Check the tire pressure with a pencil-type hand gauge. Don't depend on a gauge you might find at a car service station, because they may not indicate the high pressure common for bicycle tires, and they are often inaccurate. Hand gauges should be accurate within plus or minus 2 pounds per square inch (PSI).

Check tires for wear spots on sides and tread. As you examine the tread, look for small shards of glass that might penetrate the tire and puncture the tube. No cord should be showing through the rubber either on the tread or around the sidewall. Also, check the seating of the tire by noting the position of the mounting line (Fig. 73). The tire should be mounted to show the line evenly all the way around the rim.

TABLE N: Tire Inflation Chart

| | | Weight of Rider | | | |
|---|---|---|---|---|---|
| | | 125 | 150 | 175 | 200 |
| Tire Size | | Inflation Pressure—Pounds/ Square Inch (PSI) | | | |
| 1¼ | (26" only) | 45 | 54 | 60 | 65 |
| 1⅜ | | 43 | 50 | 55 | 60 |
| 1½ | | 38 | 45 | 50 | 55 |
| 1¾ | | 33 | 40 | 45 | 50 |
| 1¼ | (27" only) | 65 | 70 | 75 | 80 |
| 1 | (27" Hi-Pressure) | 80 | 90+ | 95 | 95+ |

WHEELS

Spin the front wheel to see if it runs true. Ask a friend to help with this check unless you have access to a rack or frame that holds the bicycle firmly while you spin the wheel. Look directly from the side to check for any out-of-round condition that will show up as a flat spot. If they are serious, out-of-round flat spots may show up as a recurring bump when you ride. A rim that is out of round needs expert attention. Take it to a bicycle shop for truing by spoke adjustment and/or actual bending of the rim into a circle.

More common is the side-to-side wobble you detect by looking directly down at the tire as it spins. Wobble may be due to loose bearing cones or loose spokes. Check for loose or misaligned cones by grabbing the tire and jerking to one side. If the wheel shakes, cones are loose. Cones are tightened by using two thin end wrenches held on the thin cones as shown in Fig. 69. Cones should be tightened until there is firm resistance, then backed off about ⅛ turn. No axial end play should remain when cones are properly tightened. (See Chapter Fourteen for instructions on cleaning and relubricating wheel bearings.) Check with fingers on both sides of the fork for wheel alignment. The axle should be firmly against the stops in the front fork for this test.

If the wheel moves back and forth irregularly between the forks as determined by the finger test, flatten the wheel by adjusting the spokes. Pinch two spokes on one side together and note how easily the rim moves to one side (Fig. 70). Truing a wheel is accomplished in two steps. First, loosen spokes on the side opposite the direction you want the rim to move. Second, tighten spokes with a spoke wrench (Fig. 71) to draw the rim away from the bump and toward the flat plane of the wheel. Don't tighten each spoke more than ½-turn at a time. Then recheck alignment. Patience and continuous small adjustments can bring a warped rim into true alignment— with rims not more than ⅛ inch out of plane around the full circumference. If you try to move the rim quickly and without patience, you'll end up with a badly warped rim. CAUTION: Any time you tighten spokes you may puncture a tire. For major realignments, remove the tire and rim liner over the spoke ends. Then, as you tighten the spokes, you can see if any spoke ends protrude into the tire contact space. If so, file ends flush or cut them back with end-cutting nippers and then file smooth.

Fig. 69—Cones are adjusted on
wheels with two thin end wrenches.
Cones and bearings should be tight
but not binding. Back off ⅛ turn
after cones are tightened to the
point where wheels resist turning.

Fig. 70—Pinching two spokes on
the same side of a wheel quickly
shows how much tightening can do
to straighten an out-of-plane wheel.

Fig. 71—Spoke wrench tightens or
loosens nipple on spokes to straight-
en wheel. Nipples should be turned
no more than a half-turn at a time
when bringing a wheel into alignment.

If you find cones loose, dirt may have entered the bearings. With the wheel off the ground but still mounted in the fork, spin the wheel and listen with an ear close to each bearing for scratchy noises. Should you detect signs of grit in the bearings, clean and re-lubricate the bearings as detailed in Chapter Fourteen. Properly tightened and lubricated wheel bearings should rotate easily under the weight of the valve stem alone. With the wheel off the floor, turn the wheel until the valve stem is at the 11 or 1 o'clock position. Allow the wheel to move under its own imbalance if it will. A wheel should rotate under the weight of the valve stem, pass bottom center and coast up the other side, then fall back—oscillating until it stops with the valve stem at or close to the 6 o'clock position.

You can feel grit and missing bearings in the wheels too by holding onto the hubs while the wheels rotate. A skipping jerk in the wheel's rotation indicates one or more balls may be missing from the bearing race. Coarse vibrations felt through the fingers indicate grit in the bearings. Remember, though, you will never detect absolute quiet.

Repeat the alignment and cone test for the rear wheel. To spin the wheel freely, spin it backwards. It will freewheel backwards with either cluster gears or one of the in-hub brakes and/or gear changers. Rear wheels with gear clusters will usually be dished; that is, the plane of the rim will not be centered directly over the middle of the rear hub. Instead, the rim will be displaced toward the rear gear cluster relative to the axle. Thus, when the wheel rim is centered, the cluster will be supported closer to the frame.

## BRAKES

Brake shoes used with caliper brakes on front and rear wheels wear in use and must be replaced occasionally. Check brake shoes to make sure the wear surfaces are spaced at least ⅛ inch away from the side of the rim around the full circumference on both sides. If you have a true wheel, see above, then you won't find the rim wobbling toward or away from the braking surface as it spins. Make sure the brake shoes bear on the metal rim and not on the tire sidewall at any point; otherwise, you can wear away the tire quickly and cause a blowout. Brake blocks should parallel the rim as in Fig. 72. If they do not, loosen the shoe attach bolt and reposition it in the slot or tip it to bear only on the rim as in Fig. 73. Check brake shoes on the rear wheel similarly. Of course, not all bicycles are fitted with brake shoes exactly like those shown in the photos. Slight differences will be readily noticeable. If brake shoes on either front or rear wheels have been recently replaced, check that the metal end is forward; otherwise, the brake shoe will shoot out the open end of the channel at the first hard braking action.

Brake handles mounted on the handlebars should be tight. If you find them the least bit loose, depress the handle to expose the mounting screw (Fig. 74). When brake handles are fully depressed with brake blocks bearing firmly on wheel rims, at least 1 inch of space should remain between handle and handlebars (Fig. 75). If the handles can be depressed all the way to the handlebars, you will

Fig. 72—Brake shoes parallel the rim and bear only on the metal. Note the mounting line on the tire about ⅛ inch from rim. This line should be even around rim when tire is mounted correctly. *Reynolds 531* decal indicates this bicycle is fitted with high-strength, lightweight forks.

Fig. 73—Brake shoe adjustment bolt permits aligning block and adjusting height to bear only on metal rim. Some designs also permit adjusting space between shoe and rim. Other designs depend on adjusting cable length to control space between shoe and rim.

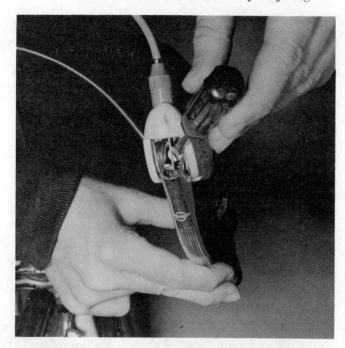

Fig. 74—Screw attaching brake handle to handlebar is exposed by pushing on handle.

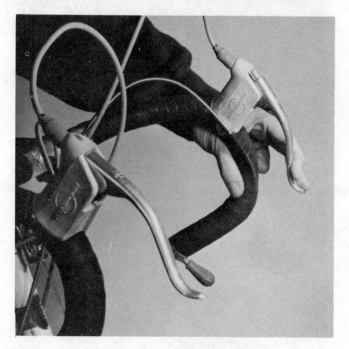

Fig. 75—When brake handle is fully depressed and shoes bear on rim, at least 1 inch space should remain between handle and handlebar.

not be able to stop quickly or possibly at all in an emergency. The handles should spring back to their "at rest" position quickly when pressure is released. If they don't, clean rotating points and oil them. If the sticking appears to be in the cable runs, see Chapter Fourteen for repair instructions or take your bike to a cyclery for correction.

Adjusting brakes is accomplished by changing the length of the cable at the brake end. As brakes are applied during riding, cables tend to stretch. Thus, you must adjust their length occasionally. Before attempting to adjust brakes, take an overall look at how brakes function. They are really quite simple. Depressing the brake handle pulls the cable. At the brake end, calipers translate cable movement into brake shoe application against the rim. Two types of brake application assemblies are in common use—center-pull and

Fig. 76—Knurled nut at end of brake cable sleeve shortens effective brake cable length.

side-pull (Fig. 77) brake calipers. Either type of brake may be adjusted either of two ways. For small adjustments, the knurled nut (B in Fig. 77) may be turned to shorten the cable by moving the sleeve relative to the cable. If the fine adjustment available with the knurled nut isn't enough, turn the nut back and pull the cable through the attach nut. The lower nut at Point E in Fig. 77 may be loosened to pull through the cable for side-pull brakes. Note that in adjusting the length with the knurled nut, the cable works against the casing. Any time a cable runs in a casing, its length is controlled. Otherwise, the cable would simply cut across the curve of the casing and shorten the distance without moving the brakes. Therefore, the casing forms an important part of the system. If the cable sticks inside the casing, you should remove the casing and replace it. Attempting to clean an existing, sticky cable is not practical except in an emergency when no replacements are available. About all you can do is remove it, blow through it to remove dirt, and apply oil.

Fig. 77—Knurled nut (B) at end of cable to side-pull caliper shortens effective cable length to both arms. If adjustment at nut is not enough, cable can be pulled through loosened clamp nut at E.

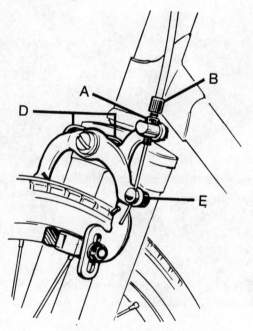

Rear wheel brakes are adjusted the same way as front wheel brakes. Fine adjustments may be made with a knurled adjusting nut. Bigger adjustments are made by pulling the cable through the clamp nut.

## BOTTOM BRACKET AND CRANK

Typical of bottom bracket, cranks, and chainwheel is the three-piece cotterless crank shown in Fig. 78. Seat and down tubes join to form a frame hub that supports the crank assembly. Two ball-bearings and cones may need tightening. Check the axle bearings in the same way as wheel cones—by feel and ear with the chain off. However, in contrast to the wheel cones, bottom-bracket bearings are adjustable from only one side. Check for looseness and end-play by pushing or pulling axially on pedal crank. The indented lock-ring may be loosened with a hammer and screwdriver if the large special wrench is not available (Fig. 79). Once the lockring is loosened, the adjustable bearing cone may be tightened or loosened to allow bearings to roll freely but not so loose as to permit end-play or to admit dirt. Adjust the cone with a large, thin wrench until the bearings begin binding, then back off ¼ turn. Cranks should turn freely in the bearings.

The crank assembly shown in Fig. 78 uses no cotters. Instead the square ends of the axle fit similar square holes in the crank for a long-lasting fit. A dust cap screws into the opening to protect the attach stud. Less expensive cranks are assembled with cotters, and these can become loose with wear. A crescent wrench can be used to tighten the nut holding the cotter pin tightly wedged in place (Fig. 80). Since considerable force is necessary to wedge cotters in place to prevent a sloppy fit, do not use a wrench with a handle longer than 6 inches, as threads on a cotter pin strip easily.

Bolts that attach the chainwheels to the crank arms and the two chainwheels for a 10-speed combination tend to work loose during pedaling. Tighten them with the adjustable wrench, as in Fig. 81. Unless the bolts holding the two chainwheels together are tight, the nut may work itself off and drop the spacers. Without all-around support, you can easily bend a chainwheel. Some chainwheel attach bolts are tightened with an allen-head wrench, usually of a metric size. If yours is one of these, keep an allen-head wrench that fits in your traveling tool kit.

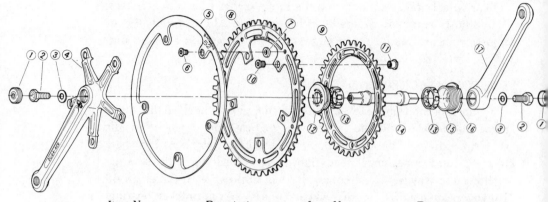

| Item No. | Description | Item No. | Description |
|----------|-------------|----------|-------------|
| 1 | Dust Cap | 10 | Chainwheel Attach Bolt |
| 2 | Attach Stud | 11 | Chainwheel Attach Nut |
| 3 | Washer | 12 | R. H. Fixed Cone Nut |
| 4 | Right Crank Arm | 13 | Ball Bearing & Retainer |
| 5 | Chain Guard | 14 | Bottom Bracket Axle |
| 6 | Guard Attach Bolt | 15 | L. H. Adjustable Cone Nut |
| 7 | Guard Spacer | 16 | Lockring |
| 8 | Large Chainwheel | 17 | Left Crank Arm |
| 9 | Small Chainwheel | | |

Fig. 78—Cotterless *Dura-Ace* crank and double chainwheel assembly. (Courtesy Shimano American Corp.)

Fig. 79— Screwdriver tapped lightly with hammer substitutes for special wrench to loosen lockring prior to adjusting cone nut of bottom bracket crank assembly.

Fig. 80—Small crescent wrench no larger than 6 inches is used to tighten nut on cotter pin to reduce play in crank assembly. If a larger wrench is used, threads may be stripped with excessive torque.

Fig. 81—Bolts attaching chainwheels to crank arms tend to work loose while riding and should be tightened occasionally. If spacers fall out, chainwheel can be bent.

## PEDALS

Two bearing cones support pedals just as in wheels. Only one of the cones is adjustable—the one opposite the crank attachment. Adjusting the one cone tightens or loosens both bearings, as in the case of the two bottom bracket bearings. Because of their position near the ground, pedals pick up dirt and are frequently splashed. Check bearing action and condition by ear and feel as with other bearings. One pedal bearing is protected with a dust cover that screws out (Fig. 82). Under the dust cap, a nut can be adjusted, preferably with a socket wrench. However, pliers can be used out of a traveling tool kit in an emergency.

Pedals screw into crank ends with a thread that tightens by turning the same direction as normal pedaling action. The pedal on the right side of the bicycle tightens in a clockwise direction. The pedal on the left side of the bicycle tightens in a counterclockwise direction. These right and left screws can cause trouble, because you may think you are removing a pedal when in fact you are tightening it. Just remember that the pedals tighten in the same direction as pedaling motion; they loosen in the opposite direction. Flats at the end of the attach end of the pedal for accepting a wrench are narrow to reduce the length of the pedal arm. Therefore, you will need a special, thin end wrench to remove or attach pedals. This is one tool you should carry, particularly if you plan to ship your bicycle partially disassembled. Pedals are usually removed when stowed in a box or plastic bag.

Check the attachment of the toe-clips to the pedals, as these screws tend to work loose when pedaling. The all-purpose 6-inch crescent wrench and a slotted screwdriver are all that are needed to tighten the attachments (Fig. 83).

## DERAILLEURS

Front derailleurs operate much more simply than rear cluster derailleurs. Let's look at a typical one (Fig. 84). The cage fits over the chain as it travels over the chainwheel. To shift the chain from one chainwheel to the other, the cage simply brushes the chain in or out in response to cable-initiated action. As the case moves out, it compresses a spring. When the cable control calls for the derailleur to move in, the cable relaxes tension on the spring and the spring forces the cage back, moving the chain with it.

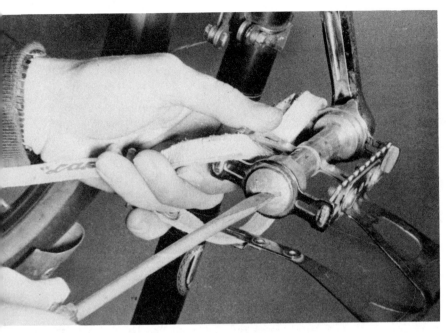

Fig. 82—Slotted screwdriver removes dust cap from pedal.

Fig. 83—With crescent wrench as back-up, screwdriver tightens attach screws for toe-clips. These, too, work themselves loose during riding.

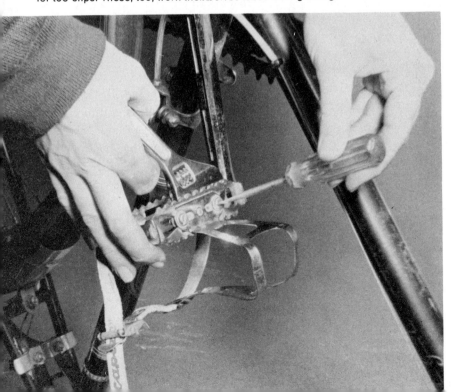

Positioning of the derailleur at each of its limit positions is controlled by an adjustment screw (Fig. 85). If you operate the front derailleur control, you can quickly follow the action and see how the limit screws stop movement at both ends of the derailleur's travel.

Your first check in working with derailleurs is—will it shift? If the chain will not shift to the large chainwheel, find the adjusting screw that is limiting movement and adjust it as necessary. Follow the same procedure if the derailleur will not shift the chain to the smaller chainwheel. The derailleur may also overshift in either direction and push the chain completely off either the larger or small chainwheel. Again, adjust the limit screws as necessary.

Cables connecting the shift lever to the operating arm of the front derailleur stretch in use just as brake cables do. A variety of shift levers will be found on different bikes, but you'll always find cable length adjustments at the derailleur end of the system. Two adjustments are provided on most systems: (1) A knurled nut permits fine adjustments. (2) A clamp nut provides for taking up cable slack and for attaching the operating end of the cable. Both adjustments are shown in Fig. 86. The knurled nut works against the sleeve to shorten the effective cable length. For larger adjustments the cable is pulled through the clamp nut and the nut is retightened.

Check the operation of the derailleur mechanism to assure smooth operation. Moving parts may be oiled sparingly occasionally. Otherwise, excess oil collects dirt.

Checking and adjusting the rear derailleur is easier with the bicycle upside down. While the rear derailleur appears much more complex than the front derailleur, it functions similarly. However, instead of brushing the chain from one freewheel to the next, the pantagraph mechanism shifts the chain with the aid of two rollers. Further, a spring mechanism on the lower roller automatically adjusts chain length according to the sprocket selected. Limit stops are controlled by adjustable screws shown being adjusted in Figs. 87 and 88. A variety of derailleur mechanisms are used on 5-, 10-, and 15-speed bicycles, but they all limit in and out movement of the shift mechanism with limit screws. You can find the limit screws on your bicycle by noting the action of the shifter as you operate the control levers. If the derailleur shifts the chain off the low gear into the spokes, adjust the limit screw as necessary. The low-gear limit screw should be ad-

Fig. 84—Forward derailleur cage bears against side of chain to shift chainwheels. (Courtesy Shimano American Corp.)

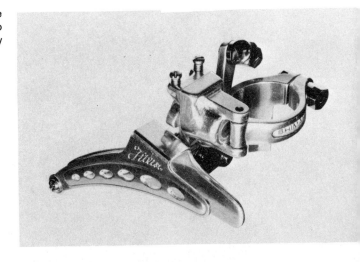

Fig. 85—Limit screws on front derailleur stop shift arm when chain is correctly centered over each of the two chainwheels. Cage should not continue to rub chain after shifting.

Fig. 86—Front derailleur cable is pulled through clamp nut to take up slack after cable stretches in use.

Fig. 87—Limit screws controlling back derailleur are adjusted with bicycle upside down. Limit screws should be adjusted to permit derailleur to shift chain to low and high gears. Improperly adjusted limit screws cause most of the problems with rear derailleur shifting.

Fig. 88—Close-up of derailleur mechanism shows low- and high-gear limit screws, knurled nut for fine adjustment of cable length, and cable clamp nut for large adjustments of cable length.

justed to permit the shifter to move the chain directly over the largest sprocket of the rear freewheel cluster. Adjust the high-gear limit stop screw in the same way. If the derailleur will not shift the chain onto the high gear (smallest sprocket), back off the limit screw until the shifter will move the chain onto the high gear.

Gear-shift cables can cause trouble several ways. When limit screws are incorrectly adjusted, attempts to shift into extreme high or extreme low gear can break a cable. Procedures for replacing a cable are detailed in Chapter Fourteen. The gear-shift cable also stretches in use and may need adjustment. If the derailleur will not shift into the high gear when the gear-shift lever is at its extreme position, check the limit screws first. If there is open space between the end of the adjustment screw and the derailleur mechanism, the cable is too long to move the shifter through its full travel. Fine adjustments can be made by turning the knurled nut at the end of the sleeve near the derailleur (Fig. 89). If the knurled nut runs out of threads while taking up the cable slack, screw the nut close to the end again and

Fig. 89—Low-gear limit screw is adjusted with chain centered over smallest freewheel.

pull cable through the clamp nut (Fig. 89). Check again to make sure the cable is not so short that the spring in the derailleur cannot shift the chain onto the low gear.

Shifter cables should slide smoothly in their sleeves. If they stick or move sluggishly, check the sleeve and the cable closely. Sticky operation may be due to frayed cable, dirt and/or hardened grease inside the cable sleeve, a kink in either the cable or the sleeve, or burrs from exposed wires rubbing inside the sleeve. All of these conditions except the dirt and hardened grease or oil will generally call for a new cable, new sleeve, or both. If you detect dirt and grease binding the cable, unhook the cable at the derailleur end, but do not pull the cable completely out of the housing—at first; instead, slide the sleeve up the cable (toward the shift lever). Wipe off any dirt or gunk. Slipping the sleeve back and forth on the cable and wiping it clean each time will remove most of the offending grime. Relubricate the cable in the sleeve area with light bike oil and reassemble cable and housing. Adjust cable length as necessary to move derailleur between both high- and low-gear limits.

If the chain will not stay on the freewheel you select but keeps slipping off to a higher gear, check the shift lever. Remember, the shift cable holds the derailleur mechanism in a specific position against spring tension. If the shift lever has worked loose, it may allow the cable to slip as you ride. Suddenly, the spring of the derailleur shifts the chain onto a higher gear. The answer is to tighten the nut holding the shift lever (Fig. 90).

Chain, chainwheels, and freewheels require frequent lubrication to alleviate wear. Occasionally, and particularly after riding through splattering mud or blowing dust, brush the chain and sprockets with a small brush. One of the sewing machine brushes works best for this job. If dirt has gummed up the rotating surfaces between side and cross links of the chain, wash out the dirt with kerosene. You can do this without removing the chain from the bicycle by disengaging the chain from the gear cluster. With the slack near the bottom, run the chain through a pan of solvent and brush out the gunk. Allow the solvent to evaporate before spraying the chain with lubricant. You can spray both the chain and freewheels of the rear cluster, as in Fig. 91. Use the same spray lubricant to quiet any high-pitched squeaks in the roller bearings of the guide and take-up rollers of the derailleur. A wide-angle spray works best on the chain

and rear cluster, but you might find a spray can fitted with a 3- or
4-inch plastic tube for directing the spray less wastefully when lubricating the roller bearings. If you carry only one can on a tour, settle
on the wide-angle spray.

Fig. 90—Nut holding shift
lever should be tight to
keep tension on derailleur
cable. Otherwise, the lever
jiggles from its desired
position and the derailleur
shifts gears unexpectedly.

Fig. 91—Lubricant sprayed
on clean gear cluster keeps
freewheels operating
smoothly. Spraying free-
wheel also lubricates chain.

## HEADSET

Two bearings support the headset, the upper end of the front wheel fork, and the connection between the fork and the handlebars through the stem. Check the headset bearings first. They operate similarly to the two bearings in the bottom bracket except that they are vertical and must absorb thrust loads as well as turning loads. Lift the frame and, with your hand on the top end of the stem, attempt to jiggle the headset up and down. If the bearings are loose, you will detect end-play. Turn the fork back and forth to detect any scratchiness that indicates dirt in the bearings.

To adjust bearings and remove end-play in the headset, loosen the locknut at the top (Fig. 92) and take up any slack in both bearings by tightening the cone nut, also with the large crescent wrench. Headset bearing cones should be tight enough to prevent end-play without binding. With the bearings tight, back off about ⅛th turn of the cone nut and tighten the locknut. If you detected dirt in the bearings of the headset, remove them, clean the bearings, and replace the headset as detailed in Chapter Fourteen.

Fig. 92—Large crescent wrench loosens locknut at top of headset in preparation for tightening bearing cones.

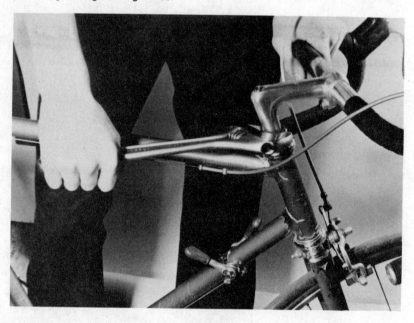

Fig. 93—Expander bolt fastens stem in headset. At least 2½ inches of stem should remain in headset for firm attachment.

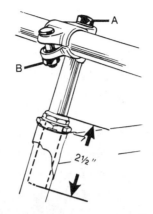

Fig. 94—Stem is tightened in headset by turning expander bolt clockwise.

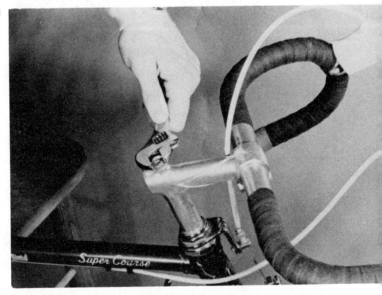

The stem controls both the height of the handlebars and their angle relative to the frame and fork. The expander bolt (A in Fig. 93) being adjusted in Fig. 94 wedges the stem at the desired position in the headset. Do not pull the stem up so far that less than 2½ inches of the stem remain in the headset (see Fig. 93); otherwise the handlebars will not be secure.

Handlebars are fastened to the forward end of the stem in a clamp controlled by a binder bolt (B of the Fig. 93). The angle of the handlebars and their tightness can be adjusted by loosening and retightening the binder bolt as in Fig. 95. There should be no loose-ness whatever between the handlebars and the clamp.

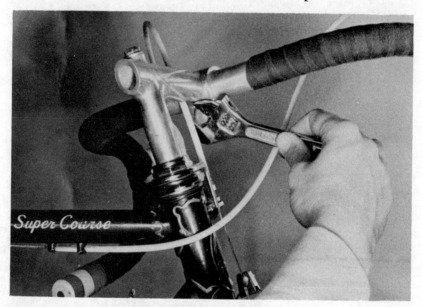

Fig. 95—Binder bolt clamps handlebars in stem. Bolt should be tight enough to prevent any movement of handlebars.

## SADDLE

The saddle clamps to the upper end of the seat post, and the position of the saddle may be adjusted through four degrees of freedom. The height of the saddle should be adjusted for your individual leg length as detailed in Chapter Two for maximum riding efficiency and touring comfort. Saddle height may be adjusted by loosening the clamp bolt at the top of the seat tube (A in Fig. 96). A minimum of 2½ inches should remain in the seat tube to provide firm support for the seat post (see Fig. 96).

The clamp that attaches the saddle to the upper end of the seat post is adjusted with a crescent wrench as in Fig. 97. This clamp adjusts the tilt of the saddle and positions it parallel with the top tube. Saddle tilt varies according to the whim of each rider, but the saddle is most comfortable at a level position or with the nose tilted slightly upward. Many saddles also provide for a fore-and-aft adjustment at the clamp bolt. On the saddle shown in Fig. 97, support bars for the saddle may slide forward or aft in the clamp.

Good touring saddles also include an adjustment under the nose for varying spring tension and, thereby, comfort of the saddle. The nut under the nose moves the spring forward or aft to tighten or loosen the tension.

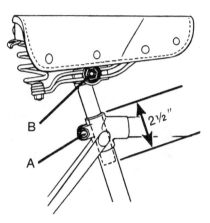

Fig. 96—Seat post is adjusted by loosening clamp bolt (A). At least 2½ inches of seat post should remain in seat tube. Bolt (B) adjusts tilt and fore-and-aft position of saddle.

Fig. 97—All-purpose crescent wrench tightens seat clamp bolt.

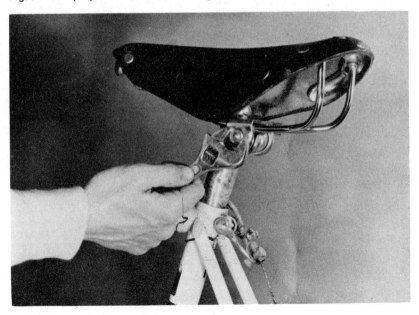

# 14.

# Repairs
# You Can Make
# Yourself

You can expect four levels of maintenance and repair or replacement for mechanical things on your bicycle. These four are:

• Routine adjustment, checks, and occasional lubrication (see Table O).

• Repair of simple problems likely to occur during riding, such as patching a flat tire, replacing a brake cable, or replacing a worn brake shoe.

• Regular lubrication of bearings in wheels, bottom bracket, headset, and pedals. A suggested lubrication schedule for these and other parts is given in Table O. During a regular lubrication, you disassemble the parts, clean them, and replace them along with fresh lubricant.

• Heavy maintenance or overhaul of assemblies or parts to correct a problem. Replacement of worn bearings or a cone damaged by sand, straightening or replacement of a chainwheel, straightening a frame or fork, or replacing a broken spring in a derailleur are examples of heavy maintenance or overhaul.

Chapter Thirteen detailed the routine adjustments and checks commonly called for to keep a bicycle in top running condition. This chapter deals with simple repairs you can make yourself with a minimum of tools. This chapter also covers lubrication of all parts that require regular attention to prevent excessive wear. Heavy maintenance or overhaul of assemblies is not covered in this book for two main reasons: First, overhaul or replacement of parts broken or worn beyond tolerances requires parts and, frequently, special tools. Unless you are a confirmed mechanic, you are unlikely to have either. Second, each manufacturer's derailleur, brake assembly, and other elements are covered in detail in available overhaul manuals that are complete books (see Appendix). These books are invaluable for the mechanic working on a variety of bicycles, but your bicycle will seldom need such attention if you give it even a modicum of care. If you should break a spring in a derailleur, or grind up a bearing because you left a cone loose, you can either note carefully the arrangement of the parts as you remove them or take your bicycle to a cyclery. The mechanically inclined bicyclist can solve most problems by observation and analysis. If you are not mechanically inclined, no book will compensate for your lack of mechanical common sense. But most cyclists can manage the maintenance activities in Chapter Thirteen or those that follow.

### TABLE O: Lubrication Chart

| Assembly | Recommended Frequency | Type of Lubricant |
|---|---|---|
| Front & rear hubs | 6 months | Bearing grease[1] |
| Internal gear changer rear hub | 30 days | Light oil[2] |
| Rear cluster (interior) | 6 months | Light oil[3] |
| Rear derailleur parts | 30-90 days | Light oil[3] or spray[4] |
| Rear derailleur rollers | 30 days | Spray[4] |
| Front derailleur | 30-90 days | Light oil[3] |
| Crank assembly (bottom bracket) | 12 months | Bearing grease[1] |
| Pedals, rubber | 30 days | Light oil[3] |
| Pedals, rat trap | 6 months | Bearing grease[1] |
| Cables | As required & new instl. | Light oil[2,3] |
| Caliper brake assemblies | 3-6 months | Spray[4] |
| Coaster brakes | 6 months | [5] |
| Headset | 6-12 months | Bearing grease[1] |

[1] Bearing grease—*Lubriplate* Low Temp, *Campagnolo* Special, or *Phil Wood* waterproof.
[2] Light oil for rear internal changer hubs—*Sturmey-Archer* or 20-weight auto motor oil.
[3] Light oil—5- or 10-weight auto motor oil.
[4] Spray Lube—*WD-40, Lubriplate* Spray-Lube A, or *LPS 3*.
[5] Special bicycle lubricant recommended.

## TIRE REPAIRS

Punctures and wear of tires call for frequent maintenance attention. You can expect to pick up a puncture sooner or later, so you should be prepared. Fixing a flat is one maintenance chore every serious cyclist should understand thoroughly.

For a flat in a *clincher tire* —

1. Remove the wheel from the frame. Quick release quills greatly simplify this chore. Otherwise, remove the attach nuts without disturbing cones.

2. Remove the tire from the wheel, using three tire wrenches as shown in Fig. 98. The tire wrenches include a slot in one end for hooking around one of the spokes; otherwise, with three wrenches and only two hands, you could have a problem. Remove only one side of the tire from the rim. Mark the valve location on the side of the tire for reference later.

3. Beginning at the valve, pull the tire to one side far enough to remove the valve and innertube and pull it out through the open side of the tire (Fig. 99). Remove the rest of the tube from inside the tire. Ordinarily, you need not remove the valve stem, as the small amount of air remaining in the innertube will not interfere with handling.

4. Find the location of the puncture. The nail or shard of glass that caused the puncture will usually be obvious. If not, pump a few pounds of air into the innertube, and with the tube close to one ear, listen for the leak. If this won't do it, immerse the tube in water and look for the bubbles. Avoid the water test if possible, however, because the tube must be absolutely dry before patching.

5. When you've located the leak, examine the tire inside and outside to make sure the nail, glass, or other object is no longer in the tire. Measure the distance from the leak to the valve on the innertube and a similar distance on the tire to locate the area for detailed examination if the offending object is not clearly visible. If the puncture is on the wheel side of the tube, examine the rim and liner (Fig. 100). Sometimes adjustment of spokes causes ends to protrude beyond the surface of the nipple, penetrate the liner, and puncture the tube. There's little point in patching a tube unless you find and remove the cause of the puncture.

6. Patch the tube using materials from a tube-patching kit. Make sure the tube is bone dry and follow these steps: Clean and roughen the area around the hole as in Fig. 101. Poor preparation of the surface accounts for more leaking patches than any other cause.

Fig. 98—Removing clincher tires begins by prying one edge of the tire over the rim near the valve. Note how the first lever is hooked over a spoke to keep it in place while the second and third levers pry the bead of the tire off the rim. After using the third lever, you can pull the tire loose.

Fig. 99—With one tire bead pulled to one side, pull out the tube, beginning at the valve.

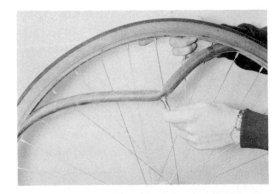

Fig. 100—Rim liner snaps into place like a big rubber band over ends of spoke nipples to protect tube from a puncture around the inside. Examine liner for breaks or holes that could lead to a puncture.

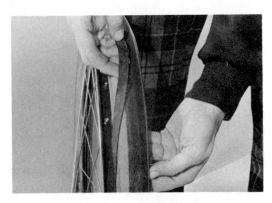

Fig. 101—First step in preparing tube for patch is to roughen surface around hole. Use either sharp-edged holes on cap from tube-patch kit or piece of coarse sandpaper. Roughing the surface removes dirt or film and exposes fresh rubber.

Spread plenty of the rubber adhesive over the roughened surface (Fig. 102). While the adhesive is drying, trim the patch to remove corners. A circular or oval patch affords no corners where the patch might start loosening. When the adhesive has dried, remove the protective cover from the patch, being careful not to touch the surface with fingers, and apply the patch immediately (Fig. 103). Thoroughly work the patch and innertube together, stretching it in all directions while pressing the patch onto the tube. This "working" action is most important in getting an airtight, long-lasting patch.

7. Replace the tube in the tire, beginning at the valve stem. If the stem is metal, run the nut onto the valve stem to hold the stem straight (Fig. 104). Otherwise, you can pull the valve stem to one side while mounting the tire. There is no way to repair a leak torn into the tube by an off-center valve stem. Tuck the innertube inside the tire all around and check the liner position again to make sure it covers the spoke nipples completely (Fig. 105).

8. "Muscle" the tire back onto the rim as far as possible without using the tire wrenches (Fig. 106). Strong boys on the Cyclemates trips could pull the tire fully onto the rim, but I use a couple of tire wrenches. Most important—keep the tire wrenches away from the tube. You can easily pinch the tube between a tire wrench and rim edge to cause an elongated puncture that is difficult to repair. Caution and patience are the key terms at this state. Otherwise, you simply insert the irons under the edge of the tire and pry it over the edge of the rim. Voila! It's on.

9. Before pumping up the tire, pull back the edge of the tire and examine the liner once again (Fig. 105). Check the position of the valve stem; it should be straight and comfortably loose in its hole. Pump up the tire, preferably with a heavy-duty tire pump. As the tire balloons out, check to see that the marker line is evenly spaced from the rim all around. Check air pressure with a hand-held pressure gauge (Fig. 107). See Table N on page 189 for the correct pressure or note the recommended pressure molded onto the sidewall of your tire.

10. Replace the wheel on the bicycle and check the cone bearings for looseness. The wheel should run true, and brake shoes should bear only on the rim, as detailed in Chapter Thirteen. From stop to start, repairing a clincher tire puncture took about six or seven minutes on the Cyclemates tours.

*Sew-up or tubular tires* call for different techniques. Finding and

Fig. 102—Apply plenty of rubber adhesive over roughened surface around puncture hole.

Fig. 103—Trim patch to round or oval shape before removing protective cover. When the adhesive has dried, apply the patch. Immediately "work the patch" by pressing on patch while stretching the tube in all directions. Otherwise, patch could spring a leak when tube is inflated.

Fig. 104—Begin reassembling clincher tire onto rim at the valve. Screw on metal valve nut finger-tight to hold the valve stem straight. With rubber valve stems, keep valve straight as you work tube inside tire around its full diameter.

Fig. 105—Before pulling tire onto rim, pull tire aside and examine tube and rim liner to make sure none of the spoke nipples are exposed and that rim liner is centered.

repairing a puncture in a sew-up tire can take several times as long as for a clincher tire—about half an hour is good time. To avoid a long break in a trip, cyclists riding sew-ups usually pack a spare tire neatly folded into a saddle bag, ready for installation. Sew-ups are so light and flexible they can be folded into a small saddle bag. On a trip you can simply remove the flat tire and replace it with a new or repaired tire and tube and be on your way in minutes. But, for a repair, follow these steps:

1. Pull off the sew-up near the valve stem (Fig. 108). No tire irons are needed, but you will need to break loose the cement holding the tire to the shallow-cupped rim and roll it off.

2. Find the leak in the punctured tube before removing it from the tire. Usually, this is no problem, as you can see the nail or glass shard in the tire. If you can't see the hole location, pump a few pounds of air into the tire-tube combination and listen, or dunk both together in a water bath to find the puncture location. The reason for finding the location before removing the tube is to avoid cutting any more stitching than is necessary. Restitching the tire together after repairing the tube can be time-consuming.

3. When you have spotted the puncture location, peel back the tape that covers the stitches about 1½ to 2 inches on each side of the puncture location. Strip back the tape to expose the stitching about 3 inches. Begin cutting the stitching at least 1½ inches to one side of the puncture using a razor blade or one of the tools used by seamstresses to remove stitching. Since you will be replacing each of the stitches cut, work with as small a hole as possible.

4. Pull out the tube and locate the hole (Fig. 109). Patch the hole in the tube following the same steps as for patching the tube in the clincher tire above (Fig. 110). All of the materials needed for patching the sew-up tire are included in a patch kit.

5. With the patch in place, tuck the tube back into the tire and work it around to remove any bulge in the patch area. With the needle and thread pick up the stitching and reclose the tire (Fig. 111). Stitches should be about ⅜- to ½-inch apart. You'll find that stitching can be tedious until you get the hang of it. Use the thimble provided in the patch kit to avoid punctured fingers—which aren't as easily patched. When the tire is restitched, cement the tape that covers the stitches back into place using rim cement.

6. Sew-up tires are cemented onto the rim to keep them from

Fig. 106—All but about the last 12 to 16 inches of tire can be "muscled" onto the rim. Use one or two tire levers to pry remaining tire edge onto rim. CAUTION: Make sure tire levers touch only the metal rim and do not pinch the tube.

Fig. 107—Check tire pressure as you pump up the tire. See Table 13A for recommended tire pressures.

Fig. 108—Repairing puncture in sew-up (tubular) tire. begins by pulling it from rim. Sew-up tires are cemented into shallow-dished rim. Sometimes, the cement resists breaking loose. Use both thumbs to gain a start, then roll the tire off progressively around the rim.

Fig. 109—Locate puncture by ear or water test before cutting sew-up tire lacing to expose tube. Note small puncture hole.

rolling off on tight turns or from working their way around the circumference and pulling the valve stem. Rim cement may not be included in the patch kit; if not, secure a tube and apply it liberally around the rim—not the tire (Fig. 112). Mounting is messy enough without fussing with cement on the tire itself. You need not remove the old cement; it helps to hold the tire and is reactivated by the solvent in the new cement. Allow the cement to dry until tacky; time will vary according to temperature—two or three minutes on a warm day. The only time a buildup of cement could cause problems would be during cycling on a very hot day. Then, the cement could soften and allow a tire to roll off and tangle the wheel, probably putting you onto the pavement.

7. Begin mounting the tire from the valve stem. With the wheel on the floor and the valve stem up, work the tire around the wheel evenly —same distance on each side from the valve stem. When the tire is on the rim except for the part near the floor, reverse the wheel. Stretch the tire as necessary to slip it onto the rim (Fig. 113). Immediately, while the cement remains tacky, flex and rotate the tire on the rim until the tread is centered. An even border of sidewall should remain showing between rim and edge of tread on each side. Inflate the tire slowly to allow it to flex on the wheel. If possible, set the tire and wheel aside to cure the cement before riding. If you are in the field and can't wait, ride carefully for a few miles and avoid turns that could roll the tire off the rim.


## SERVICING BEARINGS

Six pairs of bearings are found on every single-person bicycle—in the two wheels, two pedals, bottom bracket, and headset. They all function the same and can be serviced similarly. Servicing involves removing the bearings by disassembling the unit, washing off the old grease, checking cones and bearings for wear and flat spots, adding new grease, and reassembling the unit. Since all six bearing pairs are serviced similarly, follow step-by-step for a typical rear hub. Any variations for the other five locations will be noted later.

First remove the rear wheel from the bicycle. Two different types of removers are used to disassemble the rear cluster from the rear axle (Fig. 114). You should buy one that fits your bicycle's rear hub, as it is used often. An easy way to remove the rear cluster is to engage the

Fig. 110—Patch is pressed onto thin sew-up tube after roughening surface and applying cement similar to patching procedure for clincher tube. Work tube and patch together thoroughly.

Fig. 111—Needle and thread from sew-up patch kit are used to restitch tire together. Tape is then cemented over stitching before remounting tire.

Fig. 112—New cement is applied in a thin layer to rim—not to tire. Old cement remaining on rim need not be removed unless excessive layer has built up following repeated tire replacements.

Fig. 113—Sew-up tire can be stretched onto rim. Keep hands away from rim wherever possible to stay out of tacky cement.

remover after removing any nuts on the axle that would interfere. With the flats of the cluster remover gripped in the vise jaws, spin the wheel, and the inner nut holding the cluster in place comes off easily. When the nut is turning loose, remove the wheel from the vise and turn the nut off by hand. Remove the rear cluster for servicing as noted below.

Another nut, spacer, and a cone nut remain after removing the cluster. Remove these one at a time, using a cone wrench on the far side to hold the axle (Fig. 116). Disturb only one cone nut on either the rear or front wheels. At the other four locations, you gain access to the bearings from one end or side. By working from only one side, you spare yourself the chore of centering the axle between the cones.

As you remove the axle, watch for loose bearings. If grease remains in the bearings, the individual balls may not fall out. Individual balls in a bearing are the general rule for good quality bikes, although there are notable exceptions. If your bicycle includes a thin metal cage for holding the balls together, note in which direction the cage fits as you remove the axle. Also, if the balls fall out of the retainer cage, it and the bearings are probably worn and should be replaced. Otherwise, catch the balls in your hand as they fall through (Fig. 117). Set them aside or toss them into a container with kerosene for cleaning.

Hold the hub over a container of thinner and dab at it with a brush (Fig. 118). You could remove the bearing retainer cups on each side of the hub, but why disturb them if you don't have to? Wash out the dirt and old grease with the brush dipped in solvent. Finally, wipe the inner bearing race surfaces clean with a *clean* cloth. Wash all the axle and cone surfaces clean with solvent and wipe dry. Retrieve the bearings from the solvent dish and dry them on a clean cloth. Examine by eye and feel all bearing races and the balls for scratchy or galled areas, flat spots, or other damage. You can replace cone nuts and balls, but if the inner races are damaged, you must replace the hub.

Begin reassembly of the rear axle from the side opposite the rear cluster, that is, from the cone you left undisturbed during disassembly. Squeeze bearing lubricant into the clean, dry cone area. Count the bearing balls that came out of the bearing and place half of them in the sticky grease around the perimeter (Fig. 119). Ordinarily, an odd number of balls fit in each end. The balls will not completely fill

Fig. 114—Two typical rear cluster removers—keyed nut in foreground;
splined nut beside dark cluster. Rear
cluster bearings are lubricated through
thin opening between hub and small
freewheel.

Fig. 115—Common nut holds cluster
remover engaged. Unless remover keys
are fully engaged, remover may strip
out holes in cluster hub.

Fig. 116—Paired cone wrenches loosen
one cone nut only, preferably on right
side where rear cluster fits.

Fig. 117—Collect loose bearing balls as
they fall through hub. Some hub bearings may be restrained in metal cage;
these can be lifted out.

the space, but there should be no gaps wider than a fraction more than the diameter of one ball. The number of balls in each bearing varies according to cone diameter and individual ball size. A rear hub may include nine balls on each side. A front hub bearing may have eleven balls on each side. The number is not important, as long as most of the perimeter is filled. The sticky grease holds the balls in place as you insert the axle and turn the wheel upside down (Fig. 120). Position the remaining half of the balls in the second end after filling the bearing area with grease (see Lubrication Chart, Table O).

Turn on the second cone nut and tighten it finger-tight at first. Turn on the remaining nuts and a spacer that adjusts the position of the rear cluster. Cone tightness is critical for a smooth-running bicycle. The cones should be tight enough to prevent any wiggling or end play, but not so tight they restrict the wheel from turning freely. One trick is to tighten cones just to the point of restricting wheel motion. Tighten the lock nut behind the cone fairly tight but don't jam it. Then, back off on the cone nut 1/16 to 1/8 turn to jam the lock nut. This slight loosening should allow the wheel to turn freely, which is the ultimate test, with no detectable looseness or end play. Reassemble the rear cluster as noted below.

Lubricating and checking a front wheel hub follows the same sequence but is easier because there is no rear cluster to complicate the procedure.

The headset supports the fork and handlebars with bearings at the upper and lower end. Cleaning and inspecting the bearing races and the balls follows the same procedure detailed for the rear hub, but removing and replacing the headset follows a slightly different procedure.

Undo the brake cables at some convenient joint to allow the handlebars to be completely removed from the headset. On center-pull brakes, the easiest joint is at the top of the dividing cable. If your bicycle should be equipped with handlebar end shifters, cables should be unhitched at the lever end and the clamps holding the cable casing removed to free the handlebars.

Loosen the expander bolt three or four turns. If the stem remains tight in the fork tube, place a thin board over the head and tap it lightly to break the wedge loose inside. The handlebar should lift out easily. With a large adjustable crescent wrench, remove the lock nut at the top end of the headset (Fig. 92). A notched lock nut may be tapped off with a screwdriver in the same way as the notched lock nut is loosened on the bottom bracket (Fig. 79). Before removing the race nut, lay the bicycle on its side (front wheel off) on a large cloth or sheet to catch any loose bearing balls. Some headset bearings will be caged. If balls fall out of the cage, they or the cage is worn. Replace the bearings. Once the top race nut is loose, tip the top end to one side and collect the bearing balls. Catch the lower bearing balls the same way by pulling the fork part way out of the head frame.

Clean the bearing races and the bearing balls the same as for the rear hub (see above). Inspect the fixed and loose races for both ends

Fig. 118—Clean hub and bearing races with brush dipped in solvent. Work directly over solvent bowl to contain the mess. Kerosene is a cheap and readily available solvent that poses few fire hazards.

Fig. 119—Individual ball bearings are stuck in sticky grease previously squeezed into bearing race of rear hub. Grease prevents balls from falling through hub.

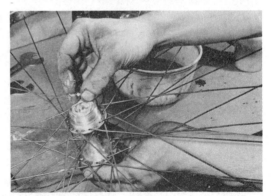

Fig. 120—Cleaned axle with one cone in position is pushed through grease and bearing in reassembly of hub. Bearing balls are positioned in grease on second side similarly.

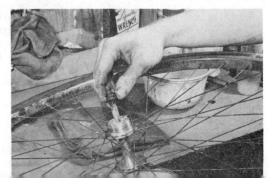

of the headset. They should be smooth and free from galling or flat spots. Replace any damaged parts. Reassemble the headset beginning at the bottom. Turn the bike upside down and fill the bearing area with grease. Fit the fork into the opening, but allow enough room for inserting the bearing balls. Place half of the balls in the sticky grease. Insert the fork and return the bike to its upright position. Place the bearings in the top end and screw the race nut on tight enough to interfere slightly with easy turning. Then back off 1/16 to 1/8 turn. The headset should turn easily but exhibit no end play. Reassemble the brake cables and any other parts removed during disassembly.

Pedals turn freely on bearings at each end of the shaft. Use a special pedal remover end wrench to unscrew the pedals. Remember, pedals unscrew in a direction opposite to the normal pedaling rotation— counterclockwise on the right side, clockwise on the left side (when facing forward in riding position).

Remove the end dust cover to gain access to the nut that jams the cone nut on the screwed axle (Fig. 121). Pedal bearings are similar to the others, thus they may be cleaned, races inspected, and reassembled with new grease as detailed above. When you reassemble the pedal to the crank, coat the treads lightly with bearing grease to protect the threads; otherwise you may experience difficulty in removing the pedal the next time. Pedals operate in a wet, dirty environment close to the ground and should be serviced regularly.

Bottom bracket supports cranks and chainwheels. Cotterless cranks, similar to the type shown in Fig. 80, will be found on better bikes. Cottered cranks are found on less expensive bikes, and one-piece cranks are used by most U.S. manufacturers. Aside from the crank design, the bearings are serviced the same as the rear hub bearings detailed above. But note these differences in removing and replacing the cranks to gain access to the bearings and races:

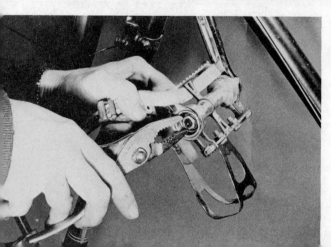

Fig. 121—Nuts at end of pedals (visible after removal of cap) may be removed by socket wrench or all-purpose pliers if on tour.

One-piece cranks do not include the inside bearing races on the crank axle. Instead a separate inside race is pressed into the outer shell. Therefore you need to inspect those bearing surfaces as well as those on the outer cones. Remove the left pedal. To remove a one-piece crank, after unscrewing the left pedal, remove the lock ring and adjustable cone on the left side. The left crank assembly can then be maneuvered through the hole in the bottom bracket. Clean, inspect, and lubricate the bearings as noted above before reassembling. If inside bearing races are damaged, knock them out with a punch from the back side (through the hole). Tap replacement races into place and make sure they are firmly seated, square with the centerline. Coat the threads of the adjustable cone, lock ring, and pedal before reassembling to prevent rust from making later disassembly difficult. Although not required to service the bottom bracket bearings, you should remove the right pedal and lubricate those threads at the same time as a precaution against rust.

Cottered cranks are so named because of a tapered pin (cotter) used to attach the cranks to the axle. Except for the cotter, the crank assembly closely resembles the bottom bracket inner assembly shown in Fig. 80. Remove both wheels from the frame to simplify handling. To remove the cotters, the first step in disassembling the bottom bracket assembly, loosen the retaining nut on the cotter two or three turns—no more, as you want to retain as many threads in the nut engaged as possible. Place the crank and axle end over a wood block. Note that Fig. 122 shows the cotter pin being assembled. Simply

Fig. 122—Cotter pin attaching crank arm to axle is assembled or disassembled with aid of two wood blocks. Bottom block supports crank to relieve crank bearings while pin is tapped in or out. Upper block protects head of cotter pin during assembly (as pictured) or disassembly when tapping nut on threaded end of cotter.

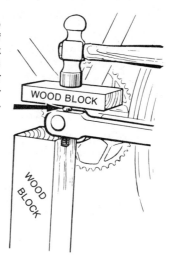

turn the crank over with the threads and nut up. With a second small block of wood on the nut, tap lightly with a hammer to break the pin loose. When the pin breaks loose, it will move only the distance of the two or three threads on the nut. Unscrew the nut and remove the pin. Mark the head R or L to note which crank each fits, as pins are seldom interchangeable. Repeat the cotter pin removal on the opposite side. Remove the lock nut, adjustable cone, and fixed cone to remove bearings and axle. Use a sheet to catch any loose balls that fall through the hole. If any roll up into the down tube or seat tube, retrieve them for cleaning and reassembly.

Clean, inspect, and lubricate the bearings as noted above. Any parts that are scratched, galled, or damaged should be replaced. After assembling bearings and axle through the bottom bracket, reassemble the cranks with the cotter pin as shown in Fig. 122.

Cotterless cranks, similar to those in Fig. 80, do not use the cotter for attaching cranks to axle. Axle ends are machined to a square or other shape, and the cranks fit snugly onto those ends. A cap covers the end, and this must be removed to gain access to the attach nut (Fig. 123). Depending on the manufacturer, a special tool may be needed to remove the nut that attaches the crank to the axle (Fig. 124). Lightweight cranks are softer than the steel axles and are often jammed on the axle. A special extractor can be used to force the cranks off the axle. The extractor screws into the cap threads and a center screw bears on the end of the axle. As you turn the center screw, it draws the crank away from the axle. If the crank does not break away after a ½ turn, tap the center screw lightly, take another ⅛th turn, and tap again. Repeat until the crank separates from the axle.

With the cranks off clean, check, and relubricate the two bearings as noted above.

Tips on bottom bracket servicing:

• Count the bearing balls that come out and make sure an equal number are reinstalled. Ordinarily, an odd number of balls fit in each side. Caged bearings simplify disassembly and reassembly, but you can use loose balls to replace caged bearings if they are worn. Bearing balls must be of identical diameter.

• Cones should be tight without restricting rotary motion. Tighten the adjustable cone until you feel resistance; then back off about ⅛th

Fig. 123—Protective cap over cotterless crank attachment is removed to gain access. Some caps screw in or out with a wide-bladed screwdriver.

Fig. 124—Special tool fits nut on cotterless crank. Each design is different; thus, you need a tool that fits your specific bicycle. A special puller may be needed to separate frozen crank from axle.

turn. Check for looseness or end play. Tighten the lock nut and test again. Or use the trick noted above for tightening hub cones: Tighten the bottom bracket bearings until you feel resistance. Turn the lock nut on tight but don't jam it. Loosen the adjustable cone another 1/16 turn, jamming the lock nut. Ideally, the bearings should be assembled with no end play or looseness—and without restricting action.

• When reassembling cones, lock nuts, and caps, grease the threads lightly. They will be easier to disassemble next time.

• After riding for a few miles, tighten the attach nuts on cotterless cranks or the nut at the end of the cotter pin. Riding tends to loosen or "work" parts, and they should be tightened to prevent further play.

## REAR CLUSTER SERVICE

The rear cluster of four, five, or six freewheels is assembled as a single unit. The freewheels in the cluster coast freely because of an internal pawl and sprocket combination. As you begin pedaling after coasting, the pawl engages the inner sprocket and drives the wheel. Ordinarily, you need not ever take the freewheel cluster apart. You may need to remove the cluster, however, and clean and oil it, service rear hub bearings, or replace spokes on the cluster side of the rear wheel (see Figs. 114 and 115).

To clean the inside of the cluster and remove any hardened or dirty oil that may be interfering with the action of the pawls, soak the entire cluster in kerosene, overnight if time permits. After soaking, swish the cluster up and down a dozen or more times in the kerosene to wash out any and all of the old soil softened during the soaking. Set the cluster aside to drain on a stack of newspapers. Before oiling the cluster, all of the kerosene should be dried out of the inside. Never use grease, as it can interfere with pawl action when temperatures are cold. Instead, use a light oil (see Lubrication Chart, Table O) at the locations shown in Fig. 114.

The cluster is replaced in the reverse order—special wrench followed by two jam nuts.

## REAR DERAILLEUR

While the rear derailleur mechanism appears to be one of the most complicated parts on your bicycle, it seldom causes trouble you can't fix. Figure 125 shows a typical rear derailleur assembly. Begin any repairs or maintenance with the idea that you will disassemble the derailleur only as a last resort.

As long as the derailleur operates through its full range, nothing is broken even if operation is sluggish. With so many moving parts free to collect dirt, sluggish operation can usually be traced to dry or dirty pivots on the parallelogram arms. Without removing the derailleur from the frame, but with the chain off the rear cluster, clean the mechanism with a stiff bristle brush. Open and close the mechanism to gain access for brushing out dirt. Using light oil, lubricate each of the joints as you move the mechanism back and forth. Keep excess oil off tires, as oil deteriorates rubber. Wipe the outside of the derailleur mechanism with a cloth to remove any excess oil.

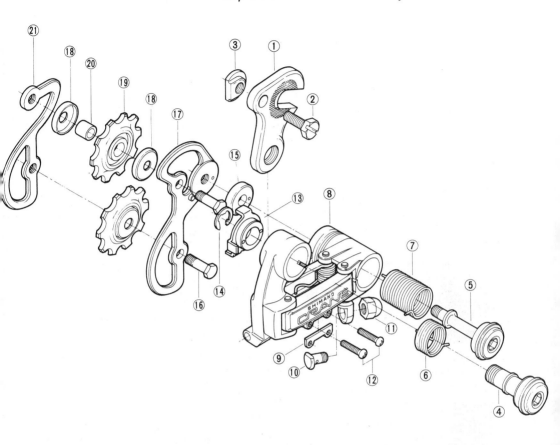

| Item No. | Description | Item No. | Description |
|---|---|---|---|
| 1 | Adapter | 12 | Adjusting Screw |
| 2 | Adapter Screw | 13 | Adapter Bushing |
| 3 | Adapter Nut | 14 | Stop Ring |
| 4 | Adapter Mounting Bolt | 15 | Plate Bushing |
| 5 | Plate Mounting Bolt | 16 | Pulley Bolt |
| 6 | B-Tension Spring | 17 | Inner Cage Plate |
| 7 | P-Tension Spring | 18 | Pulley Cap |
| 8 | Mechanism Assembly | 19 | Pulley |
| 9 | Adjusting Plate | 20 | Pulley Bushing |
| 10 | Cable Attachment Bolt | 21 | Outer Cage Plate |
| 11 | Cable Attachment Nut | | |

Fig. 125—Typical rear derailleur with springs for shifting cable position and for taking up cable slack.

If the derailleur moves the chain toward the high gear but will not return it, the spring is broken. Springs do not break often, but if you are on a tour, you could use a replacement handily. The spring on the popular *Simplex* derailleur is shown out of its normal position in Fig. 126. A protective plastic cover keeps dirt off the spring. Ends of the spring are bent—one out to fit into a hole in the derailleur frame, and the other in to fit the slot in the connecting bolt. Note how spring ends are bent in Fig. 125. As the derailleur cable forces the pantagraph arms out to move the chain to higher gears, it tensions the spring. When the gear shifter releases the cable, spring action returns the pantagraph arms toward the low gear. All derailleurs function similarly, and you can follow the action as the cable moves the arms out and the spring retracts them. If you should break a spring in the derailleur mechanism, you can manually position the chain on a middle freewheel and pedal home or to a cyclery in one gear.

A second spring takes up cable slack as the derailleur shifts from large to small freewheels. This spring may not provide enough force to keep the chain running taut. A number of derailleurs provide for adjustable tension at one of four slots (Fig. 127).

A bent derailleur frame results from rough treatment, usually when the bike falls against a solid object or pavement. Plastic frames have the facility for "remembering" and returning to their former position if

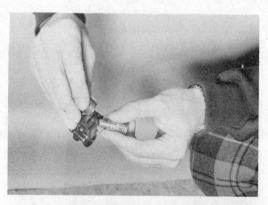

Fig. 126—Replacing a spring in derailleur. One bent end of spring fits into hole in housing; second bent end slips through slot in mounting bolt. Each derailleur design varies. Individual parts may be difficult to obtain except from a well-stocked local or mail-order source (see Appendix).

Fig. 127—Spring for take-up rollers can be repositioned to increase or decrease tension by moving end to one of four stops.

Fig. 128—A lightweight alloy derailleur frame bent from rough treatment may be bent back into alignment as shown. Force on T-wrench in allen recess bends derailleur frame outward. For this procedure to work, T-wrench must fit tightly all the way into access.

bending was not extreme. Cast or forged alloy derailleur frames can sometimes be straightened as shown in Fig. 128. Other types of derailleurs must be overhauled by replacing bent or damaged parts in the assembly. A cyclery with a supply of parts for your derailleur can rebuild it—or you can replace the derailleur with a new one, at possibly less cost than rebuilding an old, bent one. Make sure you know the cost of rebuilding before authorizing a go-ahead.

Two rollers guide the chain as it is shifted from one freewheel to the other. Simple journal-type bearings (Fig. 125) require no maintenance unless they squeak. Spraying the core of the rollers with a lubricant will generally quiet the squeak. Although the rollers turn rapidly, they carry very little load—only the tension of the spring that keeps the chain from sagging.

## CHAIN

One of the toughest and hardest-working parts of your bicycle is the chain. With a modicum of care, regular cleaning and lubrication, it will last as long as your bicycle. Most touring and general-purpose adult derailleur-equipped bicycles use a 3/32-inch chain at ½-inch pitch. Sidebars, rollers, and rivets or connector pins are hardened steel. One of the worst things you can do to a chain is to allow it to rust. A light film of oil keeps the chain working smoothly and protects the surfaces from rust. After riding in the rain, spray the chain with a penetrating oil (*Liquid Wrench* or *WD-40*).

Before riding the bicycle after a winter layoff or other period, brush the chain, rear cluster, and chainwheels to remove any dirt or grit.

Dirt becomes an abrasive that hastens wear on rollers and gear teeth. Spray the cleaned chain with a light oil (Fig. 91). While spraying, turn the chain through a full length. During regular riding sessions, brush clean and spray the chain about once a month or every 200 to 250 miles.

Stiff links may result from inadequate lubrication, rusting, or trapped dirt. Links turn back and forth on pivot pins as they roll over the gear teeth and around the small-diameter rollers of the rear derailleur. Unless links turn freely on the rivet, they fail to conform to the rollers. You can feel the jerking that results. Stiff links may be cured by working with each one individually. With the bicycle clamped in a workstand or upside down, turn the pedals slowly as you examine the chain action around the rollers. You can see any stiff links because they will stand away from the roller. Mark each of the stiff links with chalk. With the chain slipped off the gear wheels, squirt stiff link joints with oil and work it back and forth in your fingers (Fig. 129). Usually, the added oil and working will free up the joint. If that doesn't do it, dip the link in kerosene or brush the joints with a brush dipped in kerosene. Work the links back and forth as before and dip again. When the link works freely again, wipe dry, and spray with light oil.

If continued cleaning, oiling, and working between fingers does not loosen stiff links, replace the links. If you find a number of stiff links around the chain, consider replacing the entire chain. But, for one or two stiff links, use the chain rivet remover (Fig. 130) to replace a section. Two rollers or one inch of chain is the minimum you can replace because of the under- and overlapping of side links.

The hardened steel pivot, mistakenly but commonly called a rivet, is a press-fit in the outer links. To remove a pivot, simply align the rivet remover with the center of the pin and force it out through screw action. Never push the pivot all the way through; leave an edge of the pin in the opposite side.

Joining two ends of a chain or adding a new section of chain to one end reverses the pin removal procedure. Reverse the removing tool and screw the handle to force the pivot pin back into position. Enough force is generated by the screw action to break one of the side links if the pin is not properly aligned. Modern 10-speed bike chains do not include a special link for joining or breaking the chain due to the close clearances between freewheels in the rear cluster.

Fig. 129—Working chain links to remove stiffness. Before and during working, spray affected joints. Working links back and forth draws lubricant into the joint.

Fig. 130—Chain pivot remover pushes pin through all but last of four links to break chain. Reverse process for pushing pivot pin back to rejoin chain ends.

## FRONT DERAILLEUR

Continued rubbing of the chain against one or both sides of the front derailleur cage can wear a hole in it. If a bicycle's front derailleur shows grooved wear, first examine the limit stops. The adjustable screw may be stopping the cage short rather than permitting it to move slightly behond the chain's aligned running position. If so, adjust the limit stops as noted in Chapter Thirteen.

If the limit stops appear to be adjusted properly and the front derailleur is still worn, check your shifting habits to make sure you are shifting the front derailleur full throw.

With the chain off the chainwheels, shift the front derailleur back and forth to see if it moves smoothly. If not, oil the sliding mechanism and work it back and forth to work the oil into the sliding parts.

About the only breakable part on the front derailleur (other than the cable) is the spring. If the spring should break (highly unlikely), remove it, noting how it came apart. Take the spring to the cyclery and get an exact duplicate. Install the spring by reversing the take-apart procedure.

If the front derailleur won't work or works very hard, the sliding arm may be bent. You can observe this immediately by examining the sliding mechanism. There's nothing to lose by trying to bend the arm back. If it still doesn't work, replace the unit.

## CABLES

Four cables control the vital functions on your bicycle—two for brakes and two for derailleurs. If your bicycle should be equipped with a 3- or 5-speed internal hub changer, only one cable controls the gear position.

Since all cables suffer the same maladies, they will be considered together. Cables are woven or braided from flexible yet extremely strong steel alloy strands. They function only in tension or pulling. Since they are flexible, cables cannot change direction without a guide, and this is the function of the sheath or casing. As a cable moves inside the coiled spring or plastic casing, it is restricted to a fixed path in space. Changing the length of the casing, in effect, lengthens the cable because it must travel a longer path around a curve. Thus, by turning the knurled nut to adjust the casing on brake and derailleur cables, you can take up slack in the cable.

All cables stretch, and cable stretch causes frustrating problems. A derailleur perfectly adjusted works fine for a while, then won't pull the cable onto high gear—cable stretch has limited the travel of the cable. Two means are provided on most bicycles for correcting cable stretch. You are already familiar with the adjusting nuts at the working end of the cables. Turning these nuts extends the casing and takes up small changes in cable length (see Chapter Thirteen). When the knurled nut runs out of threads, you must take up another length of cable by loosening the clamp nut and pulling the cable through (Figs. 131, 132 and 133). At the same time, screw the nut down to permit another ¼ or ½ inch of fine adjustment. Because cable stretch can be so irritating, plan to protect cables once they are broken in. A new cable may continue to stretch for as long as a month when ridden daily —longer if ridden intermittently.

Fig. 131—Adjusting knurled nut at derailleur extends cable casing to effectively shorten cable and compensate for cable stretch.

Fig. 132—Nut compresses U-shaped collar over cable to attach end to derailleur. When casing adjustment nut runs out of travel, shorten cable by pulling it through loosened attach nut.

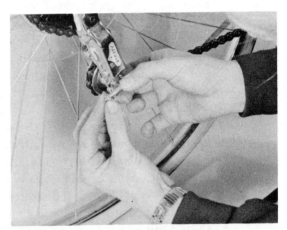

Fig. 133—Nut at caliper brake compresses cable threaded through hole in bolt.

Cables may move sluggishly inside the casings. If you find a cable sticking, slide the casing back and forth on the cable. You may need to remove clamps holding the casing to the frame to permit moving the casing. Do not remove the cable from the casing unless absolutely necessary; otherwise, you will experience difficulty in threading the cable back through the casing. Instead, wipe the cable clean, then pull the casing over the cleaned cable. Wipe off the other end of the cable. With this back and forth motion, you can remove dirt and hardened oil from inside. Add a few drops of oil to the casing (Fig. 134). Routinely oiling the cable twice a year should keep it moving smoothly through the casing.

Sticky cables may also result from a bent spring inside the casing, a broken strand or kink in the cable, or a jammed piece of dirt inside the casing. The plastic over the wound spring in Fig. 135, for example, appears cracked over a kink in the casing spring. When routine cleaning and oiling fails to clear up a case of sticky cable, loosen the cut end of the cable (opposite the end with a swaged ball at the shifter or brake handle end of the cable). Pull the cable out of the casing and cut new piece of casing the same length.

Inserting a new or cut end of an old cable into a casing can be tricky. First, cut the end of the cable square to remove any brush. Special cable cutters are available for cutting the end without smashing the strands. But sharp side-cutting pliers or wire cutters will trim the end neatly (Fig. 136). Shape the end of the cable delicately to avoid a wedge-shaped end. Insert the' cut end of the cable into the casing and push it through. When starting the cable, make sure all strands are inserted; otherwise, it will catch, bend back, and prevent the cable from slipping through the casing. Attach the new casing at the former clamps and the cable end to the clamp nut on derailleur or brake (Fig. 132).

Broken cables seldom result from a problem with the cable. Find out why a cable broke before stringing a new one through the system. Squeezing the U-shaped clamp nut too tightly (Fig. 132) may sever some of the strands of a cable near its end. With continued use, it finally breaks. Or the adjustment screws on front or rear derailleur may be improperly set, and attempting to jerk the derailleur to shift into a high gear could break a cable. Some foreign object may restrict brake-arm action, and extra pressure on brake handles breaks the cable. Whatever the cause, find it; otherwise, cables will keep breaking

Fig. 134—Light oil may be added to cable casing to relieve sticky operation and to help insert new cable.

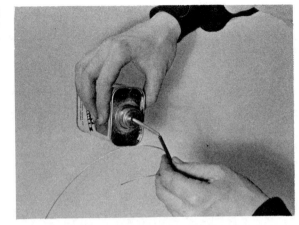

Fig. 135—Break in cable indicates a kink or worn spot causing sluggish cable operation.

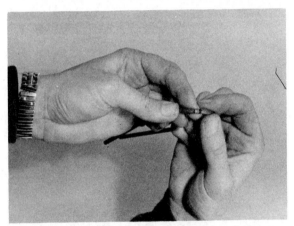

Fig. 136—Trim cable "brush" with sharp wire-cutters. To avoid wedge-shaped end, cut crisply and avoid mashing strands.

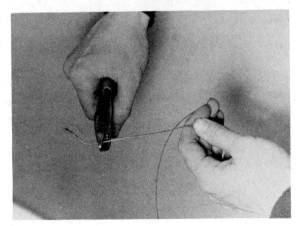

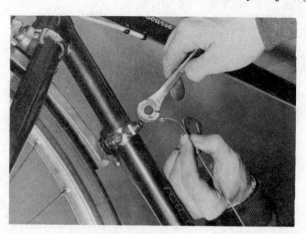

Fig. 137—Replace shifter cable by inserting swaged end in handle recess.

as fast as you install them. When touring, even for a day, you should pack an extra rear derailleur and rear brake cable along with the tools to install them. You can ride without a front derailleur or front brake, but rear derailleur and rear-wheel brakes are critical.

To replace a broken cable, begin with the forward or handle end—either shifter or brake handle. A shifter cable fastens into the base of the handle as shown in Fig. 137. Before attaching the swaged end to a brake handle, thread the opposite end of the cable through the casing that begins immediately above the center-pull or side-pull mechanisms. Then attach the handle end at the clamp nut (Fig. 133). Different manufacturers use slightly varying designs for clamping the ends, so examine the system before taking anything loose.

## BRAKES

Brake shoes wear out with use on a bicycle just as on a car. A brake shoe should not be allowed to run so long before replacement that it wears flat. Molded pillows on each pad allow water to drain through and for each individual surface to wear separately. Therefore, brake pads should be replaced when they wear within 1/16 inch of the solid base. Brake shoes may be molded from a rubber-base material or one of the new plastics. You may wish to experiment with their action and choose the one that suits you best.

When replacing shoes, you may slide a new block into the metal frame or replace the block and frame as a unit. If you slide a new block into the metal container, make certain the metal frame folds up at the

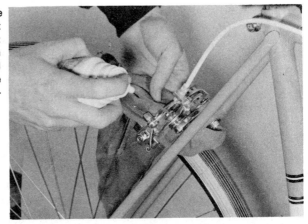

Fig. 138—Lubricate caliper brake mechanism with spray to keep it functioning smoothly. CAUTION: Protect tire from overspray with cloth behind brake mechanism. Oil deteriorates rubber and should be kept off or wiped from tires immediately.

end to keep the block from sliding out the end the first time you apply brakes forcefully. Some of the shoe frames include a turned-up edge at both ends; that way you can't install the shoe backwards.

Sluggish action of the caliper arms usually results from dirt in the mechanism or lack of lubrication. First check to be certain any sluggishness noted is not in the cables (see above). You can isolate caliper brake action by pulling on the arms, thus bypassing the cable actuation system.

Brush out any dirt that may have collected with your stiff-bristle brush. Then, spray the mechanism. Work the mechanism back and forth to work the oil into the sliding parts. You may need to repeat the spraying and the working operation. If this action doesn't free up the caliper arm operation (99 percent of the time, it will), one of the arms may be bent or a spring weakened. If you are mechanically inclined, you can disassemble the caliper mechanism to replace a spring. Otherwise, take the brake assembly to a cyclery shop for overhaul.

## HANDLEBARS

Every cyclist likes to tape handlebars to suit his own taste in colors or tape material. Two types of tape are generally available—a plastic tape that may be opaque or semitransparent and cloth or fabric tape. Both types are available in a rainbow of colors. Plastic tapes are stretched into place without an adhesive. A thin adhesive comes already in place on fabric tapes.

Some riders prefer the plastic tape. I, personally, prefer the fabric tape because it becomes less sticky when riding in hot weather. On the other hand, light-colored fabric tapes pick up grime that is difficult to remove. Plastic tape remains glossy in appearance and is easy to clean. It's your choice, but either way, taping handlebars is an easy task accomplished as in Figs. 139 through 142.

## SADDLE

Leather saddles should be treated with saddle soap three or four times a year. Leather will harden and become uncomfortable without this regular attention. Follow directions on the can.

Vinyl saddles or vinyl-covered metal saddles do not absorb moisture and do not assume the peculiar shape of the rider. They can be cleaned with a household detergent and water.

Fig. 139—Taping handlebars begins about 2 inches out from stem. Double wrap the beginning point to hold tape in place. Overlap tape half its width and stretch plastic tape tightly as you roll it around the handlebar metal! Cloth tape stretches less than plastic but includes a light adhesive to cement it in place. At the brake handle wrap tape around forward side as shown.

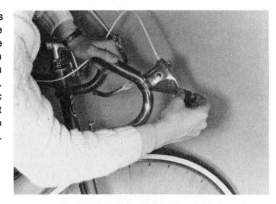

Fig. 140—Complete wrap around brake handle before continuing around curve of handlebar.

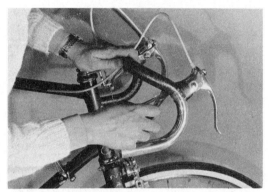

Fig. 141—Continue wrapping and over-lapping tape as you approach the end of the handlebar.

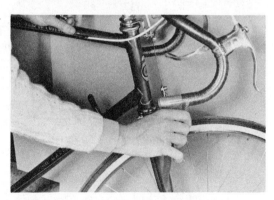

Fig. 142—While holding tape tightly to prevent it from unwinding, stuff end into handlebar. Push handlebar end cap into opening to bind end of tape.

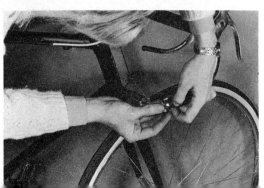

# Appendix

## ORGANIZATIONS OF INTEREST TO CYCLISTS

American Youth Hostels (AYH), National Offices, Delaplane, Va. 22025

Bicycle Institute of America, Inc., 122 East 42nd St., New York, N.Y. 10017

International Bicycle Touring Society, 2115 Paseo Dorado, La Jolla, Calif. 92037

League of American Wheelmen, P.O. Box 988, Baltimore, Md. 21203

National Safety Council, 444 North Michigan Ave., Chicago, Ill. 60611


## BICYCLING PERIODICALS

*The Bicycle Paper*, P.O. Box 842, Seattle, Wash. 98111 (7 issues per year)

*Bicycling!*, Rodale Press, 33 East Minor Street, Emmaus, Pa. 18049 (monthly)

*Cycle Touring*, 69 Meadow Dodalming, Surrey, England

*Cycling USA*, P.O. Box 1069, Nevada City, Calif. 95959 (monthly)

*National L.A.W. Bulletin*, P.O. Box 988, Baltimore, Md. 21203 (monthly)

*Northeast Bicycle News*, 12 Cherry Street, Brattleboro, Vt. 05301

## LOCAL TOURING GUIDES

*The American Bicycle Atlas*
*Bay Area Bikeways* (Northern California)
*Bicycle Tours in and around New York*
*Bicycle Touring in the Pioneer Valley* (Massachusetts)
*Bicycler's Guide to Hawaii*
*Bicycling the Backroads around Puget Sound*
*Bike Tripping Coast to Coast*

For other areas, consult Bikecentennial Routing Service, P.O. Box 8308–A, Missoula, Mont. 59807

## OVERHAUL GUIDES

*Anybody's Bike Book,* Tom Cuthbertson, 10-Speed Press, 1979 (soft cover)
*The Bicycle Manual on Maintenance and Repairs,* Robert Whiter, Laurida Books, 1972
*Glenn's Complete Bicycle Manual,* Coles and Glenn, Crown, 1973
*Richard's Bicycle Book,* Richard Ballantine, Ballantine, 1978

All of the above books are available from William Allan, Bookseller, P.O. Box 315, Englewood, Colo. 80151

## MAIL-ORDER SOURCES OF BICYCLE PARTS AND SPECIAL TOOLS

Big Wheel Ltd., 340 Holly St., Denver, Colo. 80220
Bikecology, P.O. Box 66909, Los Angeles, Calif. 90066
Bike Warehouse, P.O. Box 290, New Middletown, Ohio 44442
Cyclo-Pedia, 311 N. Mitchell, Cadillac, Mich. 49601
The Touring Cyclist Shop, P.O. Box 4009 B, Boulder, Colo. 80306
Wheel Goods Corporation (*Handbook of Cycl-ology*), 2737 Hennepin Ave., Minneapolis, Minn. 55408

## SOURCES OF CAMPING EQUIPMENT

Early Winters, Ltd., 110 Prefontaine Place South, Seattle, Wash. 98104

Eddie Bauer, 1737 Airport Way S., Seattle, Wash. 98134

Gerry Div., Outdoor Sports Industries, Inc., 5450 N. Valley Highway, Denver, Colo. 80216

L. L. Bean, Inc., Freeport, Me. 04032

Orvis, Manchester, Vt. 05254

Recreational Equipment, Inc., 1525 Eleventh Ave., Seattle, Wash. 98122

The Ski Hut, 1615 University Ave., Berkeley, Calif. 94703

# Index